INVESTING ON YOUR OWN

A CONSUMER REPORTS MONEY BOOK

INVESTING

ON YOUR OWN

A Commonsense Way to

Make Your Money Grow

DEBORAH RANKIN

AND THE EDITORS OF

CONSUMER REPORTS BOOKS

CONSUMER REPORTS BOOKS

A Division of Consumers Union

Yonkers, New York

Copyright © 1994 by Deborah Rankin

Published by Consumers Union of United States, Inc., Yonkers, New York 10703.

Library of Congress Cataloging-in-Publication Data

Rankin, Deborah.
    Investing on your own: a commonsense way to make your money grow / Deborah Rankin
    and the Editors of Consumer Reports Books.
       p.   cm.
    Includes bibliographical references and index.
    ISBN 0-89043-545-6
    1. Investments. 2. Finance, Personal. I. Consumer Reports Books. II. Title.
    HG4521.R283 1994
    332.6—dc20   94-18923
                                                    CIP

Chart on page 10 © *The Asset Allocation Decision* Slide Presentation, 1990–93. Ibbotson Associates, Chicago. Used with permission. All rights reserved.

Design by Joy Taylor

First printing, September 1994

Manufactured in the United States of America

This book is printed on recycled paper.

To Larry, Dave, and Mike
for their understanding, support, and encouragement,
even though this book is not about sports

CONTENTS

ACKNOWLEDGMENTS

My deepest thanks to Ruth Turner, the former director of Consumer Reports Books, who urged me to tackle the project. This book would not have been written without her encouragement

I also extend my thanks to the following individuals, who generously agreed to review various sections of the book for technical accuracy: John Allen, of Allen-Warren, Arvada, Colo.; William Arnone, director of retirement planning services, Buck Consultants, Secaucus, N.J.; Charles Brandes of Brandes Investment Partners, San Diego, Calif.; Marilyn Cohen of L&S Advisors, Los Angeles; James Hunt of the National Insurance Consumer Organization, Washington, D.C.; Sheldon Jacobs of the No-Load Fund Investor, Irvington-on-Hudson, N.Y.; John Markese, president, the American Association of Individual Investors, Chicago; Avery Neumark, partner in charge of employee benefits, Weber, Lipshie & Co., New York; and Peter Roberts, President, the College Savings Bank, Princeton, N.J.

Their comments greatly improved the quality of this book, and whatever errors remain are entirely the author's responsibility.

INVESTING ON YOUR OWN

INTRODUCTION

WHEN it comes to investing their hard-earned money, most middle-income folks are largely on their own. Their assets are not large enough to interest professional money managers, and most of the financial planners who might accept their business probably aren't worth consulting. So, many people end up doing it themselves, although they can be easily intimidated by the complex jargon of the financial markets.

If, like many individuals, your only experience with investing has been with bank products, such as certificates of deposit, this book is designed to take you a step further. The goal is to explain how other investments, such as stocks, bonds, and mutual funds, work so that you will feel comfortable about expanding your investment horizon. Once you learn the basics of these different types of investments, as well as their pros and cons, you'll be able to consider how to fashion an investment program that suits your particular needs.

A recurrent theme is the need for all investors, regardless of age, to go beyond the traditional safe haven of such investments as bank CDs and Treasury bills and to venture into the stock market. Even though owning stocks can be an unsettling experience in the short term, marked by huge swings in market prices, research has shown that over the long term, stocks are the only way that investors can achieve "real" growth and outpace the combined threat of both inflation and taxes.

It may be tempting to believe there is some kind of magic approach that will guarantee you success, but there really are no secrets behind savvy investing. Instead, there are just a few commonsense principles that can be very rewarding if you stick to them over the years. So, you won't find any get-rich-quick schemes discussed in this book. Instead, you'll read about some tried and true approaches that many wealthy people have used to achieve their financial goals.

Chapter 1 discusses the basic aims—and pitfalls—of investing and gives some simple, down-to-earth tips on accumulating wealth. You'll learn why it's wise to set up a systematic investment program (and how to do it), how to assemble a diversified portfolio of both stocks and bonds, and how to protect your investments from the devastating impact of inflation.

Since the primary way that most people accumulate money for investment is through savings plans at work, Chapter 2 discusses the many different approaches that are available and their considerable tax advantages. You'll learn about 401(k) plans, thrift plans, profit-sharing plans, stock purchase plans, and stock options. You'll find out which types of investments make the most sense and which types of investments to avoid.

People who are self-employed have special vehicles they can use to accumulate wealth, too. Chapter 3 discusses the tax advantages that make Individual Retirement Accounts, Keogh plans, and Simplified Employee Pension plans such attractive ways to accumulate money for retirement and other purposes.

For people with children, the main financial goal is usually to amass enough money to pay for the steadily escalating cost of college. Chapter 4 covers the impact of the "kiddie tax," the different approaches you can use to accumulate a college fund for your youngsters, and the specific investments that work best for children above and below the magic age of 14.

Because of uncertainty about the future of Social Security, and the dwindling of traditional pension plans, most people realize it is increasingly important to focus on saving for retirement well before they receive the traditional gold watch. Chapter 5 explores different investment approaches you can take today so that you'll be able to have a financially comfortable retirement tomorrow.

The rest of the book discusses specific types of investments. In Chapter 6, the role of bank products, such as savings accounts, money market accounts, and CDs, is covered. Even though these products have limited appeal in terms of their investment potential, they can still play an important role in your financial life by offering a way for you to accumulate funds for a rainy day.

Stocks, which should be the mainstay of your portfolio, are discussed in Chapter 7. You'll learn how the stock market and different trading exchanges work, how to read a balance sheet and the stock listings in the newspaper, and how to find (and deal with) a broker.

Chapter 8 covers bonds and other fixed-income investments. You'll learn about corporate, government, and municipal bonds and whether it's best to invest in individual bonds or to buy a bond fund or unit investment trust. You'll also find out how to sidestep a broker and purchase Treasury securities directly from the U.S. government at no cost.

Mutual funds have become the favored investment route for most individuals, but selecting the best ones for your needs has become more difficult as the number of funds has proliferated. In Chapter 9, you'll learn how to read a fund prospectus, how to decipher the fund listings in the newspaper, and how to choose the most appropriate funds for the different types of stock, bond, and hybrid funds that are available; you'll also find out about index funds and learn how to deal with taxes when you sell a fund.

Chapter 10 discusses the pros and (mostly) cons of life insurance investments such as whole life policies and variable annuities. You'll learn about the steep carrying costs these products typically entail, and how it can be very expensive if you decide to unload them after a year or two. But you'll also discover how they may fill a role for certain affluent investors who can benefit from their tax advantages.

It's important to bear in mind that for most of us, investing is a means to an end, not an end in itself. The path to accumulating wealth should be fairly straightforward—not filled with roadblocks and so convoluted that you give up soon after you've started.

The aim of this book is to demystify the world of investing and give you a roadmap so that you're able to embark on the journey on your own. Of course, you'll encounter setbacks along the way. But if, over time, you remain focused on your final destination and remain faithful to the route you have chosen to reach it, this book will have succeeded.

1

WHY INVEST ANYWAY?

LET'S face it, most folks don't pick up a book on investing just for the fun of it. There are plenty of other, more enjoyable ways to spend an afternoon. The impetus is usually a nagging feeling that you should be doing something—anything—to plan your financial future. Or, if you've already started to invest, to improve the way you're doing it.

Regardless of whether you're just a beginner or have been investing for years, your goal is probably to accumulate a certain amount of wealth by a certain time, not just for the pleasure of having it but because you want to do something with it. Perhaps you want to retire early to a houseboat in Florida. Perhaps you want the money for a downpayment on your first house, or to build a fund that will help put your youngsters through college. Or perhaps you want to save enough money to start your own business. In any case, investing is only a means to an end, a way to financially enable you to reach certain personal objectives.

Although the words saving and investing are often used interchangeably, there is a distinction between the two. In this book, the word *investing* is used to indicate the process of putting money into specific assets, such as mutual funds, so you can reach a long-term goal, such as accumulating a college education fund for your toddler. The term *saving,* on the other hand, is used to indicate the process of accumulating enough liquid assets, in the form of a bank savings account or a money market account, so you can weather a temporary emergency, such as the loss of your job or illness in the family.

In the chapters that follow, we'll discuss appropriate investment philosophies for the objectives that many of us share, such as a fund for our children's college education or a nest egg for retirement. None of these philosophies are get-rich-quick schemes. Rather, they represent a commonsense, down-to-earth approach to investing without a lot of bells and whistles. You won't find mention of the latest exotic products touted by Wall Street, or recommendations to use some of the more adventurous (and dangerous) trading techniques.

Instead, you'll find discussions of the basic, tried-and-true avenues that people have used to accumulate assets over the years. You'll learn why it is important to assemble a diversified portfolio of both stocks and bonds (or stock mutual funds and bond mutual funds), why it's important to follow a systematic investment program (and how to do it), and how to cope with the devastating impact that inflation and income taxes can have on the value of your investments over time. You'll also learn how to fashion an investment program that will help minimize some of the most common risks that individual investors face. Most important, you'll learn that there is nothing mysterious about investing as long as you follow a few commonsense rules.

SOME COMMONSENSE RULES OF INVESTING

• *Don't spend more than you make.* This is called going into debt. If you find that you can't keep pace with your credit card bills and installment loans, you won't have anything left to invest. The result is deficit spending, regardless of whether you're an individual or a government. The only difference is that Uncle Sam can print more money to finance the national debt, whereas your individual debt payments can soar only so high before your creditors call a halt.

• *Don't even spend all you make.* If your outgo equals your income, you also don't have anything left to invest. And the whole idea behind investing is to make do with a little less today so that you can grow that forgone income into something big tomorrow (or, more likely, 10 or 20 years from tomorrow).

• *Invest to the limit in tax-favored savings plans.* Individual Retirement Accounts (IRAs) and 401(k) plans sponsored by many employers not only can reduce your current income tax bills, but the earnings they generate can accumulate tax-free—an enormous advantage—until you start to withdraw your money years from now. Furthermore, many employers match some or all of your contributions to 401(k) plans, providing you with an instant positive return on your money.

• *Reinvest all your dividends and interest income.* As long as you don't need that money to live on, investing this extra cash will allow you to harness the enormous power of *compounding*—the process of having your investment earnings produce even more earnings. Over time, the results of compounding can be substantial. According to Ibbotson Associates, a Chicago investment research firm, a $1.00 investment in stocks grew to $12.11 over the 23-year period 1969 through 1992 if dividends were reinvested, for a compound annual total return of 11.5 percent. If the dividends were not reinvested, that same dollar grew to $4.74, or an annual return of only 7 percent.

The results of compounding were even more dramatic with an investment in long-term government bonds over the same period. A $1.00 investment grew to $7.68 if dividends were reinvested, for a compound annual total return of 9.3 percent. But if dividends were not reinvested, that same dollar grew to only $1.02, an annual return of 0.1 percent.

• *Use an automatic investment program.* Try to set aside money on a regular basis, no matter how modest the amounts. Over time, the growth in these investments can be impressive. Invest in savings, profit-sharing, or 401(k) plans at work, for example. Sign up for payroll withholding to purchase U.S. savings bonds, or enroll in an automatic investment program with a mutual fund, which will take out a preset amount from your bank account each month or each quarter. The virtue of all these plans is that the money disappears before you ever see it—or spend it.

• *Set realistic goals.* The 1980s were a terrific time for investing. Even money put into ultrasafe Treasury bills easily outpaced inflation, while money invested in stocks soared far above historic norms. But now we're well into the 1990s, and investment patterns have returned to their more normal (but less exciting) levels. Don't expect to match the performance of the previous decade by investing in something totally unsuitable. It's far better to scale back your expectations to an attainable level. The numbers tell the story: Since 1929, according to Ibbotson, small-company stocks have returned 16.1 percent annually, large-company stocks 11.8 percent, corporate bonds 4.8 percent, and Treasury bills about 4.2 percent.

• *Don't invest in anything you don't understand.* Even sophisticated people can succumb to sophisticated sales pitches, especially ones that promise spectacular results. If you can't explain the pros and cons of an investment to yourself, or to your spouse or a friend, then you probably don't understand what makes it tick—and what conditions may bring everything to a grinding halt. Don't be embarrassed if you're bewildered by a particular investment's promotional literature; it may be deliberately designed to obscure, rather than clarify, how the deal actually works. Chances are, if you really understood it, you'd say no in a minute.

A case in point is limited partnerships in such areas as real estate and oil and gas drilling, which were sold to millions of ordinary investors years ago. When these industries collapsed, so did the value of the partnerships. These days, anyone lucky enough to find someone to buy out their interest in these investments has to settle for far less than 100 cents on the dollar.

• *Don't invest in something that sounds too good to be true (it probably is).* You know the old maxim: There's no free lunch. Well, it's never more true than in the world of investing. Take the case of junk bonds, which pay much higher rates than bonds issued by blue-chip corporate borrowers. The only problem is that the quality of junk bonds is very low, sometimes so low that the bonds are not even given a rating by the major credit-rating agencies. Now, it's possible that junk bonds are quite appropriate for your portfolio. But the price for their very attractive return is the possibility that the borrower will go under and you'll be left holding a worthless piece of paper.

The Risk of Being Too Conservative

Many investors, particularly those who recall the Great Depression, spurn any investment in which they risk the loss of their principal (the money they initially invest). They limit themselves to what they consider stable, "safe" investments, such as federally insured bank savings accounts or certificates of deposit. These are known as "cash equivalent" investments because they can readily be turned into cash. Many people feel these are the most prudent of investments, because there is no risk that the interest rate they receive will fluctuate and no risk they will lose the money they invest, even if the bank fails. There's only one problem with this approach: These investors don't make much money, especially once the impact of inflation and taxes is factored in.

Historically, the "real" rate of return on those investments has been near zero, although there have been a few periods—such as the 1980s—when such investments provided an effective hedge against inflation. A $1.00 investment in Treasury bills at the end of 1969 would have grown to $5.09 by the end of 1992, or a compound annual rate of return of 7.3 percent compared to an inflation rate of 5.9 percent for the period. That meant the real return was less than 1.5 percent. Although hardly impressive, this return nonetheless represents a positive return on your money and points up why there's always a role for cash equivalent investments in your portfolio.

But if you want your portfolio to provide you with significant future growth, make sure that these "safe" investments don't make up the major portion of your holdings. After adjusting for taxes and inflation, there's only one way to go if you want an investment that provides significant real growth over time: stocks.

Consider the implications of Chart 1.1. The first set of bars to the far

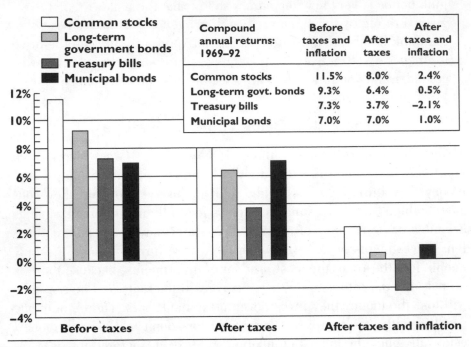

Chart 1.1 Effects of Inflation and Taxes

☐ **Common stocks**
▨ **Long-term government bonds**
▨ **Treasury bills**
■ **Municipal bonds**

Compound annual returns: 1969–92	Before taxes and inflation	After taxes	After taxes and inflation
Common stocks	11.5%	8.0%	2.4%
Long-term govt. bonds	9.3%	6.4%	0.5%
Treasury bills	7.3%	3.7%	–2.1%
Municipal bonds	7.0%	7.0%	1.0%

Before taxes   After taxes   After taxes and inflation

Source: Ibbotson Associates

left shows the *nominal,* or stated, returns before inflation and taxes for four different types of investments over the last 23 years. The compound annual return for stocks was 11.5 percent, for long-term government bonds 9.3 percent, for Treasury bills 7.3 percent, and for municipal bonds 7.0 percent.

The next set of bars in the middle shows what investors were left with after paying federal income taxes on their holdings. Common stocks returned 8.0 percent, long-term government bonds returned 6.4 percent, Treasury bills returned 3.7 percent, and municipal bonds still returned 7.0 percent (because they are not subject to federal taxes).

The final set of bars to the far right illustrates the real return of investors after both federal taxes and inflation were taken into account. After subtracting for both these items, common stocks still came out on top. They had a real return of 2.4 percent, compared to a return of 0.5

percent for long-term government bonds, minus 2.1 percent for Treasury bills, and 1.0 percent for municipal bonds.

The Risk of Being Too Adventurous

So, now you may be convinced that over the long term, stocks far outperform bonds and other fixed-income investments in terms of real growth. The trouble comes in if, like many people, you don't have a 23-year horizon but think you may need to sell some or all of your holdings before that. Depending upon precisely when you sell, you may be clobbered by the enormous price swings that are characteristic of stock market behavior. If, for example, you had panicked and sold on "Black Monday" in October 1987, you would have suffered an overnight loss of more than 20 percent in the value of your portfolio.

This points up the risk of putting all your investible funds into the stock market. In the real world, where long-term usually means having a shorter time frame than 20 years (at least for part of your portfolio), you need to have some other investments, such as bonds and cash-type securities, to cushion the volatility of stocks.

The Risk of Market Timing

How many times have you heard the lament "I'm afraid to invest right now, the stock market is too high." It's scary to contemplate putting your hard-earned money into the stock market when it's climbing to record highs. You wonder if those peaks are about to be transformed into breathtaking drops. But predicting market turns is a futile exercise. What's more, research indicates that even if you had the bad luck to buy at market peaks instead of at market troughs, the final value of your portfolio—as long as you didn't panic and sell during the downturns—would be at roughly the same level as it would have been had you been more adept at timing your purchases.

T. Rowe Price, a big mutual fund family, calculated the hypothetical performance of someone who managed to buy on the worst possible day of each of 20 years between 1974 and 1993. The study assumed this hapless investor invested $2,000 in the Standard & Poor's 500-

composite stock price index of large and medium stocks on the day the
market peaked during each year of those two decades, for a total investment of $40,000. At the end of the period, the value of the portfolio
would have grown to more than $186,000, representing a profit of more
than $146,000 (see Table 1.1). To be sure, there were plenty of rocky
periods, especially during the early years (which coincided with the
1974–75 bear market) when this hypothetical investor lost money. But
by the third year things had turned around, and by the sixth year the
investment had really started to pay off.

A big part of the problem with market timing is that it's almost
impossible to be consistently right. However, many money managers

Table 1.1 S&P 500 TOTAL RETURN
Annual $2,000 Investment at Market High

Date	Cumulative Investment	Value at Year End	Cumulative Profit & Loss
01/03/74	$ 2,000	$ 1,441	$ ($559)
07/15/75	4,000	3,903	(97)
09/21/76	6,000	6,865	865
01/03/77	8,000	8,236	236
09/12/78	10,000	10,617	617
10/05/79	12,000	14,550	2,550
11/28/80	14,000	21,225	7,225
01/06/81	16,000	22,059	6,059
11/09/82	18,000	28,793	10,793
11/10/83	20,000	37,191	17,191
11/16/84	22,000	41,490	19,490
12/16/85	24,000	56,631	32,631
12/12/86	26,000	69,097	43,097
08/25/87	28,000	74,166	46,166
10/21/88	30,000	88,377	58,377
10/09/89	32,000	118,275	86,275
07/16/90	34,000	116,409	82,409
12/31/91	36,000	153,731	117,731
12/31/92	38,000	174,704	136,704
12/28/93	40,000	186,208	146,208

Source: Performance Department, T. Rowe Price Associates

have made headlines by accurately predicting a major market turn (though they usually fail to repeat the feat again).

In one study, the investment management and research firm of Sanford C. Bernstein & Co. illustrated what would have happened if you tried to time the market between 1980 and 1992. During that period, the S&P 500 compounded at a rate of 16.0 percent a year, while Treasury bills grew by 8.1 percent (see Chart 1.2).

Chart 1.2 Difficulties of Market Timing: 1980-92

Fully Invested Returns (1980–92)	
S&P 500	16.0%
T-Bills	8.1%

Market Timing Results	
Accuracy	Return
100%	27.9%
63	16.0
50	12.0

Source: Sanford C. Bernstein & Co., Inc.

If you had a crystal ball, and the foresight to switch out of stocks (and into cash and bonds) right before every bear market and into stocks (and out of bills) right before every bull market, you would have earned an impressive return of 27.9 percent. If your switching tactics were right about two-thirds of the time (a pretty unbelievable record), you would have had a return of 16.0 percent, just about equal to what a buy-and-hold philosophy would have provided. If you were just an average forecaster and were right only half the time, you would have had a return of only 12.06 percent, significantly less than the buy-and-hold approach.

Research has shown that to profit from the stock market you have to be *already invested* in the market so you can make the most of those intense—but very brief—bursts of price increases when they do occur. The Bernstein firm found that if you miscalculated and were out of the market for the 10 best trading days of the period, your return would

Chart 1.3 Why Market Timing Doesn't Work:
Annualized Returns for the S&P 500

1980–92	
3,262 trading days	16.0%
Minus 10 best days	12.2
Minus 20 best days	9.7
Minus 30 best days	7.5
Minus 40 best days	5.4

Source: Sanford C. Bernstein & Co., Inc.

have dropped to 12.2 percent (see Chart 1.3). And if you missed the 40 best trading days (which was tantamount to being out of the market a mere 1 percent or so of the time), your return would have plummeted to 5.4 percent, and you would have been better off in Treasury bills. That's a powerful argument in favor of hanging on to stocks for the long term.

One way to smooth out the stock market's inescapable peaks and valleys is to use a technique called *dollar-cost averaging*. This involves investing a set amount of money in stocks or stock funds at regular periods, regardless of what the market is doing. Say, for example, you decide to invest $100 a month in a stock that costs $10 a share. When the market is high and the stock is selling for $12.50 a share, you can purchase only 8 shares. But when the market declines and the stock is selling for $9 a share, you can purchase 11.11 shares. In effect, dollar-cost averaging not only helps to lower the average cost of acquiring a security over time but also helps to take some of the emotion out of investing.

The Importance of Diversification

Whatever investment course you decide to pursue, be careful about going overboard on one type of investment or another. One of the secrets to successful investing is to maintain a mix of stocks, bonds, and money market securities. By diversifying your portfolio in this way, you can not only earn significantly higher returns over time than by sticking with the most conservative of investments, but you can also reduce your exposure to the risks of holding the most aggressive investments.

Not only do you want to diversify your holdings among different asset categories, but you also want to diversify your holdings within each asset group. Take stocks. You wouldn't want to own the shares of only one company (even if it's the company you work for). Rather, the best approach is to spread your holdings among a number of different companies (preferably in different industries), so that when one company or industry is in a slump, the price decline of that stock is offset by the healthy performance of your other holdings.

Similarly, the wisest course with bonds is to spread your holdings among corporate, government, and (if you're in the 28 percent bracket or higher) municipal securities and to hold a mix of maturities that run the gamut from short-term to intermediate-term and long-term issues. Even with cash investments, such as savings accounts, it's best to divide your money among several different financial institutions—particularly if you are close to the federal deposit insurance limit—so that you are not vulnerable if the institutions should suffer financial reversal.

Think International

With the globalization of the world's economies, it's also a wise idea to diversify beyond the borders of the United States. The reason is that the economies and financial markets of other countries, and other regions of the world, do not necessarily move in tandem with those of the United States. Sometimes, when our markets are up, foreign markets are up even more; sometimes they're up when we're down; and sometimes (as in the early 1990s) they're down while we're up. By deploying at least some of your assets overseas (typically by purchasing international stock funds and bond funds), you can insulate your portfolio from the declines it would otherwise experience if it were invested only in domestic securities.

For example, Bernstein & Co. found that if you had maintained a portfolio of 80 percent domestic stocks and 20 percent foreign stocks for the period 1970 through 1993, you would never have lost as much in a single year and would have earned significantly more than with a portfolio made up of domestic stocks alone. If you had kept 50 percent of the portfolio in bonds, you would have reduced your growth rate somewhat but nonetheless kept it above that of an all-bond portfolio (see Chart 1.4).

Chart 1.4 How Diversification Can Boost Your Portfolio Returns

Initial Investment: $10,000
Total Growth: 1970–93

	100% Bonds (Intermediate)	40% U.S. Stocks/ 10% Foreign Stocks/ 50% Bonds	80% U.S. Stocks/ 20% Foreign Stocks	100% U.S. Stocks
	$91,000	$125,000	$151,000	$133,000
1970-93				
	1982	1985	1985	1975
Best Calendar Year	29.1%	30.4%	40.4%	37.2%
Compound Annual Return	9.7%	11.1%	12.0%	11.4%
Worst Calendar Year	1.4%	(9.4%)	(24.5%)	(26.5%)

Source: Sanford C. Bernstein & Co., Inc.

SHOULD YOU HIRE A FINANCIAL PLANNER?

Most people don't need a financial planner. You can usually do very well on your own. It does take some time and energy to master the basics, but the dos and don'ts of successful investing are quite simple and haven't changed much over the years, even though there are many more financial products around than there used to be.

And that may explain why more investors are using financial planners. Because so many investing options are available these days, and because it takes time to understand the pros and cons of those options as well as the mechanics of finally purchasing whatever you decide on, the idea of having someone handle everything for you is very tempting.

Ideally, a financial planner should serve as a one-stop financial super-market, where you can first visit the diagnostic aisle to have the current state of your finances examined and analyzed, then load up your cart with the cures—a mutual fund here, a money market fund there, per-haps an estate tax plan at the end.

The problem is that while there are some crackerjack planners around, they are vastly outnumbered by less qualified ones. More often than not, planners are simply insurance agents or stockbrokers who have added this catchy title to their names. There is very little regula-tion in this area, although there are some organizations that offer courses and award certificates in financial planning. But just because some people have completed one of these courses doesn't mean they provide good advice. Financial planning is often nothing more than an expensive and glorified form of hand-holding. But by reading books like this one, by following the developments of investments you own in the financial press, and by monitoring the ups (and inevitable downs) of your investments, you can do an amazingly good job on your own. And you don't need an elaborate plan or a lot of fancy printouts.

If you're just beginning an investment program, chances are that you don't have enough money to interest a really competent planner anyway. The word *competent* is key here. There's no shortage of people or finan-cial services companies that will be glad to sell you a computer-gener-ated plan for a fee of $150 or so. But these plans often aren't worth the paper they're printed on.

Consider the following: A few years ago, a middle-aged investor responded to a well-known mutual fund company's request to complete a financial planning questionnaire. The investor dutifully enumerated all the holdings in the family's portfolio, which were weighted toward stocks but included a substantial holding of bonds. After a few weeks, the company's advice arrived: Put all future investments into a money market fund.

Now this advice was truly silly. The investor, who was trying to accu-mulate a retirement nest egg and college education funds for two chil-dren, didn't need any investment income to live on and was expecting to spend at least 20 more years in the workforce. Additional growth-oriented investments, such as more stocks or stock mutual funds, would have been far more appropriate than a money market fund, which is simply a temporary parking place for money awaiting investment.

Furthermore, such computer-generated plans rarely ferret out the information that makes your financial situation unique. Perhaps you have a disabled child and need to establish a fund to pay for his or her lifelong care. Perhaps you are single but responsible for looking after an ailing parent. You may be self-employed and have a difficult time forecasting your income, which can be erratic. The truth is there are very few people whose financial situation is truly "average," and trying to force them into a few predetermined scenarios isn't at all helpful.

Looking for a Planner

Even if you have substantial assets, this doesn't mean it will be easy for you to find a knowledgeable financial planner, although you will probably find many people interested in getting your business. Locating a good planner is akin to finding any other good professional, such as a lawyer, accountant, or doctor. Although you can rely on word-of-mouth referrals and recommendations from friends or colleagues in similar circumstances, it's very difficult for a layperson to evaluate the competence of specialized professionals.

At the very least, try to find someone with a solid track record. The planner should have more than just a couple of years of experience and should be more than willing to give you the names of a few satisfied clients whom you can call. Another possibility is to tap an accountant or family lawyer for planning advice or for a referral to a planner he or she has worked with.

Planner Fees

Just how planners are compensated has sparked a lot of controversy. There are several patterns: Some are paid only by fees; others are compensated only by commissions on the products they sell you; still others are paid by a combination of fees (or salary, in the case of bank planners) and commissions.

Theoretically, fee-only planners make sense because they don't profit by suggesting high-commission products that may not be appropriate for you, and they are usually paid by the hour or the job. But just because you aren't paying commissions doesn't guarantee that you're receiving good advice. On the other hand, planners who are compensated entirely by commissions on the products they sell you (such as life insurance policies or mutual funds) have a potential conflict of interest, since the products that are best for their financial health may not be the best for yours. That same potential problem exists with planners who are compensated by a combination of fees and commissions. Nevertheless, there are some fine planners who are compensated in full or in part by commissions.

Whatever type of compensation arrangement you decide upon, be aware that advice from a financial planner costs money and that you are going to pay in one way or another. It's crucial that the planner disclose up front, before being hired, how he or she will be compensated, so there will be no future misunderstandings.

2

INVESTING THROUGH WORK

A Painless Approach

SAVING 10 percent of your annual salary may seem impossibly ambitious. But most companies make it easy to achieve this goal—or even double it—by sponsoring a variety of savings plans that have additional sweeteners. Investing in these plans is relatively painless, because the money you contribute is automatically deducted from your paycheck each pay period. Once you've made the initial decision to participate, you no longer have to make a decision each time you get your paycheck about whether and how much to invest.

This automatic approach is especially appealing to people who have trouble disciplining themselves to save. The reason: What you don't see when you cash your paycheck, you tend not to miss—and not to spend. You quickly become accustomed to living on what's left over after these regular contributions are deducted from your pay. (There are ways, discussed later in this chapter, that allow you to dip into your savings in an emergency.)

Furthermore, many companies help you fatten your nest egg by "matching" a specified percentage of your contributions, up to a certain level. For example, a company might chip in 50 cents for each dollar you contribute to a savings plan until your contributions reach 6 percent of your pay. That can provide an instant return of as much as 50 percent on your contribution. As a further sweetener to encourage you to save for retirement, the federal government allows the investment earnings in these company-sponsored savings plans to accrue on a tax-deferred basis during your working years. You generally don't have to pay taxes on the investment growth within these plans until you withdraw your money.

The company-sponsored savings plan with which most workers are familiar is the *401(k) plan.* A similar, but not identical, savings arrangement, called a *403(b) plan,* is available to employees of certain tax-exempt organizations such as hospitals and to employees of public and private schools. Because of the tax advantages to both workers and their employers, these plans have now eclipsed traditional profit-sharing plans, which were their precursors.

All these company-sponsored savings plans are known as *defined-contribution plans.* With such plans, your employer promises to put away a specific amount—for example, 10 percent of your pay—every year. You are not guaranteed a specific level of benefits when you retire; how much you receive at that time depends upon how your investments have fared. The responsibility rests with you, the employee, to invest those sums wisely, within the choices provided by your employer's plan.

With *defined-benefit plans,* by contrast, your employer promises that you will receive a specified benefit—typically in the form of a monthly pension check—after you retire. Here, it is the responsibility of the company sponsoring the pension plan to invest the money wisely. You, the employee, should get your promised benefit regardless of how much the company has set aside on your behalf or how the pension plan investments have fared.

TYPES OF EMPLOYER-SPONSORED SAVINGS PLANS

There are several types of employer-sponsored savings plans, some more prevalent than others. These include profit-sharing plans, thrift or savings plans, 401(k) and 403(b) plans, and stock bonus and stock option arrangements.

Profit-Sharing Plans

Profit-sharing plans, which have been in existence for more than a century, were designed to give employees a chance to share in their companies' success by sharing in their profits. Over the years, however, the restrictions on these plans have been relaxed to the point where companies no longer need to have profits to establish such arrangements. Furthermore, companies can vary their contributions to such plans year by year. If, for example, business is good one year, a company might decide to pump in the maximum amount permissible; if business declines the following year, the company might decide to contribute nothing at all.

There are two basic types of profit-sharing plans: cash plans and deferred plans (which can be 401(k) plans). With a *cash plan,* a company calculates its profits, decides what percentage of those profits it will distribute to employees, and then pays out those contributions directly to workers in the form of cash, checks, or company stock. These contributions are considered taxable income, and you, the employee, must pay tax on them when they are received.

With a *deferred plan,* company contributions are not paid out each year but rather are "deferred" to individual accounts set up for each employee within a trust fund. These contributions, plus any accrued investment earnings, are not subject to income tax at the time they are paid into your individual account. But they are subject to tax when they are distributed, typically when you leave the company because of retirement, death, disability, or termination of employment.

If your company has a "pure" profit-sharing plan (either the cash or deferred variety), you, the employee, need do nothing at all to benefit from it. You are not required to make any contributions. You simply sit back and reap the rewards of any contributions that your company makes to your individual account. These contributions are allocated to workers' accounts using a formula that is based on each person's annual compensation.

A profitable and paternalistic company might consider making very generous contributions, but most companies today limit their largesse to what they can deduct on their federal tax returns. That limit is no more than 15 percent of the total compensation they pay to all employees covered by a profit-sharing plan. Total contributions on behalf of any one worker to all such company-sponsored plans cannot exceed $30,000 or 25 percent of the person's annual compensation, whichever is less.

Some profit-sharing plans may also permit employees to make voluntary contributions to such plans (these voluntary contributions are taken into account when determining the contribution limits discussed above). If your employer is already putting money into your account, should you be interested in contributing on top of that? Absolutely.

First, it might be the only automatic savings vehicle available to you at your company, particularly if you work for a small employer. And participating in such a forced savings program may be the only way you can save when faced with spending temptations. Second, there is a tax advantage. All the money that you contribute to your account (along with your employer's contributions) accumulates on a tax-deferred basis, along with any investment earnings, until you withdraw it.

Thrift or Savings Plans

In contrast to profit-sharing plans, which are funded by employers, thrift or savings plans are essentially funded by employees. The money that workers contribute to such plans usually comes from after-tax dollars.

If you choose to participate in a thrift or savings plan, you make periodic contributions to the plan through a payroll deduction arrangement. Typically, these contributions are matched (completely or in part) by the company, although employers are not required to contribute a penny. Both employee and employer contributions are placed in a special trust fund and the money is invested. The investment earnings accumulate on a tax-deferred basis in your individual account until you withdraw the funds, usually at retirement or because of death, disability, or termination of employment. When the money is withdrawn, the investment earnings are taxed as ordinary income, but presumably you will then be a retiree and thus in a lower tax bracket.

The major advantage of a thrift or savings plan is the tax treatment of investment earnings within the account. Faithful savers who regularly contribute to these plans over the years will see their individual accounts swell to a much larger amount than they probably would have been able to accumulate by making similar investments outside such plans. And if your company matches even part of your contributions, the return on your money is further enhanced.

401(k) Plans

In general, 401(k) plans allow you to postpone receiving a portion of your current compensation that would otherwise be paid in cash and instead allow you to contribute the money to a special retirement account. Since federal and most state income taxes are due only on the amount of pay you receive after contributing to the plan, your contributions are made on a pretax rather than after-tax basis. (Your Social Security payroll taxes are not reduced, however.) Most companies match some portion of their employees' contributions to these plans, and earnings on both your and your employer's contributions accumulate within the account on a tax-deferred basis until you withdraw the money.

These arrangements (named for the section added to the Internal Revenue Code in 1978 that sanctioned their use) are extremely popular. According to the Employee Benefit Research Institute, the number of workers participating in 401(k) plans more than doubled between 1987 and 1991, and reached 17.34 million at the end of that period.

There are several reasons for the growth of these plans:

• Contributions can reduce the amount of income taxes you would otherwise pay. Under these plans, your contribution is not treated as current income, but rather as a reduction in salary. Since your salary is lower, your federal and most state and local taxes are lower, too.

• Roughly four out of five employers match employee contributions to some extent. This means that for every dollar you contribute, your company will kick in a specified amount on your behalf. The most common approach is for a company to match up to 6 percent of your pay, at a rate of 50 cents on each dollar you contribute. This is equivalent to getting an instant 50 percent return on your money, even before you consider any investment earnings within the plan.

• The investment earnings within the plan on both the employee and the employer contributions accumulate on a tax-deferred basis until the money is withdrawn. In effect, you are postponing—sometimes for decades—the day of reckoning with the Internal Revenue Service (IRS) and betting that your tax rate as a retiree will be lower than your tax rate as an active employee.

• Because contributions to the plan are fully and immediately vested, you do not forfeit the money you have contributed (and the investment earnings on it) if you leave your job after a few years. Upon termination of employment, you can keep the money in the plan and roll over the accumulated contributions and earnings of your account into a special Individual Retirement Account (IRA). If you get a new job (and if your new employer permits it), you can roll over the proceeds into your new employer's 401(k) plan. Or, you can keep your money in your former plan. All these factors make these plans ideal for mobile workers who change jobs frequently or for parents who temporarily leave the workforce to care for young children.

Because of such advantages, the popularity of 401(k) plans has been steadily increasing. If you have such a plan and can afford it, try to contribute to the fullest extent permissible. Under federal law, the maximum amount that you can contribute is linked to the consumer price index and is adjusted annually. For 1994 the maximum employee contribution is $9,240.

To illustrate just how beneficial participating in a 401(k) plan can be, let's take the case of Ann, a 40-year-old single woman earning an annual salary of $50,000. Assuming Ann is in the 28 percent federal bracket and 3 percent state bracket, she would have to pay $9,801 in federal tax, $1,503 in state tax, and $3,825 in Social Security (FICA) tax on her income. (See Table 2.1.)

Ann decides to contribute 6 percent of her salary to a 401(k) plan. This means that instead of her W-2 Form showing $50,000 of gross income at the end of the year, it would show only $47,000 ($50,000 minus her $3,000 contribution). Her FICA tax would remain unchanged, but her federal tax would fall to $8,961 and her state tax would drop to $1,410, a total tax reduction of $933.

If Ann's employer matches her contributions by 50 cents on the dollar, the total contributions to her 401(k) account for the year would be $4,500 (Ann's contribution of $3,000 plus the $1,500 matching contribution from her employer). If we assume that the same pattern of employee/employer contributions continues every year until she retires at age 65, and that she receives annual salary increases of 4 percent and achieves an annual investment return of 6 percent, Ann would accumulate $411,799 in her 401(k) plan account by retirement.

Table 2.1 Breakdown of Ann's Gross Income in Year 1

With 401(k) Contributions			Without 401(k) Contributions*		
Gross Salary	$50,000.00		Gross Salary		$50,000.00
401(k) Contribution (6 percent)	3,000.00		FICA Tax	3,825.00	
			Federal Tax	9,800.50	
Taxable Income		47,000.00	State & Local Tax	1,502.70	
FICA Tax	3,825.00		Total Taxes		15,128.20
Federal Tax	8,960.50		Employee Savings		3,000.00
State & Local Tax	1,410.00				
Total Taxes		14,195.50	Net Spendable Income		$31,871.80
Net Spendable Income		$32,804.50			

*But saving $3,000 in after-tax money.

Source: William M. Mercer, Inc.

If, by contrast, Ann tried to save 6 percent of her salary outside the 401(k) plan, the investment earnings on her savings would be taxable each year, and she would lose the advantage of her company's matching contribution. Assuming that Ann had the same pattern of annual salary increases and investment returns as she did within the 401(k) plan, she would accumulate only $215,915 by age 65. (See Charts 2.1A and 2.1B.)

THRIFT OR 401(K) PLANS—WHICH ARE BETTER?

A major difference between thrift or savings plans and 401(k) plans is the type of money that you as an employee contribute. The basic issue is whether the contribution comes from pretax or after-tax dollars.

With a thrift or savings plan, which is essentially employee-funded, you are usually contributing after-tax dollars—the money left after you have paid federal and state taxes on your salary. With a 401(k) plan, in which employee contributions are often matched in part by employers, you are instead contributing pretax dollars—your gross salary before any income taxes have been withheld (although some plans allow you to contribute after-tax dollars as well). This means you can plow more of your current earnings into retirement investments and be left with more spendable income than if you had put the same amount into a thrift or savings plan.

So, given a choice, it is usually more advantageous to participate in a 401(k) plan than in a thrift or savings plan, especially if you expect to leave your money in the plan for a long time. However, your company may not offer a 401(k) plan, or you may need to draw on your contributions within a few years after making them. If that is the case, and the choice is between doing nothing at all or participating in a thrift or savings plan, try to participate in whatever plan is offered to the maximum extent allowed, particularly if your company matches contributions.

If your company offers *both* a 401(k) plan and a thrift or savings plan, try to contribute to both if you can afford to forgo the extra income.

Chart 2.1A Comparison of 401(k) Plan to 6% After-Tax Savings

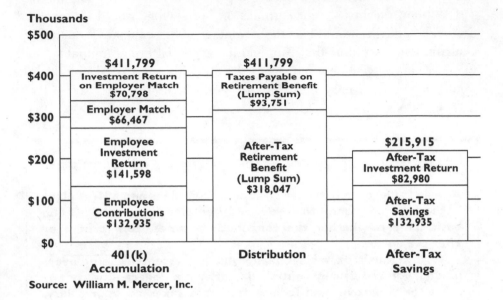

Thousands

$411,799 (401(k) Accumulation)
- Investment Return on Employer Match $70,798
- Employer Match $66,467
- Employee Investment Return $141,598
- Employee Contributions $132,935

$411,799 (Distribution)
- Taxes Payable on Retirement Benefit (Lump Sum) $93,751
- After-Tax Retirement Benefit (Lump Sum) $318,047

$215,915 (After-Tax Savings)
- After-Tax Investment Return $82,980
- After-Tax Savings $132,935

401(k) Accumulation   **Distribution**   **After-Tax Savings**

Source: William M. Mercer, Inc.

Chart 2.1B Comparison of 401(k) Plan to After-Tax Savings with Same Net Spendable Income

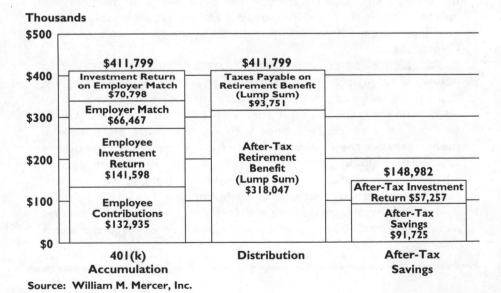

Thousands

$411,799 (401(k) Accumulation)
- Investment Return on Employer Match $70,798
- Employer Match $66,467
- Employee Investment Return $141,598
- Employee Contributions $132,935

$411,799 (Distribution)
- Taxes Payable on Retirement Benefit (Lump Sum) $93,751
- After-Tax Retirement Benefit (Lump Sum) $318,047

$148,982 (After-Tax Savings)
- After-Tax Investment Return $57,257
- After-Tax Savings $91,725

401(k) Accumulation   **Distribution**   **After-Tax Savings**

Source: William M. Mercer, Inc.

403(b) Plans

These unique tax-deferred retirement arrangements, similar to 401(k) plans, are available to employees of certain nonprofit organizations and public and private school systems. With these plans (again named for the section of the IRS code that governs their use), employers contribute a fixed percentage of salary for each participating worker, and workers can make contributions that usually do not exceed 15 percent of their pay. A growing number of 403(b) pension plans for employees of nonprofit organizations now contain a salary reduction arrangement similar to that of 401(k) plans.

The major difference between the two plans is that employees of nonprofit organizations can defer and contribute more to their 403(b) plans than employees of for-profit companies can contribute to their 401(k) plans. Employee contributions (including those to other tax-favored retirement plans) are limited to 20 percent of annual earnings or $9,500 a year, whichever is less. This limit applies until the contribution limit for 401(k) plans, which stood at $9,240 in 1994, reaches $9,500. At that point, the ceiling for employee contributions to 403(b) plans will be indexed, as is the 401(k) contribution limit.

Certain workers may be able to make additional "catch-up" contributions beyond the $9,500 annual limit, if they have worked for their employer for at least 15 years. This special provision is available to employees of educational organizations, hospitals, home health agencies, health and welfare service agencies, and churches or conventions of churches.

Should you contribute to your 403(b) plan? Absolutely. Just as it makes sense for workers in the corporate world to take full advantage of a 401(k) plan and contribute the maximum amount permitted, it also makes sense for their counterparts in the nonprofit world to do so, assuming they can afford it.

Employee Stock Plans

In addition to sponsoring savings plans that allow workers to save for retirement, many employers also sponsor plans that allow workers to acquire an ownership role in the company itself. These plans are designed to encourage employee loyalty and to give workers a financial stake in the performance of their company. The common denominator is that workers can acquire shares of company stock, sometimes at no cost at all and other times at steep discounts to the current market price.

Types

Typical arrangements for acquiring company stock include stock bonus plans, employee stock ownership plans (ESOPs), stock purchase plans, and stock options. Stock bonus plans and ESOPs are "freebies" that are bestowed on employees by their employers and require no action by them to benefit. But stock purchase plans and stock options do require workers to make a conscious investment decision in order to participate in the programs.

    Stock Bonus Plans. A stock bonus plan is a profit-sharing plan in which the benefits distributed to workers are in the form of company stock, rather than cash. The shares of stock are considered ordinary income and thus are subject to regular income tax. Such a reward can be very valuable if your company is doing well and its share price is going up. If your company's stock is in a downturn, you'd probably do better to get cash rather than the stock; however, that decision is made by the company and not by you. In such a case you can only hope that conditions will improve.

    Employee Stock Ownership Plans (ESOPs). A type of stock bonus plan, ESOPs are unique in that they must invest primarily in the stock of the sponsoring company.

    The major advantage of ESOPs rests with the sponsoring companies, which use them as powerful corporate financing tools that can provide a large and immediate cash infusion. The advantage for workers is less clear. Even though employees do not contribute their own funds to participate in an ESOP, this type of plan tends to concentrate workers' investments in the stock of their employer, and the success of the investment depends upon the long-term performance of the company and its stock. If the company and its stock prosper, participation in the ESOP is indeed a boon. But if the company does poorly and uses the

ESOP merely to prop up operations that could not stand alone, the employees probably would have done better by participating in a regular profit-sharing plan that allowed them to diversify their investments outside of company stock.

Once employees reach age 55 and have participated in an ESOP for 10 years, they can move some of their ESOP account holdings into other investments. At that point, workers usually must be allowed to diversify at least 25 percent of their total account; five years later, they must be allowed to diversify at least 50 percent. A similar rule applies to other retirement plans (such as profit-sharing plans) that invest primarily in company stock.

Stock Purchase Plans. These plans allow employees to purchase their company's stock at a discount to the open market price, without paying any brokerage commissions. Although not widespread (surveys indicate anywhere from 8 to 14 percent of large publicly held companies offer such plans), these programs can be an attractive option for employees who choose to participate.

A survey by the consulting firm William M. Mercer, Inc., found that more than half the companies that offer these plans allowed workers to purchase their company's stock at discounts of 15 to 20 percent off the prevailing market price; roughly another quarter of companies surveyed offered discounts of 10 to 15 percent. Some plans require workers to hold the stock for a year before selling; others allow them to sell immediately.

Even if your company's stock simply holds steady before you sell, participating in such a plan makes sense because you receive an instant return on your money, reflecting the difference between the market price and your discounted purchase price.

Take the case of a stock purchase plan with a 15 percent discount. If the company's stock is selling at $100 a share, you can buy it at $85. Assuming the price doesn't change in the meantime, you can later sell at $100; that's equivalent to a return of 17.6 percent on your investment (the return is greater than the 15 percent discount because your starting point for calculating it is your actual investment of $85, rather than the $100 market price). If your company does well and its stock appreciates by 10 percent to $110 a share, you'd be even further ahead financially. These numbers increase dramatically if you hold your stock for the long term—say, until retirement—and if your company and its stock continue to do well over that period.

Another reason to participate in such plans is the ease of the whole transaction. You determine at the start of the year how much of your salary you want to set aside for purchasing your company's stock. The minimum amount you can contribute is generally 1 percent of your total compensation (salary plus bonuses), and the maximum is usually no more than 10 percent. The transaction is then handled automatically, through payroll deduction. Once or twice a month, the amount you've earmarked for purchasing your company's stock is deducted from your gross pay and applied toward the stock purchases.

There are no tax advantages to stock purchase plans. The amount you have set aside for buying your company's securities is tantamount to cash compensation. As such, it is fully taxable in the year you make the purchases.

Once you've decided to participate in a stock purchase plan, that doesn't mean you are irrevocably committed to it should your circumstances—or your company's performance—change. At least once or twice during the year, you are usually permitted to increase or decrease the amount of your salary you set aside for purchases.

Incentive Stock Options (ISOs). Instead of allowing you to purchase company stock now, at a discount from its current market value, incentive stock option plans work the other way: They allow you to purchase the stock *in the future* at today's price. The expectation is that the company's stock price will appreciate over time, so that when you eventually buy the stock you'll be paying a bargain price. The idea is to give the holders of stock options a financial incentive to improve their company's performance.

With a typical incentive stock option plan, a company grants you the right (or option) to purchase a specified number of shares of company stock at a specified price within a specified period. You can exercise the option—that is, buy the shares—immediately, or you can wait until a future time when the price of the shares is higher. Regardless of when you exercise your options, you are allowed to purchase the stock at the option price—typically, the price for which it was selling on the date the option was granted.

Take the case of an executive who is granted the right to purchase 1,000 shares of her company's stock at $15 a share on January 1. A year later, the company's stock has doubled in price to $30 a share, and she exercises her option and purchases 1,000 shares at $15 a share. This means she pays only $15,000 for stock that is now worth $30,000. (If the stock had dropped to $10, she would not be required to exercise her option.)

There is a powerful tax advantage to incentive stock options: you do not have to pay tax on the difference between the stock's purchase price and its actual market value when you exercise the option. In the case of the executive above, for example, she is not required to pay any tax on the $15,000 of paper profit she reaps by exercising her stock option. But if she decides to sell a year later, after the stock has reached $45 a share, she would have to pay capital-gains tax on the difference between the selling price of $45,000 and her original purchase price of $15,000.

Incentive stock options are clearly a good deal. They were originally offered only to top-echelon executives. But recognizing just how powerful a motivator they can be, some companies are offering options to all their employees, from the mailroom to the executive suite. Hewitt Associates, an employee benefits consulting firm, says that while just 5 percent or so of corporations now offer company-wide stock option plans, it expects that number to grow so that by the turn of the century, 25 to 30 percent of companies will be offering company-wide stock options.

MAKING THE RIGHT DECISIONS: INVESTMENT OPTIONS

Once you've decided to participate in an employer-sponsored savings plan, what kinds of securities can you invest in? Even though the federal government is pushing for more investment options, the investment menu you can choose from is up to your plan sponsor—that is, your employer. Most plans offer at least four investment options, typically, stock mutual funds, guaranteed investment contracts (GICs), govern-ment-bond or other fixed-income mutual funds, and shares of your employer's stock.

Choosing the appropriate investment category (or combination of cat-egories) is the key to accumulating an adequate retirement nest egg. Unfortunately, when it comes to their own retirement contributions, people tend to opt for investments such as GICs, which guarantee a fixed interest rate for a set time period. They mistakenly think, because of the interest-rate guarantee, that such investments are safer than investing in the stock market, which can be buffeted by large fluctua-tions. But over the long term, investments in such fixed-income securi-ties have appreciated far less than investments in common stocks.

Up until recently, the vast majority of employees put their 401(k) plan money in GICs. But the popularity of these insurance products has been tarnished by the failures of two large insurance companies that left some employees unable to collect all the money they had invested in GICs issued by those companies. Belatedly, these employee-investors realized that the only thing guaranteed with a GIC is the inter-est rate, not the money they invested, which is backed only by the assets of the insurance company that issued the GIC. In some cases, employers voluntarily made their employees "whole" and reimbursed their 401(k) accounts for any losses; in other cases, the matter of who should bear responsibility for such losses is in litigation.

Some employers have become so skittish about potential problems with GICs that they have renamed these products. They have dropped the word "guaranteed" to dispel the notion of absolute safety and instead have given them names such as *assured interest* or *stable invest-ment* account.

These problems don't mean that GICs are necessarily bad invest-ments. But you should exercise some caution before you automatically stash your 401(k) plan money in one. Check with your plan administra-tor (usually someone in the employee benefits department or controller's office can help) to see if your plan has diversified its GIC holdings among several different insurance companies and if each company has a top rating from a credit rating agency such as Standard & Poor's. If the plan's GICs are concentrated with just a handful of issuers, or if the issuers have shaky credit ratings, consider moving some of your money to a money market fund, a short-term bond fund, or a stock mutual fund.

Be sure not to overweight your 401(k) investments with the stock of your employer. If your company makes its matching contributions in the form of company stock (which is the case in about half of all plans where employer stock is an investment option for employer contributions), it is particularly important for you to diversify your own contributions. In other words, invest your own money in a stock mutual fund

CHANGING THE MIX

Once you've made up your mind to invest all your 401(k) contributions in the stock market, what happens if you later have a change of heart? Perhaps interest rates have risen to record highs, and you want to direct all your new contributions into a fixed-income fund. Or perhaps you want to shift just a portion of your existing stock market investments into a bond fund. Are you irrevocably wedded to an investment decision that you may have made years before? Usually not, although the amount of flexibility you have in shifting your investment strategy differs from company to company.

Hewitt Associates reports that almost half the 401(k) plans it surveyed allow employees to change their investment mix once a quarter for both existing balances and new contributions. Ten percent allow daily changes, another 10 percent allow monthly changes, but almost 20 percent allow changes only twice a year. Depending upon how your plan is structured, changing your investment mix may involve just a telephone call to the plan administrator, or it may require completing a form.

Beware of constant tinkering with your investment mix, however. Remember, this is long-term money you are managing, and short-term fluctuations in the stock and bond markets are inevitable. Switching your investment direction with every zig and zag is bound to lead to disappointing results.

(or a bond fund if you are wedded to the idea of fixed-income investments) rather than your company's stock. That way, if your company's
stock price later plummets, the impact of the downturn will be offset to
some extent by your other holdings.

When you are determining how to invest your 401(k) plan money,
especially if you have a decade or more before reaching retirement age,
take a cue from professional pension plan managers. These investment
professionals, who bear the responsibility of wisely investing billions of
dollars of plan assets to pay for the benefits of future retirees, generally
place about two-thirds of their portfolios in common stocks and the rest
in fixed-income securities. Individual workers tend to do just the opposite—that is, they put about two-thirds of their money into fixed-income
securities and only one-third into common stocks.

HOW TO GET YOUR MONEY IN AN EMERGENCY

There may come a day when you suddenly have a need for all, or part,
of the money you've been putting away in your 401(k) plan. Perhaps
there is a medical emergency in the family, or you've finally found your
dream house and need to come up with the down payment. In any case,
you have two options: Either apply for a "hardship" withdrawal, or, if
the plan permits, take out a loan against your plan balance.

Hardship

The IRS has imposed tough rules in order to qualify for a hardship
withdrawal. First, you must show that you require the money for "immediate and heavy financial" needs and, second, this money cannot be
"reasonably available" from your other financial resources. The following items meet the "immediate and heavy" requirement:
  • Medical expenses for you, your spouse, or dependents
  • Purchase of a principal residence
  • Payment of tuition for post-secondary education for you, your
  spouse, your children, or dependents

• Payments to prevent you from being evicted from your principal residence or to prevent your mortgage from being foreclosed

If you meet one of the above four tests, the IRS also requires you to satisfy a *safe-harbor* test to determine whether or not you can get the funds from someplace else. It allows you to tap your 401(k) plan only if:

• The money you withdraw does not exceed the amount of your need.

• You first empty out all your available funds from other employer-sponsored savings plans.

• You agree not to make any new contributions to your 401(k) plan for a year after you receive the hardship distribution. Any new contributions after that period will be reduced by the amount you contributed in the prior year.

If all these restrictions do not deter you, there are other drawbacks to obtaining a hardship withdrawal. First, unless you are at least age 59½ when you make the withdrawal, you must pay a 10 percent early withdrawal penalty tax on the amount you take out of the plan. Second, you must also pay regular income taxes on the funds you withdraw from your 401(k) plan account.

Loans

Clearly, obtaining a hardship withdrawal from your 401(k) plan carries heavy restrictions and should not be entered into lightly. If you really must have the money, it is usually preferable to obtain a loan from your plan, because you get access to your funds without the hardship restrictions and the 10 percent penalty tax. But the procedure can be complicated, and you cannot borrow unlimited amounts.

Under IRS rules, the maximum amount you can borrow is generally limited to $50,000 or one-half the amount in your 401(k) account balance, whichever is less. You must repay the amount you borrow within five years. If the loan is for a down payment on a principal residence, you have a longer repayment period—10, 15, 20 years or longer, depending on what your particular 401(k) plan allows.

In addition, you must pay a "reasonable" amount of interest on the loan, and must repay it in at least equal quarterly payments over the life of the loan. (Since you are, in effect, paying interest to yourself, the IRS does not allow you to deduct it as well.)

According to Hewitt Associates, about two-thirds of 401(k) plans have loan provisions. Most of these plans allow employees to take out general-purpose loans, and the interest rate is typically pegged to either the prime rate that banks charge their most creditworthy corporate customers, or to the average rate used by local lending institutions.

3

INVESTING WITH UNCLE SAM'S HELP

PERHAPS the company you work for doesn't offer any savings or retirement plans. Perhaps you are self-employed or don't work outside the home at all. There are still ways you can invest for retirement. What's more, as long as you meet certain conditions, the federal government will foot part of the bill and even allow you to claim a tax deduction for your contributions.

There are three main tax-favored types of retirement plans for people who aren't covered by traditional pension plans at work: Individual Retirement Accounts (IRAs), Keogh plans for the self-employed, and Simplified Employee Pension plans (SEPs) for people who are self-employed or employees of small businesses.

It isn't quite as easy to save with these plans as it is with employer-sponsored arrangements, because the amounts you contribute are not automatically deducted from a paycheck. But the additional discipline these plans require is well worth it. Not only are your contributions usually tax-deductible, but, in addition, the earnings on that money accu-

mulate on a tax-deferred basis until you withdraw the funds upon retirement, disability, or death. Although you usually don't get the advantage
of an employer "match" of your contributions (as with a 401(k) plan),
the tax-deferred buildup of earnings within your account enables you to
amass a much larger retirement fund than you could outside such tax-
favored arrangements.

To make the most of these government-sanctioned tax shelters, try to
contribute the maximum amount allowed as early in the year as you can
(in effect, you're dollar-cost averaging, but on an annual, rather than on
a quarterly, basis). That way, your savings will generate more tax-
deferred earnings than if you waited until the deadline to contribute.
Also, if you've been parking that money in a taxable account, such as a
money market fund, the earlier you transfer it into your tax-free retirement account, the more current income taxes you'll save.

If you think you're going to have trouble accumulating one large
lump sum to contribute, consider establishing your retirement account
with a mutual fund family or a brokerage house that offers an automatic
investment program. With such an arrangement, you authorize whatever
financial institution you choose to act as custodian for your retirement
plan—for example, a bank or mutual fund—to debit your bank account
each month for a prearranged amount. That money is then deposited in
the account or mutual fund that you select from among the choices
offered by the custodian.

The advantage of this technique is that once you've decided how
much to set aside each month, the rest is done for you automatically.
You become accustomed to living on a smaller budget, and you're not
continually faced with deciding whether you should pay current
expenses, or use that income to contribute to your retirement fund.

TYPES OF TAX-DEDUCTIBLE RETIREMENT PLANS

Individual Retirement Accounts (IRAs)

These special savings accounts have had a checkered history. Originally created in 1974 as a retirement savings vehicle for people who

did not have a pension plan at work, IRAs were liberalized in 1981 so that all employees—even those covered by company pension plans—were eligible for them. The change meant that virtually all workers could make tax-deductible contributions of up to $2,000 a year to their IRAs. By 1985 a record 16.2 million taxpayers, representing almost 16 percent of all returns filed, claimed IRA deductions.

In 1986 the law changed again. This time it drastically restricted the availability of tax-deductible IRAs. Basically, the new rules still allow people who are not covered by pensions at work to establish tax-deductible IRAs, regardless of how much they earn. But they bar deductible contributions by workers who participate in company retirement plans if their incomes exceed certain thresholds.

Who Can Make Deductible Contributions?

The current state of affairs is this: If you are not an *active participant* (a technical term defined on page 43) in a pension plan at work, you can make a fully tax-deductible contribution to your IRA, whether you earn $15,000 or $150,000 a year. The contribution limit is $2,000 for yourself, or a total of $2,250 if you have a spouse who does not work outside the home or who makes less than $250 a year. The deadline for making these contributions is the due date for filing your tax return (April 15 of the year after the year for which you claim the deduction). Even if you request an extension, you are no longer allowed to make IRA contributions up until the date you actually file your tax return if it is later than April 15.

You probably cannot make a *deductible* contribution to your IRA if you take part in any of the following employer-sponsored plans:
- Pension plan, profit-sharing plan, thrift plan, or stock bonus plan
- 401(k) plan
- Keogh plan
- Simplified Employee Pension plan
- Federal, state, or local government retirement plan
- Tax-sheltered annuities for employees of public schools and other nonprofit organizations such as hospitals
- Certain union plans

DO IRAS HAVE A FUTURE?

As a result of government restrictions, the number of workers claiming deductions has declined steadily, according to the Employee Benefit Research Institute (EBRI). In 1989 (the latest year for which data are available), only an estimated 5.9 million taxpayers, or 5.2 percent of returns, claimed an IRA deduction. Because the income thresholds have not been indexed for inflation, the decline has been sharpest for middle-income workers and two-earner couples. Unless the law is changed, EBRI projects that by 1995, only 43 percent of middle-income workers will be eligible for deductible IRAs, and only 38 percent of two-earner couples will qualify.

The dollar limits for IRA contributions have also remained static for almost three decades, despite continuing inflation. Result: What in 1974 represented a major opportunity for many workers to invest a significant amount of money for their retirement has become an avenue that is open to a dwindling number of workers who can only save a relatively trivial amount for their old age.

If you are covered by a pension plan at work, you may still be able to make a deductible contribution to your IRA if your adjusted gross income (your income from salary and investments, minus adjustments for such items as alimony payments, but before personal exemptions and itemized deductions) does not exceed certain limits. If you are married and file jointly, you can deduct your entire IRA contribution if your adjusted gross income is below $40,000; the deduction is gradually phased out and disappears entirely once your joint income reaches $50,000.

If you are single, you can make a fully deductible contribution if your adjusted gross income is below $25,000; the deduction is gradually phased out at incomes above that level and disappears entirely once your income reaches $35,000.

Here are answers to some common questions about IRAs:

Who Is an Active Participant?

With defined-benefit plans (traditional pension plans that guarantee you a set amount of monthly income in retirement), the IRS considers you to be an *active participant* if the plan's rules say you are covered, even if you decline to participate. Only a small number of conventional pension plans require workers to participate by making their own contributions to the plans, however. With defined-contribution plans (profit-sharing plans, stock bonus plans, and 401(k) plans in which you and/or your employer contributes a set amount each period), you are considered an active participant if any money is contributed to your account during the year. But for purposes of this rule, any investment earnings allocated to your plan do not count. So, you will not be considered an active participant if the only amount that is added to your account during a year consists solely of investment earnings.

What if You File Jointly and Only One Spouse Is an Active Participant in a Company Pension Plan?

You're out of luck as far as the IRA deduction is concerned. The law treats you as if both you and your spouse participated in the company

Table 3.1 Deductible IRA Limits

Adjusted Gross Income		Limit
Single	Married	
$25,000	$40,000	$2,000
26,000	41,000	1,800
27,000	42,000	1,600
28,000	43,000	1,400
29,000	44,000	1,200
30,000	45,000	1,000
31,000	46,000	800
32,000	47,000	600
33,000	48,000	400
34,000	49,000	200
35,000 or more	50,000 or more	0

plan, and if your joint income exceeds the thresholds, you cannot make a deductible contribution. To see if you qualify, consult Table 3.1.

What if You File Separately?

In this case, the spouse who is not covered at work is allowed to claim a tax-deductible IRA contribution, regardless of how much he or she earns. However, the tax rates for married couples filing separately are much higher than for those filing jointly, and the net tax savings may be insignificant or even nonexistent. Before making a choice, be sure to work through the numbers to determine which is the most advantageous route.

Where to Invest Your IRA

Since your IRA is one of the resources you will be counting on to help support you in your later years, you don't want to be cavalier about how you invest your contributions. On the other hand, most people are needlessly cautious in investing these funds.

Too many gravitate toward "safe" investments, such as certificates of deposit offered by banks, savings institutions, and credit unions. Even though your principal (the money you turn over to a bank) is usually guaranteed with such institutions under the federal deposit insurance program, the return you receive on these investments rarely matches the return you could expect to get with stocks, at least over the long haul. Furthermore, the interest rates offered by banking institutions are often not competitive with the rates you could get on other fixed-income products, such as individual bonds, bond mutual funds, or Treasury securities (considered the safest of investments because they are backed by the full faith and credit of the U.S. government).

One reason banking institutions have been so successful in attracting IRA money is because of advertisements that stress how much money will accumulate if you leave your IRA funds there for several decades. The implication is that you'll live like royalty when you retire if you only invest your IRA with your friendly neighborhood bank. A typical ad, for example, might announce that if you contribute $2,000 a year for

20 years to an IRA earning 10 percent, you'd accumulate $143,000 by the end of the period. If you left the money there for 30 years, you'd have $442,000. The problem with such examples is that they don't take into account the impact of inflation on the future purchasing power of your IRA. Interest rates usually parallel inflation rates and leave savers a "real" return of 3 percentage points or so above the inflation rate.

To be realistic, then, the purchasing power of your IRA (after including the impact of inflation over several decades) would only be about $55,000 after 20 years and $98,000 after 30 years. Those sums are nothing to sneeze about, but they're not going to allow you to spend your retirement doing much cruising around the world on the *QE 2*, or indulging yourself in other ways, either.

Diversification is the best way to steer a prudent course between the market risk that accompanies stocks and the inflation risk that comes with CDs and savings accounts. If you maintain a portfolio that's weighted toward stocks but has a healthy portion of fixed-income investments too, you should be reasonably well protected against a downturn in either sector. Typically, when interest rates are high and fixed-income investments offer attractive yields, the stock market languishes. Conversely, stocks usually shine when interest rates are in the basement.

Zero-coupon bonds backed by Treasury securities make a smart investment for your IRA when interest rates are high or look like they're heading south (see Chapter 8). That's because you lock in the stated interest rate for the life of the bond; you don't have to worry about the rate at which you'll be able to reinvest your semiannual interest payments the way you do with conventional bonds.

Unlike conventional bonds that are issued at prices close to their face value and pay you interest every six months, zeros are issued at deep discounts to their face value and pay so-called "phantom" interest. The interest accrues on your behalf, but you do not actually collect it until you redeem the bond at maturity. The drawback, if you own zeros in your regular taxable portfolio, is that you must pay income tax on this phantom interest year after year, even though you don't actually get your hands on the money. If you own zeros within your IRA, however, no taxes need be paid on the interest that is accumulating within the account until you cash in the bonds and start withdrawing the money at retirement.

There's one type of investment you should steer clear of with your IRA: tax-free municipal bonds (including zeros) or tax-free municipal bond funds. The interest generated by these bonds, which are issued by state and local governments, is free from federal income tax and (if you live in the state or locale that issued the bonds) usually exempt from state and local taxes as well.

Municipals, or munis, make a lot of sense if you're investing for your regular portfolio outside your IRA, since you would otherwise have to pay tax on the amount of income the bonds produce. But munis make no sense for an IRA (or Keogh or SEP) because the investment earnings in such an account are tax-deferred anyway. Since municipals usually pay a lower rate of interest than comparable corporate or Treasury securities, reflecting the fact that their interest payments are tax-free, you are needlessly sacrificing yield for a tax advantage you don't need in the first place. A significant number of people, however, still persist in buying municipal bonds or municipal bond funds for their IRAs, despite warnings that these investments are not suitable.

Timing and Switching IRA Investments

Try to contribute to your IRA as early in the year as possible. The difference between making your contributions each January 1 rather than December 31 of the same year can spell thousands of dollars of additional earnings in your account over the decades. Table 3.2 illustrates the advantage of early contributions, assuming you make contributions of $2,000 a year and get an 8 percent return on your investment.

Once you've made an IRA investment, you're not wedded to it for life. You can switch investments as often as you like—without running afoul of the IRS—if you maintain your IRA at an institution, such as a brokerage house, that offers a variety of investment vehicles.

You could decide, for example, to drop your bank CD and buy corporate bonds instead. You could sell your shares of Coca-Cola and buy shares of Exxon instead. Or you could unload all your stockholdings and replace them with bonds. But frequent switching may trigger expensive transaction costs such as early withdrawal penalties and bro-kerage commissions. So keep trading at a minimum, unless you're posi-tive that you'll reap an enormous gain that will make your transaction costs fade by comparison.

If you maintain your IRA with an institution, such as a bank, that does not permit you to switch investments, the IRS allows you to roll over the funds to another institution without penalty once a year. Under this approach, you personally take possession of the money and have 60 days to move it to the new institution.

You can get around this one-year rule by doing a *trustee-to-trustee* transfer. You simply authorize the trustee of the institution that currently holds your IRA funds to transfer the money to the trustee of another institution (the institution receiving your IRA usually provides you with the paperwork to facilitate the switch). Since you never get your hands on the money—it simply moves from one institution to another—it is not considered a rollover. That means it is not subject to the one-year rule, so you can switch investments as frequently as you wish.

Note: This is a different sort of IRA rollover than one involving a lump sum distribution from a company profit-sharing or retirement plan. For example, if you take a new job and receive the accumulated balance in your 401(k) plan, you have 60 days to move it into a special "conduit" or "rollover" IRA. As a result of 1993 legislation, it's impor-

Table 3.2 Advantages of Early IRA Investing

Years of Growth	Contributions Made at Beginning of Year, January 1	Contributions Made at End of Year, December 31	Advantage of Early Contributions
5	$12,572	$11,733	$939
10	31,291	28,973	2,318
15	58,649	54,304	4,344
20	98,946	91,524	7,322
25	157,090	146,212	11,697
30	244,692	226,566	18,125
35	372,204	344,634	27,571
40	559,562	518,113	41,449
45	834,852	773,011	61,841

tant that you avoid taking *personal* possession of this distribution. If you do take possession, the new law specifies that 20 percent of the distribution must be withheld and paid to the IRS. To avoid this, ask your plan sponsor to make a trustee-to-trustee transfer of the distribution. This way, if you later take another job with a company that has a 401(k) plan and the plan allows it, you can roll over this conduit IRA into the 401(k) plan at your new company. Even if you don't roll over your conduit IRA into a plan with a new employer, it's important to keep this IRA separate from your regular IRA to preserve the special tax advantages of the distribution.

Other IRA Investment Options

You can slice your regular $2,000-a-year IRA contribution into as many pieces as you like and open IRA accounts at as many different financial institutions. You'll find, though, that many institutions impose an annual IRA maintenance fee that can range from $10 at mutual funds to as much as $50 for a self-directed IRA (one that allows you to buy and sell individual securities such as stocks and bonds). The smaller the size of your IRA, the more these charges will eat away the earnings within the account.

If your IRA is relatively modest—say, less than $10,000—you're probably best off maintaining IRA accounts at just one or two institutions. Opening an IRA with a discount broker who offers a no-transaction-fee program for trading mutual funds with a no-load mutual fund family (a group of funds that imposes no sales charge) offers the most flexibility at the lowest cost. Typically, all you have to do is make a phone call to the fund to switch your IRA money from one fund to another. And many funds offer automatic investment programs that debit your bank account for a predetermined amount each month.

Getting Your Money Out

With IRAs, freedom from income tax ends once you start to withdraw your money, usually at retirement. At that point, any distributions (money you withdraw) are considered ordinary income. And those distributions—which consist of both the contributions you made, as well as the investment earnings on those contributions—now become subject to regular income tax.

Furthermore, if you take your money out of your IRA in one lump sum, you do not qualify for the same favorable tax treatment that you get with distributions from a company pension plan or a Keogh plan. Income-averaging, which treats a large withdrawal as if it were received in smaller but equal chunks spread over five (or sometimes 10) years, is not available for IRA distributions.

To make certain that workers use their IRAs to save for retirement and not for a new sports car or trip around the world, Congress has imposed a 10 percent penalty tax on early distributions. You must pay this 10 percent penalty on top of the ordinary income tax due on the funds you withdraw, if you take money out of your IRA before you reach age 59½, unless you become totally and permanently disabled.

The only way around this early distribution penalty is to withdraw from your IRA each year a series of periodic payments that are roughly equal to what you would receive if you had bought an annuity with all or part of the money. The annual payments must be based on your life expectancy (or the joint life expectancy of you and your beneficiary). You don't have to actually purchase an annuity from an insurance company to avoid penalty. Nor do you have to withdraw the entire balance from your IRA; you can withdraw just part of it in periodic payments and wait to withdraw the rest until you reach age 59½.

To prevent people from using their IRAs as a way to pass on wealth from generation to generation, free of tax, Congress also imposes a penalty on *late* distributions. The idea is to stop affluent retirees, who don't need the income, from using these accounts as a permanent tax shelter. To prevent you from accumulating a fortune in your IRA during your lifetime and then passing it along to your heirs free of tax after your death, the law requires that you begin taking distributions from your IRA by April 1 of the year following the year in which you reach age 70½. If you don't, the money you should have withdrawn but didn't is subject to a hefty 50 percent penalty.

Do Nondeductible IRAs Make Sense?

Many people wonder if they should make nondeductible (after-tax) contributions to their IRAs. The answer is not clear-cut. The advantage is that the investment earnings within your IRA accumulate on a tax-deferred basis until you eventually withdraw the money. Over the long term, the value of this tax-deferred compounding is enormous.

The accounting firm of Weber, Lipshie & Company compared what would happen to someone who invested $2,000 a year in a nondeductible IRA earning 7 percent annually over 30 years with someone who invested that same amount, at the same return, in a regular taxable investment. At the end of the period, the person who invested in a nondeductible IRA would have a net accumulation (after paying taxes) of $110,033, compared to a net accumulation of only $96,332 for the person who made a regular taxable investment—a difference of almost $14,000 (see Table 3.3).

The only other investment that offers such a grace period from income tax is a tax-deferred annuity, available from insurance companies (see Chapter 10). However, annuities are typically less flexible in terms of investment options and often impose substantial sales charges.

The disadvantages of making nondeductible IRA contributions stem from the extra strings attached to participating in a government-sanctioned retirement plan.

The first drawback is the extra paperwork involved. You must keep track of both types of contributions, so that when it is time to cash out your IRA, you are not taxed twice. You won't have to pay any taxes on your nondeductible contributions, since you were already assessed taxes on that money before you put it into the account, but you will have to pay taxes on any deductible contributions that you made. In addition, you'll have to pay tax on the investment earnings generated by both the deductible and nondeductible contributions you made to your IRA over the years. The result is that the amounts withdrawn will be treated as partly tax-free and partly taxable.

The second disadvantage of nondeductible IRAs is that, if you have been successful in your IRA investments, you may have to pay an additional tax because of your success. The reason is that your IRA with-

Table 3.3 To IRA or Not To IRA! What to Do with
$2,000 in Taxable Earnings

Example:
28% Overall Marginal Tax Bracket
7% Pretax Return

	After-Tax Investment	Nondeductible IRA	Deductible IRA—7%
Earnings	$2,000	$2,000	$2,000
Taxes	560	560	0
Net Investment	$1,440	$1,440	$2,000
Investment Return	7.00%	7%	7%
Taxable	1.96%	0%	0%
Net Return	5.04%	7%	7%
10-Year Accumulation	$18,146	$19,895	$27,633
Tax (28%)	0	1,539*	7,737
Net Accumulation	$18,146	$18,356	$19,896
20-Year Accumulation	$47,817	$59,034	$81,990
Tax (28%)	0	8,466*	22,957
Net Accumulation	$47,817	$50,568	$59,033
30-Year Accumulation	$96,332	$136,024	$188,922
Tax (28%)	0	25,991*	52,898
Net Accumulation	$96,332	$110,033	$136,024

*Tax is only on the investment earnings and not on the nondeductible IRA contributions. For comparison purposes, distributions from the IRAs do not include the possibility of using an annuity payout to save taxes.

Source: Weber, Lipshie & Co.

drawals, along with distributions from any other retirement plans you may have, become so large they trigger what is called an *excess distribution penalty.* The penalty is usually 15 percent of distributions that, in aggregate, exceed $150,000 a year; or 15 percent of a single lump-sum distribution that exceeds $750,000.

These amounts may seem incredibly large, but they are well within reach of someone who has worked for the same company for 25 or 30 years and has been regularly investing in a 401(k) plan or IRA. For this reason, many financial advisers suggest forgoing a nondeductible IRA and instead investing in municipal bonds, which generate tax-free income but have no strings attached when they are sold.

Keogh Plans

Named for the New York congressman who sponsored the original legislation in 1962, Keoghs are one of the best retirement savings vehicles around for self-employed people, or for moonlighting employees who have a line of business outside their regular jobs. With a Keogh plan (sometimes called an H.R. 10 plan) you can invest far more money—generally up to $30,000 a year—than you can with an IRA. You can also claim larger tax deductions, build a larger fund of investment assets, and enjoy greater tax benefits when you finally take the money out at retirement.

When first established, Keogh plans were much more restrictive (and had much lower contribution limits and provided much lower benefits) than corporate retirement plans. But continuing changes in the tax law have greatly liberalized their rules, and Keoghs now operate essentially the same way that corporate plans do.

Despite these advantages, relatively few self-employed people take advantage of Keogh plans, according to the Employee Benefit Research Institute. In 1989 (the latest year for which figures are available), about 827,000 individuals—less than 12.5 percent of all self-employed people—contributed to them. However, the typical amount they contributed was substantial. The average amount deducted for Keogh contributions in 1989 was $7,677, suggesting that people who are most likely to contribute are older or have been self-employed for many years.

Table 3.4 shows what would happen if you invested $7,500 a year in a Keogh plan that earned 8 percent annually. By year 15, the tax-deferred earnings within the Keogh plan would total about $116,200, or more than the $112,500 you had contributed up to that point. By year 25, the tax-deferred earnings would be nearly $450,000, or more than twice as great as your actual contributions.

Table 3.4 Advantages of a Keogh

Number of Years	Total Contribution	Tax-Deferred Interest	Total Value
5	$ 37,500	$ 10,645	$ 48,145
10	75,000	45,365	120,365
15	112,500	116,201	228,701
20	150,000	241,213	391,213
25	187,500	447,490	634,990

What Self-Employment Means

To qualify for a Keogh, you must be self-employed. That means you cannot be someone else's employee, unless you also have another source of income—perhaps from freelance work—apart from your regular job. As more and more companies turn to temporary workers to fill even professional positions, and as more and more workers leave their jobs to become consultants to their former employers, the distinctions between the self-employed and ordinary employees are becoming increasingly blurred.

The determination about whether you are an employee or a self-employed individual is typically made by the person or company that pays you. If you receive a W-2 form, reflecting salary or wages paid, you are considered an employee; but if you receive a 1099 form, for miscellaneous business income, you are considered self-employed. You don't need to get a 1099 form to be deemed self-employed, however. You may be an artist who receives income from commissions or sales of your artwork; or a psychologist in private practice who gets fees from patients; or a writer or inventor who receives royalties from past works.

The key point is that you must show a profit from your self-employment activities in order to make a contribution to a Keogh. Technically, you must have *net earnings from self-employment* to qualify. This means you must show positive income from your self-employment activity, after deducting all your business expenses relating to that activity, before you can begin to figure your Keogh contribution. Let's say you are an architect who earned $80,000 in fees and commissions and had $35,000 in business expenses. Your net earnings for purposes of the Keogh contribution would be $45,000. But if you are a novelist who hasn't yet sold a first book, and have no income to show for your activities, you cannot contribute to a Keogh.

Types of Keogh Plans

Keogh plans come in two varieties: defined-contribution plans and defined-benefit plans.

With a *defined-contribution Keogh,* you contribute a set amount each year—for example, 15 percent of your net income (or 15 percent of your payroll if you have employees whom you must cover). How much you have available at retirement will depend on how well your investments have done during your active working years.

With a *defined-benefit Keogh,* which resembles a traditional pension plan, you contribute enough money year after year to provide you (and any covered employees) with a specific annual benefit when you (or they) retire. The amount you contribute is determined by an IRS formula and actuarial assumptions, and is based on your age and the earnings you expect to receive on investments within the plan. Let's take a closer look at Keogh plans.

Defined-Contribution Keoghs. Defined-contribution Keogh plans are themselves divided into two categories: money-purchase plans and profit-sharing plans. The maximum contribution you can make to either type of plan cannot exceed $30,000 a year per person. (To calculate your Keogh contribution, see p. 57.)

With a *money-purchase plan,* you can contribute up to 25 percent of your net income (or an employee's compensation) to the plan each year. But such a plan is subject to the IRS's minimum funding rules, which means that once you decide what percentage of compensation you are willing to contribute to the plan on behalf of yourself and any employees you must cover, you must then make these contributions each and every year thereafter, regardless of whether business is good or bad.

A *profit-sharing Keogh,* by contrast, is much more flexible. It allows you to contribute up to 15 percent of your total payroll but does not *require* you to make such contributions. In a bad year, plan contributions can be reduced or eliminated entirely. This flexibility is especially advantageous to the owners of small businesses, whose income can fluctuate substantially from year to year.

It is also possible to establish a *paired* plan, which is a combination of a profit-sharing and a money-purchase plan. This way, you retain the flexibility of reducing contributions to your profit-sharing plan if business is bad, but you also have the option of increasing your total contributions above the 15 percent limit if business is good.

Many paired plans are set up with a 10 percent required contribution into a money-purchase plan and the remaining 15 percent into a profit-sharing plan. With such an option, you must contribute 10 percent of net income into the money-purchase plan each year but can exercise your discretion about how much—if any—of the remaining 15 percent you will contribute to the profit-sharing plan.

The latest development in Keoghs is the *age-based* profit-sharing plan, a hybrid arrangement that falls between a defined-benefit plan and a defined-contribution plan. It allows you to base contributions on both age and compensation. By permitting contributions to be based on the age of a participating worker, you can make proportionately greater contributions for older employees than for younger ones earning the same salaries. The idea behind this is to allow older workers—who have fewer years before retirement—to put away enough money during that time so that they receive the same level of retirement benefit as younger workers. Result: People in their fifties might be able to contribute four or five times the amount of money each year that younger workers—who earn the same salary—can contribute.

Defined-Benefit Keoghs. Establishing a defined-benefit Keogh is much more complicated than setting up a defined-contribution Keogh. In effect, you select the amount of pension you want to receive at retirement and then work backward to determine how much you need to contribute each year to fund it. Your future pension is actually an *annuity*, or a guaranteed annual stream of income, that you purchase from an insurance company using the accumulated assets in your Keogh. Although the cost and paperwork involved in setting up such a plan can be considerable, the benefits may outweigh the hassles, particularly if you are age 50 or over. That's because you may be able to put away much larger amounts for retirement than you could with a defined-contribution Keogh.

Take the case of Harry, a 55-year-old architect with $100,000 a year in net self-employment earnings. With a defined-contribution Keogh, the most he could contribute would be $20,000 (20 percent of his earned income after taking the contribution into account). But if he establishes a defined-benefit Keogh that will pay him at age 65 a retirement benefit of $60,000 (which is roughly equivalent to the benefit he could expect to receive under a traditional pension plan), Harry could contribute as much as $40,000 a year to the plan, based on conservative actuarial assumptions. This is $20,000 more than he could stash away in a defined-contribution plan. Of course, Harry has to be in a position to forgo that money and invest it for retirement, rather than use it for current expenses.

To establish a defined-benefit Keogh, you will need to hire an actuary to determine precisely how much you can contribute. The figure depends upon your age, your life expectancy, and the expected rate of return you assign to assets in your Keogh. The older you are, and the shorter the time before you retire, the more you will be able to contribute. Also, the lower the rate of return you assume, the more you will be able to contribute.

The limit on how much you can deduct is based on the amount of your annual benefit at normal retirement age, usually 65. For 1994 you were not allowed to fund an annual benefit larger than $118,800 (a figure that is indexed annually to reflect inflation), or 100 percent of your average earnings for your three consecutive highest-earning years.

Before adopting a defined-benefit Keogh, be aware that the IRS has embarked on a large-scale examination of such plans. The government maintains that many business owners are inflating contributions to such plans, either by basing contributions on earlier-than-normal retirement ages or by using unreasonably low expectations for earnings on Keogh assets. So, establishing a defined-benefit Keogh may be inviting an IRS audit, even if you are going by the book and using very conservative assumptions.

How to Calculate Your Keogh Contribution

Figuring your actual Keogh contribution can be confusing. Before you make the contribution, you must reduce your net earnings by the Keogh contribution itself as well as by a new tax deduction for half of the self-employment tax you pay. The result is that you cannot figure your contribution based on the contribution rate stated in your plan document.

Take the case of Mark, a self-employed psychotherapist. He had $100,000 of net income in 1994 (after subtracting all his business deductions), but this does not include his Keogh plan deduction. Mark has a money-purchase plan, so the maximum he can contribute is 25 percent of his earned income. To figure out what his earned income is if he makes the maximum contribution of 25 percent, he must subtract the contribution from his net income of $100,000. This requires an algebraic computation and works out to $20,000, which represents 20 percent of his $100,000 income before counting the contribution, or 25 percent of his $80,000 net earnings after the $20,000 contribution is deducted. (Rather than do the algebraic computation yourself, use Table 3.5 to do the math for you. The table converts the maximum statutory percentage [on the left] for a Keogh contribution into the lower actual percentage [on the right] you can actually contribute once your contribution is taken into account.)

Tax Law Changes. Recalculating your earned income after taking the Keogh contribution into account used to be the only calculation you had to make. But a 1993 change in the tax law, which now allows self-employed people to claim a 50 percent deduction for the self-employment taxes they pay, has complicated matters. Even though the impact of this change is positive, in that it reduces the amount of self-employment tax you wind up paying, it has a negative impact because it also reduces the amount of money you can stash away in a Keogh plan.

Let's return to the case of Mark. Now, instead of using $100,000 as his net earnings from self-employment, Mark must reduce this figure by half the Social Security tax he pays. For 1994, that tax comes to $10,414. Half of that is $5,207, so his net earnings drop to $94,793. Now Mark can resume the old method of figuring his Keogh deduction, which is a maximum of 20 percent of $94,793, or $18,959. The result of the change is that the amount he can now put aside in his Keogh has been reduced by $1,041.

Table 3.5 *Figuring Keogh Contributions*

This percentage of earned income	is equivalent to	this percentage of net income
5		4.76
6		5.66
7		6.54
8		7.41
9		8.26
10		9.09
11		9.91
12		10.71
13		11.50
14		12.28
15		13.04
16		13.79
17		14.53
18		15.25
19		15.97
20		16.67
21		17.36
22		18.03
23		18.70
24		19.35
25		20.00

Standard and Personalized Keoghs

Most people establish Keogh plans with a bank, brokerage house, or mutual fund. These financial institutions offer standardized *master* or *prototype* plans that have been preapproved by the IRS. It's important to at least skim the major points of a prototype plan before you invest your money, because some of these plans may have design features that you won't like. For example, a mutual fund may offer only a profit-sharing Keogh, when you want a money-purchase plan. A bank prototype plan may require you to begin withdrawing money from your Keogh once you retire, even though you may wish to defer distributions until a later date.

You have the option to set up your own *personalized* Keogh plan. To do so, you must hire an attorney (and probably an actuary, if you are establishing a defined-benefit Keogh) to design a plan to fit your unique specifications. Although the extra flexibility may be worth it, such fine-tuning can be expensive. The initial legal and actuarial costs of establishing the plan can easily amount to $2,000, and the ongoing cost of such professional advice can range between $500 and $1,000 a year. This compares with a typical annual fee of $10 to $30 charged by a financial institution for a standard prototype Keogh plan. So unless you expect your Keogh assets to mount well into the six digits, it's probably best to stick with a prototype plan.

Combining a Keogh with Other Plans

Many people wonder if they can establish a Keogh if they are also covered under a retirement plan at their company. The answer is yes, as long as they have income from a sideline business.

Let's look at the case of Sally, an engineering professor who earns $60,000 from her university position and is covered under the school's pension plan. Sally has an additional $40,000 in net income from consulting fees from outside clients. If she adopts a money-purchase Keogh plan, she can make a tax-deductible contribution of $8,000 (or 20 percent of her net income) to her Keogh.

You can also set up both a Keogh and an IRA. But because you have a Keogh, you are considered an active participant in a qualified plan, so your IRA contribution will not be tax-deductible if your income exceeds the threshold.

How to Invest Your Keogh

Once you have determined what type of Keogh plan to adopt, the next major decision is how to invest the money that you contribute. Here, as with IRAs, most people are simply too conservative. According to the Employee Benefit Research Institute, almost half the money contributed to Keoghs and IRAs in 1989 went to banks, savings and loan associations, and credit unions, where it was invested in products such as money market accounts and certificates of deposit. Although those investments are usually insured by the federal government, they pay interest rates that barely outpace inflation over the long term and lag well behind the return on stocks.

To reap the maximum advantage from your Keogh plan, it pays to funnel a sizeable portion of your contributions into stocks, especially if your retirement is still in the distant future. But you also want to be sure to avoid putting all your eggs in one basket and to diversify Keogh investments with a sprinkling of bonds or bond funds.

When to Invest in a Keogh

The earlier you establish and start contributing money to a Keogh plan, the more you'll accumulate in your retirement pot. Most of the growth will come about through the power of compound interest—or the successively larger investment earnings that your contributions generate over the years. These earnings build up year after year on a tax-deferred basis until you withdraw the funds at retirement.

The IRS and Keoghs

It used to be that all self-employed people with Keoghs, regardless of how much or how little they had in their plans, had to contend with a daunting IRS form every year. Among other things, sole proprietors and partners with Keoghs were required to report how much their Keogh investments had grown during the year. But the rules have been relaxed, and that burdensome paperwork is now reserved for the relatively wealthy.

If you (or you and your spouse) are the only participants in your Keogh plan, and if the assets in your Keogh are $100,000 or less at year-end, you no longer have to complete Form 5500EZ. But if your plan assets exceed that amount, or if the plan covers more people than just you and your mate, you must file an annual information return with the IRS by July 31 of the following year.

As long as you have established your Keogh plan by December 31 of the year in which you plan to make a contribution, you do not have to put the money into the plan until April of the following year. The rule is that you have until the April 15 due date for filing your federal tax return—plus any extensions—to fund the plan. This means that if you request an automatic four-month extension, you have until August 15 to make your contribution. If you request, and the IRS approves, an additional two-month extension, you have until October 15 to make your contribution.

Despite this flexibility, it is in your interest to make your Keogh contribution as early in the year as possible to reap the maximum benefit of tax-deferred growth within the plan. The sooner the money is in the plan, the more tax-deferred earnings it can generate for your retirement.

Simplified Employee Pensions (SEPs)

If you didn't make the deadline for establishing a Keogh, all is not lost in terms of adopting a retirement plan. The alternative is to establish a Simplified Employee Pension plan, or SEP. You have until the April 15 due date for filing your tax return, plus any extensions, to set one up. This means that if you obtain two filing extensions, you can make a contribution to your SEP as late as October 15 and, in effect, reduce your prior year's tax bill with a transaction that doesn't occur until $9\frac{1}{2}$ months after the close of that year.

SEPs were really designed for small employers—those with 25 or fewer workers. But they work just as well for employers with only one employee: you.

With a SEP, an employer makes contributions to the separate IRAs of each of its workers, instead of contributing to a traditional pension plan. Workers own and control the investments in their SEP-IRA accounts, even after they have left the job. Sole proprietors and partners who have no employees are permitted to establish SEPs for themselves and their spouses.

SEPs have one important advantage over IRAs: Their contribution limits are much higher. If you (or your employer) are incorporated, the maximum annual contribution is 15 percent of compensation or $30,000 a year, whichever is less, compared with only $2,000 a year with an IRA. If you (or your employer) are not incorporated, the maximum contribution is 15 percent of your net income after taking the contribution into account; this works out to an effective contribution of only 13.043 percent.

If you are an employee covered by a SEP, and if your company plan allows it, you may also be able to make voluntary contributions to the SEP over and above what your employer contributes. The limit for such voluntary contributions is $9,240 for 1994, or 15 percent of your compensation, whichever is less. But your contributions combined with those of your employer cannot exceed $30,000, or 25 percent of your compensation, whichever is less.

When it comes to investing your SEP, follow the same approach as you would with an IRA or Keogh. Don't be too cautious, especially if you have a while before retirement. Earmark a substantial portion of your money for individual stocks or stock mutual funds, which offer the potential for maximum capital growth; put a lesser amount into fixed-income securities such as bank CDs, bonds, and money market funds, which offer greater stability of principal but may not outstrip inflation. You have the same array of custodians to choose from as with other retirement accounts: banks, savings institutions, credit unions, mutual funds, brokerage houses, and insurance companies.

When it's time to start withdrawing funds from your SEP, you're subject to the same rules as with IRA withdrawals. This means, for example, that if you withdraw the money before you reach age 59½ (unless you become totally disabled), you're subject to a 10 percent penalty tax on the amount you take out. And SEP distributions do not qualify for favorable 5- or 10-year income-averaging, the way Keogh distributions do.

Despite these drawbacks, SEPs may be the ideal savings vehicle for harried small business people who just didn't get around to setting up a retirement plan before the close of the previous year. SEPs truly live up to their name because they are cheap and easy to administer. You can use standard forms provided free by the IRS and don't need to hire a lawyer or actuary to establish them. Moreover, they're one of the rare plans in which you are not penalized by the IRS for procrastinating.

4

INVESTING FOR COLLEGE

FOR people with children, probably the biggest single expenditure they will make, outside of purchasing a home, will be sending their youngsters through college. During the 1980s, college costs rose more than twice as fast as the general inflation rate, and this trend shows no sign of reversing. College administrators say that the average cost of four years at a public school in 1994 was about $33,000 and estimate it will jump to about $73,000 by the year 2005. If your child attends a private college or university, the cost could be almost 2.5 times that and approach $184,000. By the year 2010, at present rates of college inflation, a four-year education at an average private college could cost nearly $264,000 (see Table 4.1).

With such enormous numbers, how can a middle-class family hope to even come close to saving enough to finance a four-year stint at a private college, especially if there are two or more children to educate? The truth is that most families won't amass enough from private savings but rather will scrape together the money from a variety of sources—savings, loans, scholarships, and current income from jobs held by the students' parents and the students themselves. However, just because the goal seems formidable doesn't mean that you shouldn't attempt to save as much as you reasonably can for your children's college education.

Obviously, the earlier you start investing, the better. That's because the more years your investments have to grow, the bigger the pot at the

Table 4.1 College Cost Table*

Year Child Will Enter College	Projected Future Cost of Four Years at a Private College	Projected Future Cost of Four Years at a Public College
1994	$82,930	$33,172
1995	89,150	35,660
1996	95,836	38,335
1997	103,024	41,210
1998	110,751	44,300
1999	119,057	47,623
2000	127,986	51,195
2001	137,585	55,034
2002	147,904	59,162
2003	158,997	63,599
2004	170,922	68,369
2005	183,741	73,496
2006	197,522	79,009
2007	212,336	84,934
2008	228,261	91,304
2009	245,381	98,152
2010	263,784	105,514
2011	283,568	113,427
2012	304,836	121,934

*Note: Annual increases are estimated. Actual college costs may vary. Source for 1993–94 private college costs: The College Board's Independent College 500 Index. Source for 1993–94 public college costs: U.S. Department of Education.

Source: College Savings Bank

end. But changes in the tax laws have complicated the plans of those conscientious parents who want to start a college investment program while their children are still toddlers, making it more difficult for them to put away money for their education on a tax-favored basis.

THE KIDDIE TAX

It used to be that parents could shift income within the family—and cut the family's taxes—by establishing what was known as a Clifford Trust. Under this approach, parents would temporarily turn over assets (such as cash or securities) to a trust for a 10-year period, naming their children as beneficiaries. Earnings generated by those assets during the trust period would be taxed at the children's lower rate rather than the parents' higher rate. At the end of the trust period, the parents—having saved a decade's worth of higher taxes—would regain ownership of the trust assets. The 1986 tax law put an end to that arrangement, however, imposing what is known as the *kiddie tax.*

The kiddie tax created two classes of children: those age 13 and under, and those age 14 and over. Parents who wish to begin an early college investment program for the younger set are penalized, in effect, by the tax. The law says that if children age 13 and under have "unearned" income (from sources such as bank interest or stock dividends) that exceeds a modest level, the income above that level will be taxed at the parents' higher rate rather than at the children's lower rate.

But once children reach age 14, they attain the magic age of tax independence: They can have any amount of unearned income and pay tax on it at their own rate, rather than their parents' rate. For purposes of this rule, it doesn't matter when a child turns 14. Even if the birthday doesn't occur until December 31, the child is taxed as if he or she were 14 for the entire year.

How the Tax Works

For 1993 there is no tax at all on the first $600 of the unearned income of a child below age 14, because $600 equals the amount of the standard deduction. (The standard deduction is an amount that can be deducted by any taxpayer from income, regardless of the size of the individual's actual deductions. The deduction is increased periodically to reflect inflation.) The second $600 of a child's unearned income is subject to a flat 15 percent tax, the lowest of the current five income tax brackets. If a child has unearned income above $1,200, he or she is taxed at the parents' top marginal rate, which could be as high as 39.6 percent.

Incidentally, even if your children have no income at all, the Internal Revenue Service wants to know all about them. If you report your child as a dependent on your tax return and the child is over age one, you must list the child's Social Security number on your return—even if the child didn't earn a penny in interest or dividends. And children under age 14 with $600 or more in unearned income must file a tax return— even if they owe no tax.

The only way around this paperwork is to add your child's unearned income to your own and report the combined figure on your personal tax return. The government offers parents this option to spare them the burden of having to file a separate tax return for each child. Taking this shortcut may not be the wisest course, however. By adding your child's investment income to your own income, you may wind up increasing your *adjusted gross income* (AGI) to the point where it will have a negative impact on your overall tax situation. For example, a higher AGI may mean you cannot make a deductible contribution to your IRA, or claim deductions for medical expenses, casualty losses, or miscellaneous itemized expenses (all must exceed a percentage of your AGI before they can be written off).

Investments for Children 13 and Younger

As you can see, the current tax law penalizes investments for young children that produce more than $1,200 in interest or dividends annually. So the best investment strategy for the 13-and-younger set is one that emphasizes growth over income. That's because any appreciation (or increase in the market value) in securities that your child holds is not taxed until the investments are sold. By purchasing non-dividend-paying growth stocks or growth mutual funds for your youngster and holding on to them for a decade or so while they increase in value, you get the advantage of capital appreciation without a current tax bill. The strategy is to postpone selling these growth stocks or growth mutual funds until your child turns 14 or reaches college age. That way, any capital gains resulting from the sale are taxed at your child's lower rate rather than added to your income from other sources and taxed at your own higher one.

This doesn't mean that you should completely forgo fixed-income investments for your preteen. In fact, your child should own just enough CDs, bonds, or Treasury securities to generate the amount of unearned income that escapes the kiddie tax. At the end of 1993, when long-term interest rates were about 6 percent, this translated into about $20,000 worth of bonds (since the annual interest on those bonds came to roughly $1,200). Another alternative is to purchase zero-coupon munic- ipal bonds or U.S. savings bonds for your child.

Investments for Children 14 and Over

The same tax and practical considerations that govern investments for younger children apply to older children, but in reverse. In other words, the investment strategy for the 14-and-over set should be slanted toward income rather than growth. The reasons are twofold: First, once your child reaches age 14, he or she can have up to $22,100 in unearned income (at 1993 rates) and still fall into the 15 percent bracket. A year earlier, if your child had more than $1,200 in unearned income, any excess would have been added to your income from all sources and taxed at rates as high as 39.6 percent.

Second, there are fewer years remaining before the teenage child heads off for college. This shorter investment horizon calls for more conservative investments. Say, for example, you have concentrated 17-year-old Tommy's portfolio in stocks and plan to liquidate the holdings as he enters college. What happens if the stock market takes a dive just as Tommy is about to begin freshman year? He'll wind up with a lot less money available than had been anticipated, and you may have to search for funds from other sources to make up the shortfall.

HOW TO GIVE MONEY TO YOUR CHILDREN: CUSTODIAL ACCOUNTS AND TRUSTS

Regardless of whether your child is over or under age 14, or whether you're transferring cash, stocks, or bonds, the best way for parents (or grandparents) to transfer money to a minor child is to establish a custodial account for the child at a bank, brokerage house, or mutual fund.

There are two types of custodial accounts: a *Uniform Gifts to Minors Act* (UGMA) account and a *Uniform Transfers to Minors Act* (UTMA) account. A UGMA account lets you transfer cash and securities to a child, whereas a UTMA account allows you to transfer a broader range of assets, including partnership interests, real estate, and collectibles. Usually, no special fee is associated with establishing such accounts.

With either a UGMA or a UTMA account, the property turned over to your child is an irrevocable transfer. You, the parent, can no longer use it for your own purposes, even to pay for parental obligations, such as summer vacations, music lessons, or day camp. Another adult, whom you designate as custodian of the account, handles the investment of the transferred property until your child reaches the age of majority.

At this point, one of the big drawbacks of transferring substantial amounts of money to a custodial account comes into play. Once your child reaches the age of majority (which is usually 18, but sometimes 21, depending on the state in which you live), the child has the right to do with that money whatever he or she wants. If 19-year-old Charlie decides to spend it on a Ferrari instead of four years at your alma mater, or your daughter Candy decides to seek guidance from a guru in India rather than a liberal arts degree, there's nothing you can do to prevent it.

One solution may be to establish a so-called minor's trust. Known as a 2503(c) trust, this arrangement permits parents to retain more control over the transferred funds than does a custodial account. But the legal fees can be steep, depending on the complexity of the trust and the area of the country in which you live. So, establishing a minor's trust probably isn't worth the cost unless you plan to transfer a substantial sum of money—say, $100,000 or more. For this reason, some parents will turn over a limited amount of money to their children and, despite the negative tax implications, will invest the rest in their own names. At least this way, they can continue to control the purse strings.

The second drawback of a custodial account is that if you are the donor (that is, if you are the parent giving the property) and if you also serve as custodian of the account, the property transferred will be included in your taxable estate should you die before your child reaches the age of majority. A relatively simple solution here is to name a responsible and financially competent relative or friend as custodian.

The final negative of a custodial account is that it may disqualify your child from receiving college financial aid. Generally, students are expected to contribute as much as 35 percent of their assets toward college costs, while parents need contribute less than 6 percent of their assets (up to a certain level). If your child is a likely candidate for financial aid, consider cutting back on donations to a custodial account once your child enters high school. At that point, it's probably smart to start saving more in your own name.

INVESTING WITH SERIES EE BONDS

Series EE bonds are the plain vanilla savings bonds issued by the U.S. government. For years, they were considered a stodgy investment that well-meaning but financially unsophisticated relatives gave children on their birthdays or for graduation. But these bonds have been revamped, and they now offer an after-tax return that is competitive or sometimes even better than the return on comparable investments, such as bank certificates of deposit. Furthermore, savings bonds are safe, easy to buy, and available in a wide range of prices that can fit just about any family budget.

Savings bonds are issued at discounts to their face value, or what they will be worth when they are redeemed (or cashed in) at maturity. They are sold in denominations of $50 to $10,000, but buyers pay just half of their face amount; the difference is the equivalent of interest. However, this interest is not paid out semiannually, the way it is with traditional bonds. Rather, interest accrues on a tax-deferred basis, and you do not receive it until you redeem the bonds.

One approach might be to have the maturity dates of an EE bond coincide with the dates you expect your child to be attending college. Assume, for example, you buy a $20,000 savings bond to finance part of the cost for the first year of college for your newborn daughter Jennifer. Your purchase price for that bond would be $10,000, or half its face amount. Based on the current minimum guaranteed rates, the bond will mature in 18 years, when Jennifer is ready to start freshman year, and can be cashed in for its full face amount of $20,000. When Jennifer is a year old, you could buy another $20,000 savings bond that would mature at the start of her sophomore year in college, and do the same for her junior and senior years as well.

Although you can redeem savings bonds at any time after six months of purchase, it makes sense to hold them for at least five years. That way you can collect the higher of two possible interest rates: a guaranteed minimum rate in early 1994 of 4 percent a year over the lifetime of the bond, or a "market-based" rate that is 85 percent of the rate that five-year Treasury securities earned during the period you owned the bonds. The market-based rate is adjusted twice a year, each May 1 and November 1, and stood at 4.25 percent in November 1993. People who sell their EE bonds after six months but before five years elapse get the minimum rate.

Escaping the Tax Bite

For some middle-income parents, a major advantage of making series EE bonds a mainstay of a college investment plan is that they may be able to escape paying federal income tax on the interest income that the bonds have accumulated over the years (savings bond interest is exempt from state taxes in any case). To qualify for the federal income tax exemption, you must meet several tests. The bonds must have been issued after December 31, 1989; you, the purchaser, must be age 24 or older; and you must use the bond proceeds for tuition and fees for college expenses for yourself, your dependents, or your spouse.

Furthermore, you can exclude the accumulated interest on savings bonds only if your *modified adjusted gross income* in the year you redeem the bonds does not exceed certain modest limits. For 1993, married couples filing jointly can exclude all the interest if their modified AGI (from salaries, dividends, and interest—including the accumulated interest on the savings bonds themselves—minus adjustments for such items as alimony payments and Keogh contributions) does not exceed $61,850; the interest exclusion is gradually phased out at incomes above that and disappears completely when the joint modified AGI reaches $91,850. Singles or heads of household can claim the full exclusion if their modified AGI is $41,200 or less; the exclusion phases out at higher income levels and disappears when modified AGI reaches $56,200. (These limits may be raised if a technical correction bill pending before Congress is enacted.)

Even though these income limits are adjusted annually to reflect inflation, you still need to be able to accurately project your family income a decade or more into the future if you expect to cash in the bonds without paying federal income tax. Bear in mind that the accumulated interest on the bonds—which can be significant since it can amount to half their face value—must be added to your income from other sources in the year that you redeem the bonds. Result: By simply cashing in the bonds, you may find that you no longer qualify for the exclusion.

Nevertheless, savings bonds can play an important role in investing for college, even if you wind up paying taxes on the interest. Like securities issued by the U.S. Treasury Department, savings bonds are backed by the full faith and credit of the U.S. government. You can purchase them at most banks without having to pay a transaction fee or brokerage charge. You may also be able to buy them through a payroll-deduction plan at work.

But it's doubtful that savings bonds alone will enable you to accumulate enough wealth to send your children through college, especially if costs continue to rise at twice the general inflation rate. Investing part of your money in EE bonds is prudent, but a substantial portion of your savings for younger children should be earmarked for growth stocks and stock mutual funds that historically have produced a much higher rate of return.

INVESTING WITH ZERO-COUPON BONDS

Bonds

Like savings bonds, zero-coupon bonds, or zeros, are issued at deep discounts to their face value. And, like savings bonds, zeros do not pay semiannual coupons the way traditional bonds do (see Chapter 8). Instead, the interest earnings on zeros accrue invisibly year after year until the bonds reach maturity. The difference (unless you buy zeros that are issued as tax-free municipal bonds) is that you must pay federal income tax on this phantom interest income year after year, even though you don't get your hands on a penny of that money until the bonds mature.

Why would you want to buy a bond that subjects you to a continuing current tax burden without any current reward in the form of tangible interest? Primarily for the peace of mind that comes with knowing exactly what you'll wind up with at the end of the holding period. Assume you buy a zero that pays 6 percent interest and matures in 10 years. If you plunk down $5,525 today, you'll receive $10,000 a decade from now. That's security. As with savings bonds, one approach would be to purchase zeros whose maturity dates coincide with the years during which you expect to be paying your child's college tuition. If you expect that five-year-old Maggie will be in Yale's class of 2009, for example, you might want to buy zeros with a total face value of $200,000 that will mature over a four-year period starting in 2005.

Zero-coupon bonds can be a very attractive investment for a college portfolio if you buy them at a point when interest rates are relatively high. The reason is that the initial interest rate you receive on your investment is guaranteed to continue during the entire life of the bond, even if rates subsequently fall. In effect, you've locked in your initial interest rate regardless of what happens later. With traditional bonds that pay out interest twice a year, by contrast, you don't know what your future reinvestment rate will be. Depending on market conditions, the rate at which you can reinvest your semiannual interest payments will be higher—or lower—than the original rate.

Treasury Zeros

Zeros come in several different forms. There are Treasury zeros, corporate zeros, and municipal zeros.

Treasury zeros are probably the safest investment for your child's college tuition fund for two reasons. First, Treasury zeros are backed by the full faith and credit of the U.S. government. This means you don't have to worry about whether or not the issuer—Uncle Sam—will still be around and able to repay your principal and accrued interest when the bonds mature decades hence. With corporate or municipal zeros, you count on the fact that the company or municipality that issued the bonds will still be viable and able to make good on its IOU in 10 or 20 years.

Second, you generally don't have to worry about Treasury zeros being "called" (redeemed before maturity for a prespecified price). An issuer typically exercises a call provision when interest rates are falling, and this can be bad news for you, the bondholder. Not only do you lose out on the high interest rate that you had anticipated, but you may not even get back a full return of your principal and accrued interest, depending upon how the call provision is structured. This won't happen with Treasury zeros.

But even Treasury zeros are not a foolproof way to save for college. For one thing, the future cost of college may rise faster than the interest rate you're getting on your zeros. And, because the prices of zeros are much more volatile than the prices of conventional bonds, you may not get back the book, or accreted, value of the bonds if you are forced to sell your zeros before maturity.

If you decide to purchase Treasury zeros, you have to ask for them under the brand names used by the brokerage houses that package and sell them. Treasury zeros go under proprietary names, including TIGRS (Treasury Investment Growth Receipts) and CATS (Certificates of

Accrual on Treasury Securities). The prices of the bonds, which are usually sold in minimum face amounts of $1,000, include the brokers' fees and so can vary significantly. It pays to shop around for the best deal.

Zero-Coupon Mutual Funds

Another way to purchase zeros is through a mutual fund that invests in zero-coupon Treasuries (as of March 1994, only two fund families, the Benham group in California and the Scudder group in Boston, offered such options). Structured as trusts that will terminate on set "target" dates, such as 1995, 2000, and 2005, the funds hold zeros that will mature on those dates. By investing in a fund, rather than in individual zeros, your return will be fractionally lower because of the fund's management fees. But the convenience of bypassing a broker may be worth the cost, especially if you don't have a brokerage account.

The biggest risk with a zero-coupon mutual fund occurs when you sell your holdings before the target maturity date (and this may happen if you need the money to pay for tuition bills that do not coincide with the target date). If interest rates have risen since you bought the fund, you may wind up with a big loss and find the fund just as risky as if you had invested in a speculative growth fund. So the most conservative course is to hold the funds until the target date (unless interest rates plummet and you can pocket big capital gains).

State Baccalaureate Bonds

To encourage parents to start their college savings programs early, a dozen or so states offer *baccalaureate* bonds. These are basically zero-coupon municipal bonds issued in small denominations. The interest income from them is generally exempt from federal and state taxes if the buyer resides in the state that issued the bonds. Baccalaureate bonds may be a smart investment if you're sure that the inflation rate at the school your child attends will be less than the interest rate you're receiving on the bonds.

PREPAID TUITION PLANS

Another approach adopted by some states is the *prepaid tuition plan.* The idea is to pay now, in a single lump sum, for college tuition bills that won't come due for years. Since the state school (or private college, if it sponsors such a plan) has the use of your money in the intervening period, you need turn over just a fraction of what your child's ultimate tuition costs will be.

If, for example, you assume that three-year-old Susie will attend your alma mater, State U, you might have to pay only $5,700 now to cover four years' worth of tuition bills starting in 2007. The major drawback to this approach occurs if little Susie decides to attend a different college, or if she is not admitted to State U. Some schools refund only your initial investment and keep the accumulated interest for themselves. In such cases, you would have done better putting your money in a bank passbook account.

Also, the issue of whether or not parents (or students) are liable for taxes on the accumulated earnings within such plans is still unclear. In a case involving the state of Michigan, a federal district court has ruled that the investment earnings of the state's plan are taxable. Michigan has appealed the ruling. Other states with similar plans are closely watching the outcome of the litigation.

THE COLLEGESURE CD

This special CD is sold by the College Savings Bank, a federally insured bank in Princeton, New Jersey. Its interest rate is linked to an index of college inflation.

If you invest $10,000 or more, the interest rate you earn on the CD is 1 percentage point less than the rate of inflation in college costs (room, board, tuition, and fees), as measured by an annual survey of 500 independent colleges conducted by the College Board. If you invest less than $10,000, the interest rate you earn is 1.5 percentage points less than the college inflation rate.

Say, for example, you invested $10,000 and college costs rose 13 percent the following year; you would be credited with 12 percent interest on the money. If college costs rose again by 15 percent the next year, you'd be credited with 14 percent interest for that year. But if college costs were to hold steady in the second year, you would get a guaranteed "floor" of 4 percent interest on your CD.

The major appeal of the CollegeSure CD is peace of mind. Once you make the initial investment (or series of investments), you have the security of knowing that when Junior is ready to go to college in 10 or 15 years, you'll have accumulated approximately enough to pay the bills (assuming you invested a large enough sum at the start), regardless of how high college costs soar.

On the other hand, once you take into account the fact that you'll be receiving an interest rate of 1.0 or 1.5 percent less per year than the actual college cost inflation rate, you may do better with higher-yielding investments, such as stocks and corporate bonds. Also, since there is a hefty 10 percent penalty for withdrawing your principal during the first three years and a 5 percent penalty thereafter (until the final year, when it drops to 1 percent), be sure you intend to leave your money on deposit before you invest a penny.

5

INVESTING FOR RETIREMENT

MANY people are ambivalent about the notion of retirement. On the one hand, retirement is billed as a time for you to finally leave your work-a-day cares behind, and pursue the hobbies, traveling, and reading you've never had time for. On the other hand, retirement can be a time of ill health, loneliness, and isolation. Those concerns, while all too real, are beyond the scope of this book. Our goal here is to help you fashion an investment plan so that your retirement is not a time of scrimping and poverty.

Paradoxically, the best time to start saving for the day when you are no longer able to work is when you are just starting to work. The longer your money has to grow, the more you'll have in the pot at the end. But retirement is a dim vision for most people in their twenties and thirties. Fresh out of school, perhaps repaying college loans, they're far more likely to take whatever money is left after taking care of the rent and car payments to spend rather than save. They often prefer to furnish an apartment, buy new clothes, take a vacation, and eat out a lot.

The reality is that you probably won't start saving seriously for retirement until middle age. The middle years are what financial planners call the "accumulation years," when your salary is nearing its peak and you may have met your major financial obligations, such as paying off the mortgage and putting your children through college.

Actually, investing for retirement should take a twofold approach: investing while you're still working so that you'll be able to afford to retire, and investing *after* you're retired so you'll be able to maintain the lifestyle you want for as long as you live.

Contributing to tax-favored retirement accounts, such as 401(k) plans, Individual Retirement Accounts (IRAs), and Keogh plans (see Chapters 2 and 3), is one of the best ways to save for retirement while you're still working. In effect, you set aside pretax rather than after-tax dollars, and your investment earnings compound tax-free until you start withdrawals at retirement. But faithfully contributing to these plans probably will not be enough to guarantee a financially comfortable retirement, even if you expect to be working for another 15 or 20 years. It's virtually a foregone conclusion that you'll need to supplement such plans with a personal investment program of your own.

SOURCES OF RETIREMENT FUNDS

No one has a crystal ball that can predict what life will be like for future retirees, but it's almost certain that current workers who plan to retire in the year 2000 or beyond will have a much more difficult time supporting themselves than today's retirees. The reasons are many, but all relate to the "three-legged stool" of financial resources that are supposed to help support the nation's elderly during their nonworking years: Social Security, private pensions, and individual savings.

Social Security, which provides a major financial cushion for current retirees, will probably not be so generous in the future. For one thing, there will be fewer active workers around to contribute to the Social Security system, which at the same time will be struggling to support record numbers of retirees.

Private pensions, which used to be a significant supplement to Social

Security, are becoming less generous. First, the corporate downsizings of the 1980s and 1990s have forced millions of American workers into early retirement. This means they are receiving pensions that are smaller than if they had remained working for the same company until normal retirement age.

Second, the types of pensions that companies are sponsoring for their workers still on the job are changing. Instead of traditional defined-benefit plans that promise workers a set monthly check at retirement, many employers have switched to defined-contribution plans, in which they simply promise to contribute a set amount each year to each eligible worker's retirement account.

Defined-contribution plans shift the investment responsibility for pension plan contributions from the company to its workers. Unfortunately, most workers opt for investments they think are safe. These tend to be fixed-income investments, such as guaranteed investment contracts, Treasury securities, and money market accounts.

Fixed-income investments tend to have relatively low returns, so workers have to worry about the impact of inflation, which will erode the purchasing power of their nest egg over time. Stocks are the only investment category that has been shown to outpace inflation over the long term, but most workers avoid stocks for fear of the periodic downturns in the market.

So, that leaves the final leg of the stool—private savings—supporting a much greater share of weight than it used to. Unfortunately, most people tend to be just as conservative with their individual investments as they are with their defined-contribution-plan investments. Again, they usually spurn stocks, which have the greatest potential for growth but also the greatest potential for short-term risks, in favor of fixed-income investments.

All too often, the result is that the combined income from Social Security, company pensions, and individual savings simply is not sufficient to support people in their older years. Retirees are increasingly being forced to scale back their standard of living or to add a fourth leg—a return to work, either full- or part-time—to the hypothetical retirement stool.

Many of these folks may have believed some popular retirement myths (see box).

THE FIVE MAJOR FINANCIAL MYTHS OF RETIREMENT

Most people believe that when they retire, it's time to play it safe with their investments because they can't afford to take any risks. In fact, you can't afford *not* to take some risks. The biggest danger is that you'll have such a long, healthy retirement that you'll out-live your savings. The only way to beat that risk is to be a little more adventurous with your money and invest it so that it will grow fast enough to support you (and your spouse) as long as you live. Believing that you can or should avoid all risk is as much a retirement myth as are the following:

1. *Myth: You should immediately switch all your assets from stocks to bonds.* The newly retired can expect to live for a long time, and even modest inflation will eat away at the purchasing power of a bond whose yield is fixed. If, over 15 years, inflation runs at an annual rate of 4 percent, $30,000 of current interest income will buy only $16,658 worth of today's goods by the end of the period. So, instead of limiting yourself to bonds or bank CDs, allocate a significant portion of your portfolio—perhaps as much as half—to stocks. Their appreciation (or price increases) plus dividends should more than outpace inflation.

2. *Myth: Never, ever dip into your principal.* The idea here is to keep your savings intact, so they can continue to generate interest income for as long as you need. This approach may be fine as long as interest rates are in the double digits. But as millions of retirees discovered to their dismay in the early 1990s, high interest rates are not a sure thing. A much better approach is to create a diversified portfolio of stocks and bonds (or stock mutual funds and bond mutual funds). If the yield on the bond portion of your portfolio later drops, you may need to "sell some growth," which involves selling some stocks (or shares of stock mutual funds) whose price has increased over the years. If you've been a patient long-term investor in the stock market, chances are that the equity portion of your portfolio has grown handsomely. Taking some capital gains now and then should have a negligible impact on its total size.

3. *Myth: CDs and bonds are your best sources of steady income.* That may be true in a no-inflation environment, but how many people have experienced that in this century? Instead, we feel

lucky when the inflation rate is "only" 3 or 4 percent. While that seems modest, 4 percent inflation means that $1 will buy only 68 cents' worth of today's goods a decade from now. So the best way to generate steady income and preserve your purchasing power is to invest at least part of your nest egg in dividend-paying stocks or stock mutual funds, which have growth potential as well as earnings potential.

With individual stocks, look for companies that have a history of steadily increasing dividends and the promise of future capital gains. Utility stocks, which traditionally have been considered a reliable source of dividend income, are another possibility. With mutual funds (see Chapter 9), consider growth-and-income funds (which aim for a "reasonable" return based on a combination of capital appreciation and dividends), equity-income funds (which split their portfolios between dividend-paying stocks and fixed-income securities), and utility funds (which invest in the stocks of dividend-paying utilities).

4. *Myth: Your retirement income should last you about 15 years.* That used to be true when the average life spans of Americans were much shorter. But if you're 65 now, you can expect to live another two decades. If you're 75, you can expect to live for another 12½ years. And if you're 90, you'd better have enough money to last another 5 years. Unless your parents died of heart disease in their thirties and you smoke two packs of cigarettes a day, you'll need to amass a bigger nest egg than you thought you'd ever need.

5. *Myth: You can live comfortably on 60 to 75 percent of your former gross income.* That may be true during the first few years of retirement. However, even though your mortgage may be paid off, property taxes have been rising more rapidly than income taxes, and there's no sign that their climb has leveled off yet. You may find that certain expenses, such as a business wardrobe and transportation to and from work, may decline, but other costs—primarily those relating to health care and medical insurance—may soar. You may also discover that in your newfound leisure you want to travel more. And nobody ever said vacations were cheap.

INVESTING AFTER RETIREMENT

Most people who have just received their gold watch or the equivalent tend to err on the side of safety when they readjust their investments after stopping work. What they don't realize is that becoming too conservative too soon can be a risky investment strategy, too. Although it may seem comforting to know that you'll receive a steady stream of income from a corporate or Treasury bond for the next 20 or 30 years, the truth is that the "real" return of such fixed-income investments has lagged behind inflation for most of the last half of this century. Stocks have been the only investment with enough growth potential to outpace inflation over time.

The Dangers of Inflation

The threat that inflation poses to your financial security is silent but real. For example, if inflation averages 4 percent annually (a fairly conservative assumption), a dollar of income will lose more than half its value over 20 years, which is the average life expectancy for someone who retires today at age 65. Since the interest payments and principal amounts of bonds are fixed for life, they don't provide any opportunity for you to outpace inflation if you hold them to maturity, which is what most individual investors tend to do. Only stocks, whose prices and dividends tend to rise along with corporate earnings, offer this chance.

Because stocks can have enormous year-to-year (and sometimes decade-to-decade) fluctuations, they shouldn't make up your entire portfolio in retirement. You need to have other types of investments that can cushion a temporary slump in stock prices. So, your portfolio should be diversified among stocks and bonds, with stocks constituting a relatively greater piece of the pie the younger you are.

SETTING UP A RETIREMENT PORTFOLIO

There aren't any precise rules about how much the newly retired should invest in stocks. Some professionals suggest at least a 30 percent portfolio weighting in stocks. Others say you should subtract your age from 100 and use that number as the appropriate percentage for stock ownership. The point is, even if you've never bought stocks up until now, you should consider doing so.

The actual percentage of money that you allocate to the stock market (through either individual stocks or stock mutual funds) depends on many factors, such as your age (and your parents' ages, since that's considered a good indication of family longevity), your health, and any other sources of income you have. If, for example, you retire at 62 but your mother and father lived into their late nineties, chances are that you've got to make sure your assets last for at least three decades. That may be more time than you spent working during your entire career.

If you were lucky enough to retire on a full pension that pays you about half of your former salary, you have a lot more leeway than if you don't receive a pension at all or receive only a modest one. Let's assume, for example, you used to earn $80,000 a year and now receive a $40,000 pension, as well as the maximum monthly Social Security payment. If that is enough to allow you to meet your monthly expenses, you could treat those two sources of monthly income as if they were fixed-income investments and allocate the rest of your holdings to stocks—not speculative start-up companies, of course, but solid dividend-paying stocks (or stock mutual funds) with a good record of steady, if nonspectacular, earnings growth. That way, the dividends could cushion any slump in the stock market and allow you to survive a temporary downturn without being forced to sell at the bottom.

On the other hand, if you don't receive a pension at all and you qualify for only modest Social Security benefits, you need to be much more conservative in your investing. A major portion of your money should probably be earmarked for fixed-income investments, such as corporate bonds and Treasury securities. Nevertheless, you should allocate something—even if it's only 10 percent—of your savings to dividend-paying stocks. That's the only way you'll be able to grow your money fast enough to preserve its purchasing power for the rest of your life.

Investment Strategies

Here are some different investment strategies that were devised by professional money managers for their individual clients. There's nothing magic about any one approach, and each has its pros and cons. We don't necessarily endorse these investment techniques, but we present them here to give you an indication of the many different ways you can manage your retirement money.

The 50-50 Solution

This is a way to have your cake and eat it, too. Basically, this approach involves achieving most of the high return of stocks while minimizing much of their short-term volatility (or the likelihood they will fluctuate in value). Neuberger & Berman, a New York City investment firm, studied returns for the period 1960 through 1992 for various types of investments, including short-term Treasury bills, 2- and 5-year Treasury notes, 30-year Treasury bonds, and a broad array of stocks (represented by Standard & Poor's 500 Composite Stock Price Index). Annual average returns ranged from a high of 10.26 percent for stocks, to a low of 6.21 percent for three-month T-bills. The study found that stocks were extremely volatile and on average moved (up or down) by 16 percent a quarter, while Treasury bills were far less mercurial.

By fashioning a hypothetical portfolio that was equally split between stocks and one-year Treasury bills (a 50-50 stock/debt mix), Neuberger & Berman achieved 88 percent of the return of the S&P 500 with only 53 percent of its volatility. The mix of one-year bills and stocks produced a compound annual return of 9.08 percent for the period, with a volatility of only 8.4 percent. Changing the mix to give stocks a greater weight did boost the portfolio's return, but it also increased the volatility. A 60-40 stock/debt mix, for example, provided 91 percent of the return of the S&P 500 with 62 percent of the volatility.

You might think that extending the maturity of Treasury securities beyond one-year bills would have boosted the return of this portfolio, while still reducing its volatility. The study found, however, that putting half the portfolio into long-term Treasuries not only reduced overall return slightly, it also *increased* volatility. Putting half the portfolio in long-term Treasury bonds reduced the return to the same level as if the money had been placed in one-year Treasury bills, but it increased the volatility by almost 4 percent.

Now, don't think that to benefit from this research you must put half your money in one-year bills and the other half in an index fund (a stock fund that matches the makeup of the S&P 500). If you're in your thirties or forties and have a long way to go before retirement, heavily tilting your portfolio toward stocks makes a lot of sense, because you have decades to ride out the periodic turbulence in the market. On the other hand, if you are already retired, placing half your investments in the stock market may make you understandably nervous. You may be far more comfortable allocating only 40 percent of your portfolio to the stock market.

The point is that a 50-50 mix can significantly boost your returns over those of a 100 percent fixed-income portfolio while smoothing over a lot of the peaks and valleys of the stock market. People who want to reach for greater returns should be in a position to ride out greater short-term fluctuations in their portfolios.

The 4 Percent Strategy

This approach involves investing for long-term growth by purchasing a healthy dose of stocks and then liquidating a modest portion of your holdings each year to pay for your living expenses. Its name is derived from the expectation that your "real" rate of return on your investments (after taxes and investment expenses) will average at least 4 percentage points above the inflation rate. If it does, and if your annual withdrawals are fairly reasonable, then your nest egg should last decades into the future.

A 4 percent real return may sound modest, but it can be an exceedingly tough target to meet on a regular basis, year in and year out. The longer your real rate of return exceeds that benchmark, the longer you'll have money to spend, save, or give away. But the higher the rate of inflation or the larger your annual withdrawals, the less money there will be for you.

Assume, for example, that inflation is running at an annual rate of 5 percent; your aim would be to achieve at least a 9 percent rate of return. If inflation drops to 3 percent, your aim would be at least a 7 percent rate of return. Historically, that has been a reasonable goal with stocks. A $1.00 investment in common stocks on December 31, 1969, grew to $12.11 by the end of 1992, producing a compound annual rate of return of 11.5 percent, according to Ibbotson Associates, a Chicago research firm. By contrast, a $1.00 investment in long-term bonds would have grown to $7.68, producing a compound annual total return of 9.3 percent. After adjusting for inflation, the common stock investment would have returned 5.2 percent, while the long-term bond investment would have returned 3.1 percent.

Assume you want to put the 4 percent strategy into operation. Financial planner John Allen, of Allen-Warren in Arvada, Colorado, provided the following example using a hypothetical stock portfolio worth $200,000 (see Table 5.1). During your first year of retirement, you decide you need to withdraw 5 percent, or $10,000. That would leave you with $190,000 to invest. If inflation is 3 percent and you earn 7 percent on your portfolio, you would have $203,300 ($190,000 principal plus $13,300 in earnings) at the end of the first year.

At the beginning of the second year, you would recalculate the amount you need to withdraw, increasing it slightly to compensate for the impact of inflation. For purposes of this example, we'll assume inflation remains at 3 percent. So, you would withdraw $10,300 (3 percent more than the previous year's amount) to meet expenses. That would leave you $193,000 to invest.

At the beginning of the third year, assuming inflation was still 3 percent and you continued to earn 7 percent on your investments, you would do a similar calculation. You would have earned $13,510, increasing your nest egg to $206,510. You would then withdraw $10,609 (3 percent more than the previous year), leaving you with $195,901 to invest. If you kept on at this pace, your money would last you more than 36 years.

Table 5.1 How Long Will Your Money Last?

This table shows how long $200,000 will last, depending upon different inflation rates and different net rates of return (the return you get on your investments after subtracting taxes and investment expenses).

To find out how long your money will last, first select an inflation rate you think is reasonable for the future from the inflation rates shown in the far left column. Next, select a net rate of return you expect your investments to earn from the column of net rates of return that runs along the top of the table, from left to right.

Finally, read down from the net rate of return until you reach the inflation rate you have selected. This will tell you the approximate number of years that $200,000 will last if you withdraw $10,000 in the first year (and that withdrawal is gradually increased each year to keep pace with the inflation rate you have selected).

$10,000 Initial Withdrawal (subject to annual increase to reflect inflation).

Inflation Rate	Net Rate of Return (after taxes and investment expense)					
	3%	4%	5%	6%	7%	8%
0.00%	29.55	37.39	62.40	#NUM!	#NUM!	#NUM!
1.00%	25.07	29.39	36.95	59.43	#NUM!	#NUM!
2.00%	22.13	25.00	29.23	36.53	56.98	#NUM!
3.00%	20.00	22.10	24.94	29.08	36.14	54.91
4.00%	18.37	20.00	22.08	24.87	28.93	35.77
5.00%	17.06	18.38	20.00	22.06	24.81	28.79
6.00%	15.99	17.08	18.39	20.00	22.04	24.75
7.00%	15.09	16.02	17.11	18.41	20.00	22.02
8.00%	14.31	15.12	16.04	17.13	18.42	20.00
9.00%	13.64	14.35	15.15	16.07	17.15	18.43
10.00%	13.05	13.68	14.38	15.18	16.10	17.17
11.00%	12.53	13.09	13.71	14.42	15.21	16.13
12.00%	12.07	12.57	13.13	13.75	14.45	15.24
13.00%	11.64	12.10	12.61	13.17	13.79	14.48
14.00%	11.26	11.68	12.14	12.65	13.20	13.82

#NUM! for years means principal will last forever.

Source: Allen-Warren, Inc.

Now, let's take a more realistic view. Assume that you weren't an investment whiz and that your investments produced a return of only 5 percent during the first year. That would leave you with $199,500 at the beginning of the second year. At that point, you would have several alternatives, and all would involve reevaluating your financial situation. You could try to earn more by changing your investment mix. Or you could tighten your belt and try to maintain the 4-point spread between your actual investment return and the inflation rate by increasing your second-year withdrawal by only 1 percent.

That would mean you could withdraw $10,100, leaving you with a nest egg of $189,400. If you continued to earn 5 percent, you would have $198,870 available at the start of the third year. At that point, you could withdraw $10,201, or 1 percent more than the previous year. At this reduced rate of withdrawal, your money would last you about the

9%	10%	11%	12%	13%	14%	15%
#NUM!	#NUM!	#NUM!	#NUM!	#NUM!	#NUM!	#NUM!
#NUM!	#NUM!	#NUM!	#NUM!	#NUM!	#NUM!	#NUM!
#NUM!	#NUM!	#NUM!	#NUM!	#NUM!	#NUM!	#NUM!
#NUM!	#NUM!	#NUM!	#NUM!	#NUM!	#NUM!	#NUM!
53.12	#NUM!	#NUM!	#NUM!	#NUM!	#NUM!	#NUM!
35.41	51.55	#NUM!	#NUM!	#NUM!	#NUM!	#NUM!
28.65	35.08	50.15	#NUM!	#NUM!	#NUM!	#NUM!
24.69	28.51	34.75	48.91	#NUM!	#NUM!	#NUM!
21.99	24.63	28.38	34.45	47.78	#NUM!	#NUM!
20.00	21.97	24.58	28.26	34.15	46.76	#NUM!
18.45	20.00	21.95	24.52	28.14	33.87	45.82
17.19	18.46	20.00	21.93	24.47	28.02	33.60
16.15	17.21	18.47	20.00	21.91	24.41	27.90
15.27	16.18	17.23	18.48	20.00	21.89	24.36
14.51	15.30	16.20	17.25	18.50	20.00	21.88

same number of years as in the first scenario. If, instead, you opted for larger withdrawals in order to keep pace with 3 percent inflation, you would run the risk of depleting your assets during your lifetime.

Now, let's assume that you were an investment ace and managed to earn 10 percent on your stocks the first year, which would have swelled your portfolio to $209,000. At that point, you could opt to increase your withdrawals to reflect your investing success or keep them at a rate that just matched inflation. The second course is probably the most prudent—unless it resulted in unnecessary skimping—because it provides maximum flexibility in meeting future expenses.

Even though stocks offer by far the greatest chance to accumulate wealth over the long term, you can be severely affected in the short term by enormous year-to-year price swings. In 1974, for example, the value of stocks plummeted by 26 percent; the following year, the stock market soared by 37 percent. If you had embarked on the 4 percent strategy in 1974, the value of your portfolio would have dropped by more than one-fourth in just 12 months, a severe test for even the most stout-hearted investor.

Because real life is anything but predictable and stock market returns can be expected to gyrate from year to year, this approach is best for people with other resources, such as a company pension or sizable holdings of bonds or bond funds. These additional assets enable you to pay your bills without having to liquidate some stock holdings at bargain-basement prices. Although the concept behind the 4 percent strategy is easy to understand, it's not so easy to achieve on a regular basis.

The Cadence Strategy

Developed by financial planner Dennis J. Kelly, of the brokerage firm Janney Montgomery Scott, this strategy is tailor-made for ultraconservative investors who don't want to risk a penny of their hard-earned money. The plan involves buying short-term Treasury bills, which are issued at a discount to their face value, and then using this cash discount to purchase stock mutual funds. Since Treasury bills (see Chapter 8) are backed by the U.S. government, you don't have to worry about losing any of your original principal. This safety net allows you to be more adventurous with your equity investing and gives you the freedom to perhaps choose growth or aggressive growth funds rather than more conservative growth-and-income funds. Although the Treasury bill portion of your portfolio remains fixed at the original dollar amount, the equity portion of it gradually increases over time until it represents a significant portion of your holdings.

Here's a hypothetical example of how the Cadence approach has worked in the past. Assume you sold your business in 1985 and had $200,000 to invest. Rather than buying just one-year Treasury bills with this sum, you divided the money into batches of $50,000 each and staggered the maturities of bills you purchased. With one batch you bought T-bills maturing in three months, with another batch you bought six-month maturities, and so on. Short-term rates were about 6 percent at the time, which meant, in effect, that you could purchase one-year T-bills for 94 cents on the dollar. For every $10,000 of bills purchased, you'd get a $600 check (representing the discount) from the U.S. Treasury. When the bills reached maturity, you'd get back your full purchase price and reinvest it in new Treasury bills. If you purchased $50,000 of bills each quarter, you'd get a check for $3,000 every three months.

You would then use the $3,000 to purchase shares in a stock mutual fund. Because you would be purchasing shares in the stock market every three months with your discount check from the Treasury, you would be dollar-cost averaging into equities, which is the most cost-effective way for small investors to enter the stock market. The example assumes you purchased a no-load index fund that mirrored the performance of the Standard & Poor's 500 Composite Stock Index, and that you reinvested all your capital-gains distributions and dividend income from the fund in additional shares. Six years later, at the end of 1990, your original $200,000 investment would have grown to $303,895. Stocks would represent about one-third of the portfolio, and your average annual return would have been about 8 percent.

To be fair, the 1980s were an unusually good time for stocks (despite the crash of 1987), and there's no guarantee that stock returns in the 1990s will approach those of a decade earlier. Also, the Cadence approach works best when interest rates are relatively high, as they were in the 1980s. The higher the T-bill rate, the bigger your discount and the more you can plow into stocks. Short-term rates in the early 1990s were less than half the level of a decade earlier, which meant you had received a much smaller discount check and hence had much less money available to invest in equities.

Nonetheless, this is an attractive approach for people who worry about the volatility of the stock and bond markets and want to protect their capital base. It's not a get-rich-quick scheme, nor is it designed for retirees who need the income from their Treasury holdings to meet current expenses, since that income is plowed into the stock market. Rather, it's best for people who don't need the income from their portfolio to live on. Since the income from Treasury bills is subject to federal income tax (though it is exempt from state and local taxes), and the dividend and capital-gains distributions from stock mutual funds are fully taxable, this strategy works well with tax-favored accounts such as IRAs and Keogh plans.

YOUR PENSION: PAYMENT OPTIONS

If you're covered by a company pension plan when you retire, you may have several choices about how you'll receive your pension check. With traditional defined-benefit pension plans, the starting point is to determine the amount of your monthly pension check (technically known as an annuity) that you are entitled to receive for the rest of your life. This option is called a *single life annuity,* and it provides for no benefit payments to any survivors after your death. A single life annuity is the normal form of payout when calculating pension plan benefits.

If you are married, however, your plan must offer a *joint-and-survivor option.* This means that you'll get slightly less while you're alive, but if you die before your spouse, your partner will automatically receive at least half the pension you would have received had you been around to enjoy it. It is also possible to provide your surviving spouse with 100 percent of the benefits you both received during your lifetime, but the trade-off is that you get a much lower monthly pension check.

It is possible to waive the joint-and-survivor option and receive much larger pension checks as long as you live; however, exercising this option means that your spouse will receive no further pension payments at all after you die. Because of abuses in this area (often by husbands who unilaterally opted for larger pension benefits during their lifetimes but failed to inform their wives, which meant these women did not receive any pension checks after their mates died), federal law now requires a spouse to sign a witnessed or notarized consent form, agreeing to waive the joint-and-survivor option.

Unless your spouse is independently wealthy, has an adequate pension of his or her own, or is in such poor health that he or she is unlikely to survive you, waiving the joint-and-survivor option is usually a poor idea. If you are the spouse who is asked to sign such a form, think long and hard before you do. You may be giving up a major benefit that will affect your financial well-being for the rest of your life, assuming your spouse dies before you do.

Lump-Sum Payment

You may also have the option of taking your pension as one large lump-sum payment that is equal to the value of the annuity payments you would have received if you had decided to receive a traditional monthly payment instead. The lump sum is determined by a number of different factors that are spelled out in your plan document. The key factor for you to learn is the *discount* rate of interest that the plan used to calculate the amount of your pension. You must be able to invest the lump sum at that same rate in order to equal the monthly pension payments you would have ordinarily received. To reap even greater returns, you need to invest the lump sum at a rate higher than the plan's discount rate.

Opting for a lump-sum payment is generally not a smart route for most retirees. At this stage of your life, the consequences of any investing mistakes can have a devastating impact on your standard of living. Most folks are simply not equipped to invest such a large amount as ably as the professional money managers who direct the pension plan's investments.

In addition, new tax rules require that 20 percent of the lump sum be withheld and sent to the IRS if you personally take possession of the payout. To avoid this withholding, you must arrange for a trustee-to-trustee transfer of the distribution from the plan directly to another tax-qualified plan, such as a *conduit* or *rollover* IRA (see Chapter 3). Finally, unless you are very, very disciplined, you may find it impossible not to dip into that lump sum every now and then. You might have some unexpected expenses, like a new roof on the Florida condo, or want to splurge on one of those special once-in-a-lifetime occasions, such as a fiftieth wedding anniversary cruise. Whatever the reason, to the extent that you diminish your lump sum by withdrawals, you will have less money to support you in your old age.

Opting for a lump sum *does* make sense if you have other substantial sources of income and can live on that money without touching the earnings generated by investing the lump sum. Or you may be an experienced investor, relatively sure you can do better than the plan in investing that money. Or you may plan to use the lump sum to finance a business that you have been operating for some time on the side, and in which you have considerable experience.

Beware of Pension Max

In recent years, some life insurance companies have been touting a concept that calls for waiving the joint-and-survivor option and taking the single-life annuity instead. Dubbed *Pension Max* (short for pension maximization), the idea is to use the higher monthly income that you receive under a single-life annuity to purchase an insurance policy. Your spouse then invests the proceeds of the policy after your death and presumably generates more income on these investments than he or she would have received under the joint-and-survivor option.

It may sound appealing, but watch out. In general, the only time Pension Max makes sense is if your spouse dies before you. In such a case, you could stop paying the insurance premiums, collect the cash value (if any) of the policy, and continue receiving your full pension. If, instead, you had chosen the joint-and-survivor option, you would have permanently reduced your pension in a no-longer-needed attempt to protect your spouse. If you are male, the odds are that your spouse will outlive you and that Pension Max will be an unwise purchase.

There are other reasons to steer clear of this arrangement. First, you should be relatively young when you purchase the insurance; otherwise, the premiums may be too high to justify the plan. And if you're in less than perfect health when you retire, you may not be able to purchase the coverage at any cost.

Second, even if you're in excellent health, buying a traditional whole life insurance policy (which has an investment element in addition to providing death coverage) is usually expensive at any age. An insurance company must pay its usual expenses, including the agent's first-year sales commission, to put the policy on its books. These expenses can run as high as 100 percent of the policy's first-year premium. A traditional pension payment, by contrast, already includes any administrative expenses.

Third, in comparing the costs of the two different approaches, be sure you're comparing apples to apples. That means that you must consider how much additional income you'd have left, after taxes, by choosing the single-life payout versus the joint-and-survivor option. Then you have to figure future payments from the two different approaches on a present value basis. This allows you to compare the cost of insurance purchased with today's dollars against benefits that will be paid tomorrow. All these calculations can be complicated, but they almost always make the case for Pension Max much less compelling.

If those drawbacks don't deter you, there are several other potential risks:

• *Interruption of the plan.* If you divorce after retirement, you may decide you no longer wish to continue paying premiums on a life insurance policy that names your ex-spouse as beneficiary. Or you may become absent-minded as you grow older, and simply forget to mail in the premiums. Or your expenses may grow faster than you expected, and you may not be able to afford to pay the premiums. Under all three scenarios, your surviving spouse (or ex-spouse) may wind up without any income at all after your death.

• *Long life expectancy.* These plans are based upon a projected life expectancy for your spouse. What if your spouse lives longer and the retirement fund runs dry? You can eliminate this problem by having your spouse purchase an annuity that provides a set annual payment during his or her lifetime. But there's no guarantee the annuity will provide the same stream of income that was originally projected under Pension Max.

• *The insurance company goes under.* With Pension Max, the insurance company becomes the guarantor of your spouse's retirement income. If the company fails, which is not so far-fetched these days, your spouse may face long delays in collecting the insurance proceeds, and those proceeds may be far less than the face value of the policy. Traditional pensions, by contrast, are backed by the Pension Benefit Guaranty Corporation. (If you are receiving a generous pension, however, your spouse may not get the full amount if your company pension plan were to fold.)

• *Loss of other benefits.* Some pensions offer cost-of-living adjustments, which allow retirees to keep pace with inflation. Although it may be possible to purchase similar protection under some Pension Max arrangements, it will be costly to do so. Also, if your widow (or widower) abandons the company pension plan, she or he may also sacrifice health insurance coverage.

6

INVESTING IN BANK PRODUCTS

FOR many people, investing is synonymous with putting their money in the bank. Maintaining a savings account or certificate of deposit is the ultimate security blanket for such individuals. Their reasoning typically runs along these lines: When you put your money in the bank, you know exactly what you're going to earn on that money, and your deposit is protected no matter what. You can get your hands on your money quickly in an emergency, and making the investment is as simple as strolling down to the bank branch on the corner.

The problem with this approach, however, is that over the long term, the return on bank deposits is anemic compared with the return on stocks. Even though your money is safe with a bank (as long as your bank is federally insured and you keep your deposit within the federal insurance limits), the purchasing power of that money usually won't keep pace with inflation, especially after the impact of federal and state income taxes is taken into account.

All too often, though, people fasten only on the interest rate they expect to earn. In the early 1980s, for example, when interest rates climbed into the double digits, people flocked to the bank, even though inflation also was so high that it eroded the purchasing power of their savings. When rates dropped into the low single digits in the early 1990s, those same people complained, even though inflation had subsided and the purchasing power of their savings was actually greater than a decade earlier.

THE PROPER ROLE OF BANKS

Regardless of where interest rates are at any point in time, there is a role for banks as custodians of your money. But it's important to make a distinction between savings and investments when you consider just what that role should be.

Savings are funds you set aside for the proverbial rainy day. Banks are ideal places to stash this money because it's easy to get at your money quickly, and your funds are safe. Investments, on the other hand, are a way of making the money you don't need to live on eventually grow into substantial amounts for future use, such as buying a new house or paying for your child's college tuition. Banks usually are not the ideal places to keep this money, because your money won't grow fast enough to outpace inflation and taxes.

Everyone needs to set aside some money to ride out an unexpected reversal, whether it is the loss of a job, serious illness, or some other setback. Banks are tailor-made for this purpose.

The size of your financial reserve should be determined by individual circumstances. The conventional wisdom used to be that your emergency fund should equal at least three to six months' worth of expenses, should your income suddenly evaporate. But two-career couples might need less than that, since it's likely that one spouse would remain employed even if the other suffered a job loss. Other families might need a larger reserve, especially if they do not have health insurance or if they support elderly parents as well as young children.

Banks and their brethren—savings banks, savings and loan associations, and credit unions—are also good places to park money that is temporarily awaiting investment. You might, for example, have received some proceeds from the sale of a house or from the sale of some stock. Or you could be accumulating money that will be used for the down payment on a house. In such cases, you want to make sure that your funds are liquid—that is, easy to get at—and that the money is earning some interest until you finally decide to invest it or to spend it.

You can choose among a variety of products, such as savings accounts, money market accounts, and certificates of deposit.

TYPES OF BANK PRODUCTS

Savings Accounts

Years ago, the major vehicle for savings was the passbook savings account. A pocket-size booklet recorded entries of your deposits, your withdrawals, and the interest earned on that money. Although some institutions still offer passbook savings, most of these accounts have been supplanted by statement savings accounts, which resemble the monthly statements you get with a checking account. Instead of reporting your checking activity, they report your savings activity, reflecting deposits and interest on that money. You don't have the ability to write checks with statement savings accounts the way you do with checking accounts, however.

The rates paid on passbook and statement savings are usually on the lowest rung of all bank rates. As a result, they're usually best for children and others with just a modest amount of money—$1,000 or less—to deposit. People with more cash on hand would do better to investigate other, higher-paying bank products.

If you choose to open a savings account, carefully review the rules and restrictions. Make sure, for example, that you will not be subject to an inactivity fee if you don't make deposits or withdrawals during a specified time, or a maintenance fee for the privilege of leaving your money with the institution (so it can then relend it). In some cases, these fees can erase any interest earnings on the account.

Bank Money Market Accounts

Bank money market accounts pay interest that is pegged to rates in the short-term money markets, where securities with less than a year's maturity are traded. Although they are much like regular checking accounts, bank money market accounts are more restrictive and may not be practical for your day-to-day checking needs.

First, bank money market accounts generally require a substantial minimum balance (sometimes $2,500 but occasionally as much as $25,000) that is much higher than the balance required for regular checking accounts. Second, you are allowed only minimal usage of the account. Typically, you are restricted to six transactions a month—three by check and three "other" transactions, such as in-person visits or use of automated teller machines. If you write more than three checks a month, you can be assessed a penalty of as much as $5 to $10 per check. However, a big plus of these accounts, compared to money market mutual funds, is that they are typically federally insured for up to $100,000.

Bank money market accounts go by a myriad of proprietary (and forgettable) trade names that can make it difficult to distinguish them from regular interest-bearing checking accounts. The real difference is that interest-bearing checking accounts generally have smaller minimum balance requirements and more generous check-writing privileges, but they also pay a lower rate of interest than bank money market accounts.

Although an interest-bearing checking account may be fine for routine needs, a money market account is more appropriate for those times when you need a temporary parking spot for large sums of money. Sometimes, the best deals may not be at your neighborhood bank but rather at some out-of-town institution that is soliciting funds from around the country. Before you open an account at a bank, whether local or national, compare the provisions of that institution's money market account to a money market mutual fund.

Money Market Funds

These mutual funds pool the money of thousands of individuals and invest in short-term money market obligations, such as Treasury bills and securities issued by large banks and corporations. They are not a bank product like the other investments discussed in this chapter, but they are similar to bank money market accounts in a number of ways. For example, they require investors to maintain specified minimum balances and often set limits on the number of checks that can be written each month and the minimum size of those checks. A major difference is that the money you put in these funds is not covered by federal deposit insurance. Although investors have not yet lost money because a money market fund has failed, there is always that possibility. To compensate investors for that additional risk, money market funds generally pay somewhat higher rates than bank money market accounts.

Is the potential for loss worth the extra yield? It all depends on your tolerance for risk. Money market funds run the gamut from conservative, lower-yielding funds that invest only in Treasury securities to more aggressive funds that invest in more exotic but higher-yielding securities. There are also tax-exempt funds that invest in municipal securities issued by state and local authorities, and "double tax-exempt" funds that invest only in municipals floated by issuers within a single state. This latter type of money fund makes sense only if you are a resident of that state and are in a fairly high tax bracket.

Certificates of Deposit (CDs)

CDs are a type of savings contract between you and the bank. They set forth the terms under which you agree to lend the bank a certain sum of money for a certain period of time; in return, the bank agrees to pay you a specified interest rate for that period. Generally, the longer you agree to leave the money with the bank, the higher the interest rate. Typically, rates on short-term CDs are about the same as you would get on a bank money market fund, whereas rates on longer-term CDs are slightly higher than on Treasury securities of the same maturities.

Be sure to find out what kinds of penalties, if any, a bank imposes if you have an emergency and need to get your hands on the money in a CD before it matures. Even though banks are no longer required to impose these penalties, most still do so.

Look for the best CD rates by checking the business pages of a big city newspaper that carries weekly lists of rates paid on a variety of bank products by local institutions, as well as those that accept out-of-state deposits. Don't automatically cross off institutions that are located far away from you. As long as they are federally insured, and you stay within the $100,000 limit, you should be safe. It may be difficult to monitor the financial health of a distant institution, however, and if it fails you may be one of the last to know.

Be suspicious if a bank's rates seem too good to be true. If a bank is aggressively seeking out-of-state money by paying way above the competition, it may be because it is unable to attract local funds at market rates. Should the bank later fail and be taken over by another, the acquiring bank has the option of paying you a lower interest rate on your money or returning your funds without penalty.

Also, be on the lookout for uninsured CD look-alikes that often pay higher rates than their traditional counterparts. Some institutions market what they call "thrift certificates" or "investment" certificates to unsuspecting customers. These may appear to be identical to CDs in that they pay a set rate of interest at regular intervals, but they are not "deposits" at all. And the entity that is borrowing the funds from you may not be the bank but some totally unrelated corporation. Most important, you may not be covered by federal deposit insurance if the borrower—whether a leasing company or a bank holding company—goes bankrupt. In such cases, you may wind up in line with the company's other unsecured creditors and have to wait months, even years, before you get back some or all of your money. So before you leap at a higher rate, make sure that your money is protected in the event of a business failure.

Brokered CDs

Because rates can vary significantly from region to region, you may wish to consider "brokered" CDs if rates in your area are relatively low.

This is particularly important if you live in a rural area where one or two institutions have a virtual monopoly on the banking business and don't have to worry about what the competition is paying.

A *brokered CD* is a bank certificate of deposit that is sold through a securities broker. Institutions use brokered CDs as a way to solicit funds that they are unable to raise locally. Because brokerage firms have the wherewithal to search for the best rates in the nation, the rates you get on a brokered CD may be significantly higher than the rates you can obtain from a local institution.

In the past, some troubled savings and loan associations raised money for risky real estate ventures by selling brokered CDs. After the institutions collapsed, the federal insurance system had to cover the cost of repaying depositors. Under a new law designed to strengthen the troubled banking industry, only the healthiest banks are allowed to sell brokered deposits without limits on what interest rates they can pay, and without permission from federal regulators. To protect itself against a repeat in the future, the Federal Deposit Insurance Corporation (FDIC) now allows weak institutions to hold brokered deposits only until they mature, but prohibits them from selling new ones.

The broker's commission is built into the rate you get when you purchase a brokered CD from a securities firm. But you may do slightly better—and get as much as a quarter of a percentage point more—if you contact the issuing bank on your own. The question is whether you are willing to pay for the convenience of patronizing a broker close to home or are prepared to spend the extra time to seek out the highest yields. To find the best deals, check the business section of your local newspaper or *The Wall Street Journal* for listings of banks across the country that pay the highest rates.

Alternatives to certificates of deposit, whether you buy them yourself or through a broker, include corporate or municipal bonds, Treasury securities, U.S. savings bonds, and short- or intermediate-term bond funds offered by mutual fund groups (see Chapters 8 and 9). Although these investments frequently offer better yields, they are not covered by federal deposit insurance or (except for Treasuries and savings bonds) backed by the full faith and credit of the U.S. government.

New Banking Products

As interest rates dropped to record low levels in the early 1990s, banks scrambled to keep the business of customers who were looking for better returns elsewhere. The result was that banks spruced up the menu of investment products they sell. Many now offer mutual funds that are either proprietary funds run by the banks themselves or ones run by big mutual fund companies. The drawback is that most of these bank funds impose a load (an up-front fee) that compensates the salesperson who helps you to choose a fund. Studies indicate that there's no real difference in the performance of funds sold by brokerage firms and those sold by banks. But all other things being equal, you'll have more money left to invest if you purchase a no-load fund that is sold directly to the public without any sales charges to compensate brokers or other salespeople. (It may seem like belaboring the obvious, but you should know that bank mutual funds—unlike bank CDs and savings accounts—are *not* deposits and are not covered by federal deposit insurance.)

Another new development is an equity-linked CD that is designed to soften the risk of owning stocks. Essentially a cross between a stock and a certificate of deposit, these products allow small investors to participate in the price gains of a stock market index (typically the Standard & Poor's 500) with zero risk of losing their principal at maturity.

These products sound great, but they are extremely complex and have hidden tax ramifications. Furthermore, even if a given index rises sharply, it may be very difficult to calculate how much, if at all, you'll benefit. In many cases, you may be able to do as well—if not better— by purchasing traditional stocks and bonds, or stock funds and bond funds.

HOW TO FIND THE BEST DEAL

Since the deregulation of the banking industry, all banking institutions are free to pay depositors just as much or as little as they choose. The government no longer sets maximum or minimum rates. As a result, interest rates can vary considerably from region to region, from block to block, and from institution to institution. And just because a bank pays the highest rate on a two-year certificate of deposit doesn't necessarily mean it will pay the highest rate on a money market account. A bank's rate on different products reflects its need for different types of deposits—that is, whether it requires long-term or short-term money— and that need can fluctuate from week to week. So, it's extremely important to comparison shop for the best deal on the precise bank product you want just *before* you open a new account.

Comparison shopping should be somewhat easier as a result of the 1993 Truth-in-Savings legislation (see box). This law means there should be more uniformity in the way savings yields are presented in advertisements. All institutions will be required to use a standardized "annual percentage yield" figure in their marketing materials, though banks are still fighting this provision. It will be harder for institutions to lure you with high initial rates that automatically plummet after a month or two. The law also simplifies the tricky way that banks mathematically compound interest, and it prohibits some banks' nasty habit of "reserve-adjusting," or not paying interest on a portion of your account to compensate for the non-interest-bearing balances that banks themselves must maintain with the Federal Reserve Board.

Credit unions, which were set up as savings cooperatives for workers who didn't have enough money to interest regular commercial banks, often offer the best deals for both depositors and borrowers. Because they have no shareholders, they don't have to make a profit. Also, they tend to be shoestring operations with pared-down offices and limited office hours, so their overhead is generally lower than their for-profit competition. The hitch is that to become a member of a credit union, you usually must have some sort of common bond, such as working for the same employer, living in the same town, or attending the same church or synagogue.

You may also get a higher rate by patronizing a small local bank rather than a large, nationally known one. Small banks do not have the expenses of maintaining a sprawling branch-office network and are often more flexible in setting rates than their larger competitors.

THE TRUTH ABOUT TRUTH-IN-SAVINGS

As a result of the Truth in Savings Account law, which went into effect in June 1993, you no longer have to worry whether 4 percent interest compounded daily is better or worse than 4.25 percent compounded annually. You'll be able to find out the real yield on your bank account and be able to compare it to the yield at the bank across the street. Today, all banks must:

• **Use a standardized rate called the Annual Percentage Yield, or APY, in their advertisements.** The higher the APY, the better.

• **Use a "blended" rate on tiered accounts,** ones that pay a low rate on balances up to a certain dollar level and a higher rate on balances above that level. The new blended rate that banks must use in ads must combine both the low and high rates. For example, banks that offer "step-up" CDs, which pay a low initial rate but then increase it periodically, must use a blended rate in their ads. Banks that offer "come-ons"—such as a one-year CD that pays 10 percent for the first 30 days and then drops down to 3 percent for the other 11 months—must also advertise using the blended rate.

• **Pay interest on the full balance in your account each day,** not just on the lowest balance for the month or on the "investable" balance, which subtracts certain deposit insurance fees the bank must pay and is equivalent to paying interest on only 88 percent of your deposits.

• **Notify you before your CD is slated to mature.** Only a few states used to require such a wake-up call. But now all banks must comply with a 20-day notification period for CDs that are about to come due. If, for example, a bank gives you five days' grace after the deposit matures to decide whether to roll over the account or withdraw your money, it must now notify you at least 15 days before the CD comes due. And if the institution offers no grace period on rollovers, it must notify you 30 days—not 20 days—before the rollover date.

• **Really mean it when they advertise "free" checking.** There can't be any hidden costs, such as a monthly maintenance charge, a minimum-balance requirement, or a fee for using an ATM or for writing checks.

Unfortunately, the law doesn't apply to ads for other interest-bearing securities, such as bond funds and money market funds. So you still can't easily compare the yield on a bank money market account to the yield on a money-market mutual fund.

Regardless of whether you open an account at a small bank or large one, at a credit union or an S&L, be sure the institution is federally insured.

FEDERAL INSURANCE:
YOUR PROTECTION AGAINST LOSS

In the aftermath of the savings and loan bailout of the late 1980s, it's more important than ever to make sure that the organization you do business with is federally insured. The government reported that bank failures fell to a 12-year low in 1993, totaling 42. This was a sharp drop from the peak of 169 failures in 1990.

Most banks, savings banks, and savings and loan associations are covered under the umbrella of the Federal Deposit Insurance Corporation (FDIC) up to a maximum of $100,000 per account per bank. Similar coverage is available at many credit unions through the National Credit Union Administration. Both insurance organizations are independent agencies of the U.S. government.

In addition, private deposit insurance is available in some states, although it is not always a guarantee of safety. Even though a private fund that covers Massachusetts-chartered savings banks has protected thousands of depositors in that state since its founding in 1934, a private Maryland fund collapsed in 1985, and a Rhode Island fund went under in 1990.

How FDIC Coverage Works

Despite the billions of dollars in taxpayer money that has been spent in recent years to prop up the troubled savings and loan industry, the federal deposit insurance system remains generally intact. Its broad outlines are the same as they've been for decades, and the basic insured amount for a depositor is still $100,000.

Since accrued or anticipated earnings are included when calculating insurance coverage, it's important to keep large deposits under the

$100,000 ceiling. If, for example, you had $98,000 in a one-year CD paying 4 percent, your anticipated interest earnings of $3,920 would be added to your initial deposit and bring the total amount to $101,920. If the bank were to fail, $1,920 of your money would be uninsured at the end of the period.

Because deposits in different institutions are insured separately, it's possible to obtain coverage far in excess of $100,000 by splitting up your deposits among several different institutions. It's also possible to increase your coverage by splitting up deposits in a single bank into different ownership categories. The most common categories are single (or individual) accounts, joint accounts, and testamentary accounts.

Within one bank, all the different *single* accounts of one individual, such as a savings account, a checking account, and a certificate of deposit, are added together to determine whether the person has exceeded the $100,000 coverage limit. If, for example, you had a $10,000 checking account, a $35,000 savings account, and a $75,000 CD, you would have $120,000 in single accounts and $20,000 of that would be uninsured.

Joint accounts are accounts that are owned by two or more persons. The FDIC uses a series of calculations to determine the amount of coverage for multiple joint accounts in the same bank. It is possible to get more than $100,000 in protection, depending upon how the accounts are structured.

Testamentary accounts pass to named beneficiaries after the death of the owners. These accounts are sometimes known as *tentative* or *Totten trusts, revocable trust* accounts, or *payable-on-death* accounts. Because they are in a different ownership category than single or joint accounts, testamentary accounts are insured separately as long as the named beneficiary is the account owner's spouse, child, or grandchild.

This last point emphasizes the need to meticulously observe FDIC rules when opening new bank accounts. Don't depend on advice you receive from bank personnel. In early 1993, the FDIC had to issue a special advisory to top executives of participating institutions after it received a complaint from a depositor in a failed bank who lost funds because he was misinformed about coverage for a revocable trust account.

This customer had been told that funds held in a revocable trust account, of which his mother was the beneficiary, would be separately insured from his individual account. But FDIC regulations state that such an account is insured separately *only* if the beneficiary is a child or grandchild, not a parent. Moreover, the misinformation the depositor received was not an isolated occurrence. He told the FDIC that he had posed the same question to 32 other banking institutions and in every case was given the same inaccurate advice.

FDIC Changes in Coverage

Bank personnel may also be unaware of some recent restrictions in FDIC coverage of retirement accounts. In the past, if a company invested its retirement plan assets in a bank certificate of deposit, every person in the retirement plan was individually protected up to $100,000 each. A 20-person plan, for example, would have been insured for $2 million.

But now, in an attempt to improve the financial health of the FDIC, this protection is granted *only* to those plans that invest their assets in strong, well-capitalized banks. If your plan assets—a company pension, profit sharing, or other tax-favored employee benefit plan—are invested with a weak bank that later fails, the FDIC will pay only $100,000 maximum, regardless of whether 2 or 22 employees are covered. To protect yourself, ask your employer or the plan administrator (typically, the employee benefits department) for written assurance that any plan funds on deposit with banks or thrifts remain federally insured.

Another change reduces the total amount of FDIC coverage for retirement accounts, such as IRAs, self-directed Keogh plan accounts, section 457 plan accounts (set up by some state and local governments and not-for-profit organizations), and self-directed defined-contribution accounts (set up by some corporations). In the past, you could get up to $400,000 coverage for all these accounts maintained at the same bank. Now, the amounts in these different accounts will be added together and insured for only a maximum of $100,000. If your retirement accounts exceed this figure, the solution is to split them up among several different institutions.

Commercial Insurance

The latest development in private deposit insurance is *Depositsure,* a nationwide program developed by commercial insurers to cover amounts in excess of FDIC limits. To participate in the program, you must apply by mail to Centrex Underwriters of Memphis, Tennessee. Only after sending in a written application will you learn if deposits in the bank you are considering qualify for coverage.

Although it is still in its infancy, Depositsure already has several potential drawbacks. First, the coverage will run for only six months at a time, and must be renewed after that. This means that if, for example, you purchase a one-year CD, you could buy protection only for the first half of the time period. If your bank's financial health declines after you make the initial deposit, you might not be able to obtain coverage for the remaining six months.

A second negative is that the insurance is being issued on a first-come-first-served basis. The total coverage for any one bank will be $5 million, and that maximum could be quickly exhausted if the bank is offering an attractive deal and is swamped with customers. Also, you will not get an immediate answer about whether the bank qualifies for coverage; by the time you get a reply in the mail, the good deal you were attracted to may have expired.

Third, even though the cost is modest—one-eighth of 1 percent of the deposit amount in excess of the FDIC limit every six months (the equivalent of one-fourth of 1 percent a year)—it can nibble away at your return when interest rates are very low, as they were in the early 1990s.

7

INVESTING IN STOCKS

WHEN you buy stock, you acquire an ownership stake in a going business. This is known as an equity interest, and for that reason stocks are often called *equities*. Even though your stake in a company may be minuscule, you nonetheless own a piece of everything the company owns, from its buildings and land to its equipment, products, and inventory. Of course, you also own a slice of what it owes, to the extent of your investment. As a stockholder, you also get to share in the profits (or losses) of the company.

Stockholders also have a say in how the company is run, at least theoretically. Generally, each share of stock has one vote, so the more shares you own, the greater your voting power. Every year at annual meeting time, you have a chance to cast your votes. You can vote in person, or you can cast an absentee ballot by completing a proxy. The proxy allows you to vote on matters such as nominees for the board of directors, approving the company's auditors, or items such as a change in the compensation plan for the company's key executives. Votes cast by individual shareholders typically do not carry much weight, however. If you are dissatisfied with how a company is being run, usually the only recourse is to simply sell your stock.

STOCK MARKET BASICS

Most investors buy stock to make money in one of two ways: by receiving a stream of dividends, or cash payments, from the company while they hold the stock; or by selling the stock for more than they paid for it, because the stock has increased in value.

Companies issue stock to raise money, often to finance expansion. The first time a company issues stock to investors, it is said to be *going public.* The selling of shares in the marketplace is known as an *initial public offering,* or IPO.

Companies can issue two types of stock: common and preferred. *Common* stock represents the basic ownership of a corporation and is the first type of stock to be issued. Owners of common stock share in the financial fortunes of the issuing company. If the business is doing well, they may benefit through rising dividend payments and a rising stock price; if it is doing poorly, the dividend may be cut or even eliminated, and the stock price will probably fall.

A company issues *preferred* stock only after common stock has already been issued. Owners of preferred stock, as the name implies, receive preferential treatment. They receive dividends before the owners of common stock do, for example. These dividends are fixed and do not increase, even if company profits skyrocket. If a company must cease business and sell off its assets, owners of preferred stock are entitled to receive the money they've invested before the owners of common stock get anything. Preferred stock is much like a bond with no fixed maturity.

Stock Exchanges

The stocks of major companies are traded on two principal stock exchanges, both located in New York City. The 1,900 or so oldest, largest, and best-known companies are usually traded on the New York Stock Exchange, which is variously called the NYSE or the Big Board. About 900 smaller, younger companies are traded on the American Stock Exchange, also known as the AMEX.

Stock listed on the NYSE or the AMEX is not necessarily bought and sold in New York. Instead, it can be traded at any one of the 14 regional stock exchanges located around the country. The results of stocks traded on all these different exchanges are combined at the end of each trading day and listed as *composite trading* results, regardless of where the purchase and sale took place.

The vast majority of American stocks—more than 20,000 of the smallest and youngest companies, many of them high-tech types of businesses—are traded not on a stock exchange but on an electronic marketplace known as the Over-the-Counter Market, or OTC. Traders in the OTC market don't cross swords face-to-face, the way traders and specialists do on the Big Board. Instead, they operate a national computer network and trade by telephone. The trading results of these stocks appear under the NASDAQ (National Association of Securities Dealers Automated Quotations) results carried in daily newspapers.

Some newspapers, such as *The Wall Street Journal,* list the most actively traded NASDAQ stocks under the heading "National Market Issues." Smaller, less frequently traded stocks sometimes appear under the heading "NASDAQ Small-Cap Issues." And the least frequently traded stocks are not listed in the newspapers at all. Instead, their results are collected on pink sheets that are distributed daily to brokers.

Stocks as an Investment

Over the long term, stocks represent the best bet for people who want their money to grow faster than inflation and taxes will erode it. According to studies by Ibbotson Associates, stocks grew by an average annual rate of 10.5 percent for the 24-year period 1969 through 1993, compared to 9.0 percent for long-term government bonds and 7.1 percent for Treasury bills.

Looking at a longer time period provides even stronger evidence of the growth potential of stocks. Chart 7.1 shows what would have hap-

STOCK MARKET BUZZWORDS

Every profession has its jargon, and financial markets are no exception.

Over the years, the stock market goes through different cycles, climbing upward for a period of time and then falling back again. A declining market is called a *bear market,* for the bearskin traders who used to speculate on a drop in the price of pelts and sell skins before the bears were actually caught. A rising market is called a *bull market,* supposedly from the ancient bull and bear baiting contests, with the bulls representing the opposite of the bears.

The top tier of U.S. stocks are sometimes called *blue chips* (for the most valuable chips used in poker). These are considered the elite stocks of American industry, and membership is constantly being shuffled and reshuffled. Currently, it includes such giants as AT&T, General Electric, and Exxon. *Fallen angels* are former blue chips that have fallen from favor in the marketplace, such as Merck and IBM.

Secondary issues are smaller but solid, well-established businesses that receive less attention than do the blue chips. *Growth stocks* are often the new start-up companies, with lots of potential for the future but no track record of performance and earnings, although some long-established companies are sometimes considered growth stocks, too. *Penny stocks* are for speculators only. These are shares in risky new companies that literally sell for pennies (or sometimes fractions of a penny) per share and are real long-shot investments.

Large-cap stocks are established companies that have large market capitalizations, generally above $1 billion. (A company's *market capitalization* is the total value of its stock, which is determined by multiplying the total shares outstanding by the price per share. A company with 100 million shares outstanding currently trading at $20 a share would have a market capitalization of $2 billion.) *Small-cap stocks* are, as the name implies, smaller companies that have market capitalizations of somewhere between $50 and $500 million.

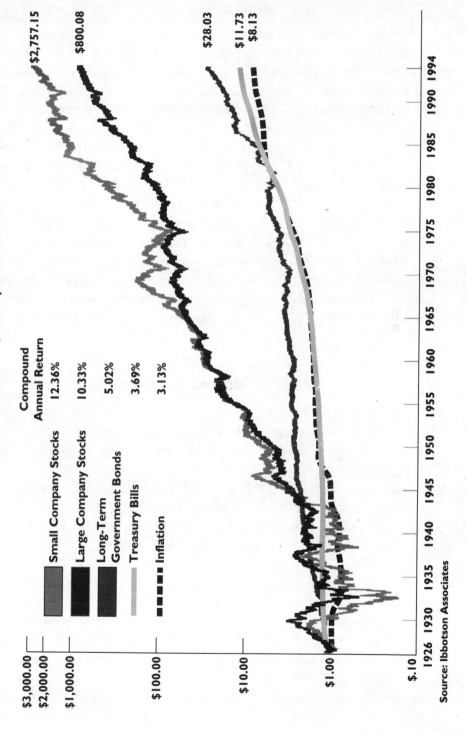

Chart 7.1 Stocks, Bonds, Bills, and Inflation 1926–94

	Compound Annual Return
Small Company Stocks	12.36%
Large Company Stocks	10.33%
Long-Term Government Bonds	5.02%
Treasury Bills	3.69%
Inflation	3.13%

$2,757.15

$800.08

$28.03

$11.73

$8.13

Source: Ibbotson Associates

pened if $1.00 had been invested in five different asset classes on December 31, 1925, and remained in that asset category through 1993. A $1.00 investment in the Standard & Poor's 500 Composite Stock Price Index would have increased to $800.08. If it had been invested in small stocks, the dollar would have grown to an even more impressive $2,757.15. Fixed-income investments, by contrast, provided only a fraction of the growth of stocks. The $1.00 investment in long-term government bonds would have grown to $28.03, while a similar investment in Treasury bills would have grown to only $11.73. The inflation index would have grown to 8.13 over the period, thus stripping these fixed-income investments of much of their modest purchasing power.

Stocks do have their down times—occasionally for many years in a row—but they nonetheless offer you a far greater shot at accumulating real wealth than do "safer" investments, such as bank certificates of deposit or Treasury bills. Furthermore, the longer your investment horizon, the lower the risk.

What Influences Stock Prices?

Stocks do not have a fixed, inherent worth. Their prices fluctuate, reflecting not only what people think about a particular company and industry at a particular time but also what they think about the financial markets in general.

Take the case of Philip Morris, the big tobacco and food company that was a favorite of investors during the late 1980s. When profits from its popular name-brand cigarettes began to fade, and the tobacco industry as a whole began to falter in the early 1990s, the stock fell from favor.

Even when a company and the industry in which it operates are in good shape, investors may nonetheless forsake the stock market as a whole because other financial markets are more attractive at the time. When interest rates soar, for example, the stock market often languishes because many people prefer to put their money in higher-yielding investments, such as bonds.

How do you figure out what a particular stock is worth? There are many different techniques, but most focus on a company's profitability.

Investors look for companies with the best prospects for strong, sustained earnings. Expectations of future earnings, rather than the current level of earnings, are a major factor in investment decisions. Good indicators may include the desirability of a company's products or services, how well it is doing in relation to its competition, the availability of new markets for its products or services, and the skill of the company's top management.

There are three major schools of thought about how to select stocks and invest in the stock market. Some analysts practice *fundamental analysis,* which focuses on the basic yardsticks of a company's financial condition, such as the state of its balance sheet, the ratio of its debt to its equity, and the expected growth of its earnings. Others practice *technical analysis,* which ignores the business fundamentals and instead concentrates on technical charts that map historical performance. This approach looks at things such as price movements and changes in performance of industries and the market as a whole. It's an attempt to predict future movements of the stock market in general, as well as those of individual stocks.

A third school of thought holds that it is difficult, if not impossible, for an investor to beat the market consistently. This is called the *efficient market theory.* It argues that all known information about a stock is fully available to both buyers and sellers, and that this information is fully reflected in a stock's price. The implication is that any investor can do as well as a professional money manager, simply by throwing darts randomly at a page of stock tables and assembling a portfolio made up of stocks picked out by the darts. Also known as the *random walk* theory, this approach to stock selection has many adherents. Studies show that random stock choices often do as well, if not better, than professional picks.

One outgrowth of this theory is passive equity management, also known as *indexing.* Indexing simply aims to match the returns of a particular segment of the market, such as the S&P 500, by passively holding a portfolio representing all the stocks in that segment or index, rather than trying to beat the market by actively buying and selling certain selected stocks. If you find this theory persuasive, you might consider buying shares in a stock index mutual fund (see Chapter 9).

Should You Own Stocks?

The first decision to make is whether you should own individual stocks. Stocks represent one of the riskiest short-term investments around, so you need an adequate financial cushion before plunking down a penny in the stock market. Realistically, that means having at least three to six months' living expenses put aside in a money market fund or a bank CD. These securities can be easily liquidated in case of an emergency.

After that, how much of your available funds you put into stocks depends upon your age, your tolerance for risk, and your other investments. If you're 25 years old and can live on your salary alone, you could invest most of your extra money in the stock market, with a heavy weighting of growth stocks. If, on the other hand, you're 65 years old and depend upon the interest income generated by your bond holdings to meet your monthly living expenses, then you will probably be better off putting just a modest portion of your available funds—say, 10 to 15 percent—into stocks.

Regardless of your age, unless you have at least $50,000 to invest, you're probably better off buying a stock mutual fund rather than buying individual stocks. If you have $50,000 or more and want to buy individual stocks, plan to split that money among 8 or 10 stocks in different industries—for example, retailing, cars, computers, financial services, oil and natural resources, chemicals—rather than sinking everything in just one or two stocks. The more diversified your stock portfolio, the better positioned you are should a few companies in your basket of stocks suddenly slump.

The Growth of Mutual Funds

Since the late 1980s, individual investors have gradually been deserting the stock market. Institutional investors, such as banks, insurance companies, pension funds, and mutual funds, are now the dominant players. Many small investors are too intimidated to venture alone into the market, particularly given the enormous drop in stock prices during the 1987 market crash. Instead, more and more are choosing to invest through mutual funds (see Chapter 9), which offer professional management and instant diversification. This may be the wisest course, unless you have the money, time, and inclination to invest in and keep tabs on individual stocks. If you do, read on.

How to Trade Individual Stocks

There is no formal requirement that you need a broker to buy or sell stocks, but as a practical matter it is hard to trade without one. So, you must decide what type of broker to use: a full-service broker or a discount broker.

A *full-service broker* is affiliated with one of the major brokerage firms, such as Merrill Lynch or Dean Witter. The advantage of such brokers is that they can provide investment advice as well as execute trades. The broker, backed up by recommendations of the firm's research department, can suggest which stocks to buy and sell, thus relieving you of the need to do most of the basic research on your own.

It's a mistake, however, to blindly follow the recommendations of a broker without doing some independent evaluation. Remember, no broker will look after your money with the same care and attention that you do. The courts have seen many cases where people took the advice of their brokers and purchased investments that were patently unsuitable for their objectives. "Churning" an account—that is, recommending numerous trades that produce generous commissions for the broker but are questionable from an investment standpoint—is a common issue in many other cases.

Discount brokers, such as Charles Schwab or Fidelity, don't offer advice. Instead, all they do is execute orders, buying and selling stocks (or bonds) as directed by the customer. In return for this no-frills approach, your cost per trade is usually a lot less, sometimes more than 50 percent less, than it would be with a full-service broker. If you are comfortable with making your own investment decisions and do not need the hand-holding that a traditional full-service broker provides, then using a discount broker is probably a smart move.

Trouble with Your Broker

One way to head off potential problems with a broker is to be careful in completing the seemingly innocuous *brokerage account form,* which must be completed when you open an account with a brokerage house. It is typically the only written document the stockbroker has about you, so it can become extremely important if a dispute later arises.

When completing the form, be sure that you don't exaggerate. If you try to impress your broker by inflating your income, your net worth, or your investing experience, you may be removing your best defense if you suffer losses because you follow your broker's advice and buy unsuitable investments. If, for example, you indicate that your salary is double its true level and you have had years of experience in investing (when in fact this is your first foray into the market), the broker may legitimately assume you are a seasoned investor who is able to tolerate severe periodic market downturns without significant loss to your overall net worth.

It's also not a good idea to give a broker complete discretion over your investments. You've probably worked hard to amass the money you now have, so don't give someone else the right to invest that money without your prior approval.

To check out your broker's closet for skeletons, call the National Association of Securities Dealers (NASD) toll-free at (800) 289-9999. This organization can tell you if there were any disciplinary actions taken against the broker or the broker's firm by the securities industry or by federal or state regulators, and if any criminal convictions were handed down. This information is disclosed by letter, not over the phone, and it does not cover any *pending* complaints against brokers or their firms.

Another source of help is the North American Securities Administrators Association in Washington, D.C., (202) 737-0900. Although this organization does not have information about individual firms or brokerage houses, it will provide the telephone numbers of securities regulators in your state (unfortunately, their numbers are not toll-free). These regulators have access to the same disciplinary data as the

NASD but are sometimes more forthcoming and will often provide disciplinary histories over the phone.

What if you have honestly and carefully completed the brokerage account form, have diligently checked out your broker, but nonetheless experience problems? First, complain to the broker directly. If you get no satisfaction, contact the branch manager of the brokerage house and finally the head office of the firm.

If you remain dissatisfied with the handling of your complaint, contact your state securities regulators (see above), who may be more helpful. Or take your problem to the regulator of last resort, the Securities and Exchange Commission (SEC), the branch of the U.S. government responsible for regulating the securities industry. Complaints must be in writing and sent to the Consumer Affairs Branch, SEC, 450 Fifth Street, N.W., Washington, D.C. 20549. (For the fiscal year ended September 30, 1993, the SEC received 16,500 consumer complaints.)

If the SEC is unable to resolve the matter, you may have no other choice but to have your case heard by an arbitration panel. The account forms used by many brokerage firms require customers to agree to binding arbitration, rather than use the legal system, as a means for settling any disputes. Even though the arbitration process is quicker and cheaper than going to court, some critics maintain arbitration is stacked against individual investors. As a result, arbitration has been subject to continuing legal challenges.

THE DANGERS OF MARKET TIMING

Some money managers believe they can anticipate peaks and valleys in the stock market by practicing what is called *market timing*. This involves exiting the stock market—and taking profits—when stocks appear to have reached unsustainably high levels and then reentering the market when prices appear to have reached their lows. In effect, this is every investor's dream: buying low and selling high.

But several recent studies have shown market timing to be just that: a dream. The reality is that patient long-term investors who have the fortitude to withstand intermittent market declines almost always do better than market-timers.

A study by the investment firm of Sanford C. Bernstein & Company compared the results of market timing to a buy-and-hold strategy for the period 1980 to 1990. It compared a hypothetical market timing plan that switched between investing in the S&P 500 and 3-month Treasury bills, and was based on which asset class had a better return for the quarter. If you had been 100 percent accurate in predicting market turns (a feat that would border on the miraculous), you would have had an impressive average annual total return of 29.1 percent for the period. But if you had correctly predicted market performance only 50 percent of the time—an extremely optimistic but much more likely possibility—you would have failed to match the average return of a buy-and-hold strategy. Another study of market timing success found that newsletters espousing this strategy beat a broad-based market index no more than 30 percent of the time.

An important implication of the Bernstein study is that there is little room for error when incorrectly predicting market performance. The main danger lies in missing a market rally, since the biggest stock gains are typically concentrated in a relatively small period of time.

Since professional money managers have a hard enough time correctly calling market turns, it's unlikely that individual investors will do better. The most prudent course, therefore, is to leave market timing to those who choose to ignore the evidence and believe they possess the crystal ball necessary to accurately predict the future course of stock prices.

GROWTH VERSUS VALUE INVESTORS

Analysts and professional money managers generally follow two different investment styles: growth or value. *Growth investors* are risk-takers who comb the equity landscape looking for companies they think will have above-average rates of earnings growth in the future. The expectation is that over time, the price of these companies' stock will rise along with their earnings, and that investors will be able to sell their holdings for far more than they paid for them. *Value investors,* on the other hand, are like shoppers in a discount store looking for bargains. They seek companies that are selling at cheap prices in terms of their underlying values. Their hope is to buy these unpopular companies at rock-bottom prices and hold them until the market recognizes their true worth; at that point, they expect to sell their holdings for more than they paid.

Because these different investment philosophies go in and out of fashion, it's a good idea to have a foot in both camps and to own some growth stocks and some value stocks (or stock funds). By diversifying your portfolio in this way, you'll protect yourself against a decline when one investment style or the other is temporarily out of favor.

Growth Investing

This aggressive and adventurous approach to investing typically (but not always) focuses on small, rapidly growing companies. The dream is to find the next Microsoft or McDonald's before everyone else. Although these companies can be found in any industry, they are often clustered in the science and high-technology areas. The consumer sector, such as fast food, low-cost motels and video rentals, is also fertile ground. Regardless of what industry they operate in, growth companies share three characteristics:

Size

The size of a growth stock is fairly small, with market capitalization usually somewhere between $50 million and $500 million. This pared-down size can make them much more nimble competitors than giant corporations laden with entrenched bureaucracies. Small companies generally find it easier than large companies to adapt to sudden changes in the marketplace, for example. Because their overhead is usually less than that of large companies, small companies may also be able to retain a larger chunk of their revenues as earnings.

Earnings

The earnings of growth stocks are anticipated to grow at a faster rate than those of the "average" company. Although investors use different criteria, growth companies are often expected to have at least three years of consecutive increases in both per-share earnings and return on equity, and projected earnings increases of at least 15 percent a year for the next three to five years. Some analysts look for stocks with an earnings growth rate that is at least twice that of the typical company represented by the S&P 500.

Dividends

Growth stocks usually do not pay out any dividends but instead reinvest profits in the business to finance product development and expansion. The lack of dividends removes an important cushion that can shield investors from the impact of a sharp fall in a stock's price. This makes emerging growth stocks far more volatile than larger, more established companies.

Despite this volatility, many investors flock to growth stocks because they offer the opportunity to make a killing in the market. Over time, small-cap growth stocks have handily outperformed their more conservative cousins—dividend-paying large-cap stocks. Their prices tend to rise higher than those of established large-cap stocks during a bull market, but they also tend to fall much lower during a bear market.

Their turbulent behavior makes growth stocks well suited for fairly young investors in their twenties and thirties who have the long-time horizon needed to shrug off their jagged performance pattern. They are far riskier for older investors, such as retirees, who may be living off their capital and cannot afford to see it eroded by temporary market fluctuations. No matter what your age, you need to have the psychological makeup and the patience to endure the inevitable roller-coaster rides that go along with owning growth stocks.

Value Investing

A much more conservative approach, value investing is akin to trying to buy a mink coat at the price of a rabbit jacket, or a luxury car for the cost of a subcompact. Rather than buying the most popular (and most expensive) stocks, value investors try to buy the most cheaply priced stocks today, relative to their long-term value.

Maintaining a long-term horizon is key: Value investors don't expect a quick profit. Instead, they usually plan to hang on to their purchases for at least three to five years. A 10-year holding period is often preferable.

Focusing on low stock prices alone can be dangerous, however. Sometimes, there are good reasons for a stock's depressed price. A company may be facing tough new competition, for example, or its industry may be on the brink of a downturn. In other cases, though, a company may be unfairly penalized. It may be part of an industry that has fallen on troubled times, but the company itself may be well positioned to survive a temporary decline that drives out weaker competitors. Such a company may become undervalued in the marketplace. Savvy investors may buy and hold its stock until the market eventually recognizes the company's true worth and is willing to pay a higher price for the shares.

The theory of value investing is easy to grasp, but doing the actual research to make it work can be difficult. The hardest part is determining if a company's stock price fully reflects its problems, and whether the reasons for its price decline are temporary or more intractable. Analysts use several different ratios to ferret out real bargains:

Low Price/Earnings Ratio

To calculate a stock's price/earnings (p/e) ratio, divide the stock price by its earnings per share. Take a company whose price is $50 a share and earned $5 a share. It has a p/e of 10, which means investors are willing to pay $10 for each $1 of earnings. If a stock has a p/e that is significantly below that of its peers, the market as a whole, or its own historic pattern, that may indicate a value situation.

Some analysts turn the p/e ratio upside down to get a company's earnings yield, and then compare it with long-term interest rates. In the above example, the company's earnings yield would be about 10 percent (1 divided by 10). If long-term rates were about 7 percent, the company would have a higher earnings yield than long-term rates and might represent a value situation. Because there are many ways for companies to manipulate earnings, some analysts prefer to look at price/cash-flow ratios instead of price/earnings ratios.

Low Price-to-Book Ratio

Book value is what accounting rules say a company's assets are worth, not necessarily what they could be sold for in the open market. The book value of assets such as land and buildings purchased decades ago is often understated, because these assets must be carried on a company's books at their original acquisition cost minus depreciation, rather than at their current (and usually higher) market value. So a price-to-book ratio tells you whether a stock's price accurately reflects the accounting value of company assets. A ratio of 1 means the stock's price is the same as the book value of its assets. A ratio of below 1, or below that of a company's industry or its own historic norm, may indicate a value situation.

High Dividend Yield

A stock's dividend yield is calculated by dividing its annual cash dividend per share by its price per share. For example, a stock that pays an annual dividend of $.50 a share and is selling at $10 a share would have a 5 percent dividend yield ($.50 divided by $10). If a stock's dividend yield is significantly above its own historic norm or that of its competition, this may indicate a value situation.

One advantage of using the value approach to purchasing stocks is that it can limit your losses in a bear market. That's because, having paid a relatively low price for your holdings, you reduce the risk of overpaying for a stock; your exposure should be less than if you had purchased more expensive growth stocks near the peak of their popularity. Also, value stocks tend to pay higher dividends than growth stocks. So, the more generous stream of income you receive can help cushion a temporary decline in the stock price.

Value investing also has disadvantages. First, doing your own research may be time-consuming; you may wish to turn over the job to a professional and do your value investing through a mutual fund that follows this approach. Also, while value investing may seem to imply a buy-and-hold approach, it really involves a buy-until-the-price-appreciates-and-then-sell philosophy. You must constantly monitor your holdings and, once you achieve your target price, be prepared to sell and start looking for new stock bargains.

Finally, even if you are a successful value investor, you should know that this investment style—like all others—periodically waxes and wanes and is not successful 100 percent of the time. When growth stocks are booming, value investing will tend to be eclipsed. Don't automatically dump your value stocks at that point, but be prepared to ride out the storm and hang on for the long term.

INTERNATIONAL INVESTING

If you're interested in the extra diversification that foreign stocks provide in today's global economy, you can buy them—not by stepping on a plane, but by simply picking up a phone and calling your broker. Such stocks are available through *American Depositary Receipts,* or ADRs. Each ADR represents one share or a specified number of shares of a foreign stock and is issued by a U.S. bank, which holds the underlying foreign shares. You can generally purchase ADRs for only the largest foreign companies, such as Japan's Sanyo and Toyota; Britain's Glaxo Holdings, Hanson, and British Petroleum; and the telephone companies of Mexico, Hong Kong, and Spain. (You can also invest in foreign stocks through international mutual funds. See Chapter 9.)

ADRs are denominated in U.S. dollars and traded on the New York Stock Exchange and the over-the-counter market. Just because ADRs are priced in dollars and purchased in this country doesn't mean they are immune from foreign currency swings, however. The dollar price of an ADR will fluctuate, reflecting any changes in the value of the greenback against currencies such as the Japanese yen or British pound.

STOCK TRADING BASICS

When you're ready to buy your first shares of stock in a company, it's helpful to know the lingo. Most stocks are bought and sold in *round lots*, or multiples of 100 shares at a time. Large trades, those over 10,000 shares, are called *block trades*. But many individual investors will trade in *odd lots*, or orders of less than 100 shares. For example, someone who has $750 to invest and wants to buy stock in Associated Gizmo, currently trading for $75 a share, would purchase an odd lot of 10 shares.

The most common way to trade in the stock market is to place a *market order*, which indicates you are asking for the best current buy or sell price. Sometimes, you may wish to give your broker more direction. Then you can place a *limit order*, which tells the broker the specific price at which you will buy or sell the stock. In the case of Associated Gizmo, for instance, you might be expecting a slight price drop, so you tell your broker you want to place a limit order to buy once the price declines to 72. Sometimes, when the market or a specific stock is dropping sharply, you may wish to protect yourself against further losses by placing a *stop loss order*. Such an order instructs your broker to sell once the stock reaches a certain price. In the case of Associated Gizmo, you could place a stop loss order to sell if the stock reached 60.

You can also put time limits on these special instructions. When you place a limit order or a stop loss order, for example, your broker will usually ask whether you want it to be "good until canceled," which means the order will remain in effect until the trade is completed (even though that could take weeks or months) or until you yourself cancel it. Or you can tell the broker that it is a "day order," which means that it will either be filled that day or automatically canceled.

Market Indexes

Investors often use *market indexes*—averages that track price changes in various types of stocks—as benchmarks against which to measure the performance of the particular stocks they own. There's no one

READING THE STOCK TABLES

If you're not familiar with stock tables, your first encounter with newspaper stock listings may be daunting. But once you understand how the tables are organized, they are simple to decode.

• *Stock name.* Determine the exchange—that is, the **NYSE**, the **AMEX**, or **NASDAQ**—on which your stock is listed and then locate the name of your stock in the tables. Company names are abbreviated and listed alphabetically. Following the name is the company's ticker symbol.

• *52-week high/low.* This figure appears to the left of the company's name and tells you the price range of the stock over the last year.

• *Div.* Even though dividends are paid quarterly, the figure in the table is an estimate of the anticipated yearly dividend per share for the coming year. If the dividend column is blank, as is the case for many emerging growth companies, that indicates the company does not pay cash dividends.

• *Yld.* This figure expresses the dividend as a percentage of the price of the stock, and allows you to compare at a glance the current income you receive from a stock with the flow of income you could receive from a fixed-income investment such as a bond or a bank **CD**.

• *p/e.* This number stands for price/earnings ratio and indicates how much investors are willing to pay for a given stream of earnings. A stock's p/e ratio is calculated by dividing the price of a share of the company's stock by the company's earnings per share. If a company sells for $50 a share and has earnings of $5 a share, its p/e ratio would be 10.

• *Vol 100s.* This figure indicates the number of shares bought and sold that day, measured in hundreds of shares. If, for example, the figure listed is 422, this means that 42,200 shares of a particular stock changed hands that day.

• *High/Low.* These two columns give a stock's high price and low price for the day. Stock prices are expressed in fractions of dollars. So, if a stock's high price was $32\frac{1}{8}$, that means the stock sold for as much as about $32.13 that day; if the low was $31\frac{1}{4}$, that means the stock sold for as little as $31.25.

• *Close.* This figure indicates the price of the stock at the end of the trading day.

• *Net Chg.* Although this is the final column in the tables, it is often the first column many investors read. It shows how much the price of a stock rose or fell compared to the final price on the previous trading day.

"right" index for all investors, and which one you follow is a matter of your own investment objectives and holdings.

The *Dow-Jones Industrial Average* is the most widely quoted index and is what most people think of when stock market averages are mentioned. The Dow, as it is called, is a formula based on the stock prices of 30 major industrial companies, such as American Express, AT&T, Coca-Cola, IBM, Sears Roebuck, and Philip Morris. The 30 companies are chosen from industry sectors considered to be the most representative of the country's financial health but they are all mature, long-established, consumer-oriented companies. Because it does not include any small or medium-size companies, the Dow is not necessarily indicative of the stock market's behavior as a whole, and it can experience much more dramatic swings than some other averages.

Many professional money managers measure their performance against the *Standard & Poor's 500 Composite Stock Price Index* (widely known as the S&P 500). As its name indicates, it tracks 500 large, well-established companies that are traded on the New York Stock Exchange, the American Stock Exchange, and the Over-the-Counter Market. The S&P 500 represents more than 70 percent of the total market and is weighted by market value, so that each company's stock influences the index in proportion to its market importance. A rough rule of thumb during a broad move in the market is that the S&P 500 will move 1 point for every 7-point move in the Dow.

Other indexes include the *Russell 2000,* which represents about 2,000 small-cap stocks, and the *Wilshire Small Cap Index,* which tracks about 250 small-cap stocks. The *Ibbotson Small Company Index* follows about 2,700 companies constituting the smallest one-fifth of stocks traded on the New York Stock Exchange. The *Wilshire 4500* covers all U.S. exchange-traded stocks, minus those on the S&P 500, and the *NASDAQ Composite* follows about 4,000 small- and medium-cap companies.

These smaller-company indexes, which mirror price changes in emerging growth companies, do not always work in tandem with the Dow and the S&P 500. Instead, they often shine at times when investors are optimistic about the earnings growth potential of small companies, while the Dow and S&P 500 often do better when investors are concerned about the economy and gravitate toward the security of larger, well-established companies.

Dividend-Reinvestment Plans

The cheapest way to buy and sell stocks is to deal directly with the company yourself. You can do this by participating in the direct-purchase and dividend-reinvestment plans sponsored by more than 1,000 companies. Under these plans, you can purchase a set amount of stock each year—sometimes as much as $20,000—or reinvest your quarterly dividends in additional shares of stock rather than taking them in cash. Sometimes, you can even purchase the stock at a discount. If, for example, a company offers a 5 percent discount on purchases made through its dividend-reinvestment plan, this means a $100 dividend will purchase $105 worth of stock.

In effect, dividend-reinvestment and direct-purchase plans allow you to buy straight from the company store, thus eliminating or greatly reducing the brokerage commissions you would normally pay and saving you hundreds of dollars a year.

Details vary from plan to plan. To participate, you must own at least one share of company stock, and preferably more, to outweigh the brokerage cost associated with making your initial purchase. If you already own stock in a company that sponsors such a plan, but it is held by your broker in "street name," you must have the registration changed to list yourself as owner before you can participate.

A few companies, such as Exxon, Texaco, and W. R. Grace & Co., will sell you your initial shares directly. They tend to have minimum purchase amounts that hover between $200 and $250.

One plus of dividend-reinvestment plans is that they force you to dollar-cost average, which means you automatically invest a set amount every quarter, regardless of how a company's stock or the market as a whole is performing. Over time, this approach should reduce your cost per share below what it would have been had you invested your money all at once. And these automatically reinvested dividends will purchase an increasing number of shares that will generate even more dividends every successive quarter.

The disadvantage of these plans is their lack of timing flexibility. You have no control over the dates on which your direct purchase of new shares and reinvestment of dividends into additional shares takes place; these dates are usually preset and may not coincide with the best times to make a purchase. For example, if a company is experiencing significant financial difficulties, you may not wish to make additional investments in it. Also, when it comes time to sell your shares, you must give the company sufficient advance notice so it can prepare stock certificates for the shares you have purchased through the plan, and then send those certificates on to you.

The pluses of these plans generally outweigh the minuses. And dividend reinvestment can be a real boon for investors who might otherwise have difficulty forcing themselves to invest in the stock market on a regular basis.

For further information, contact Evergreen Enterprises, which publishes a quarterly guide and annual directory of almost 1,000 companies that offer dividend-reinvestment and direct-purchase plans. The cost is about $30. (For further information, see References and Resources.)

Investment Clubs and Other Sources of Help

If selecting stocks on your own seems too complicated, consider joining company with other investors in an investment club. More than 9,400 clubs are affiliated with the National Association of Investment Clubs (NAIC), 1515 East Eleven Mile Road, Royal Oak, Mich. 48067, (313) 543-0612. The cost of an individual membership is $32.

Most clubs are made up of groups of about 15 people who invest a set amount (the average is about $45 per person) each month. After discussing where to invest their pool of money, a club then executes the group's decision. Clubs share a few basic tenets, such as the importance of a long-term holding period, an emphasis on growth stocks, a belief in dividend reinvestment, and the necessity of thorough research. Even though the association stresses that club membership is not a get-rich-quick scheme, members have accumulated very respectable holdings:

The average member had an individual portfolio of about $225,000 at the end of 1992.

The association publishes a raft of helpful technical materials to help clubs get started. It has an investor's manual that discusses techniques for portfolio management, and suggests how to compare similar companies and when to sell a stock. It also offers information on how to organize and run an investment club (including how to handle the bookkeeping).

Don't expect instant success, however. Most clubs lose money for the first year or two, partly because they must produce enough profits to offset the cost of brokerage commissions, which can be high in relation to relatively modest initial investments. But after that, most clubs tend to equal or exceed the performance of the S&P 500—a record that most professionally managed mutual funds don't match.

Another helpful organization is the American Association of Individual Investors, 625 N. Michigan Avenue, Chicago, Ill. 60611. A yearly membership costs $49 and covers a monthly journal and annual guide to no-load mutual funds. The association, which assumes its members are familiar with the basics of investing, has about 150,000 members and 54 local chapters across the country. It also publishes a journal on computerized investing and offers a variety of one-day seminars on a broad range of investment issues, which are held periodically in major cities around the country.

HOW TO READ AN ANNUAL REPORT

For many investors, a company's annual report, a brochure or booklet in which the company reports on its performance during the previous year and discusses its future prospects, is the first official financial information they receive as stockholders. The report, which must be filed 90 days after the end of the company's financial year, usually begins with a letter from the president or chairman of the board to shareholders, explaining why the company performed as it did. The letter is sometimes as revealing for what it doesn't say as for what it does. The tone is invariably positive (even though the financial statements which follow may be negative). So, take the prose with a grain of salt (look out for phrases such as "despite the" or "except for," which may be red flags indicating some major underlying problems), enjoy the pretty pictures, and then flip to the heart of the report: the financial statements, which include the balance sheet and the income statement.

The Balance Sheet

The *balance sheet* is a snapshot of the company's financial position on a particular day—the final day of its fiscal year. It's divided into two parts: One side reports the company's assets and the other side reports its liabilities and stockholders' equity. Stockholders' equity is determined by subtracting a company's liabilities from its assets; it represents the dollar value of what stockholders own in the company. The final numbers on both sides must always be in balance, that is, equal.

Assets

Assets are cash, securities, inventory, products manufactured by the company, office buildings, plants, land, equipment, and other items of value that can be sold off if the company ceases operations.

Current assets are those that can be turned into cash within a year from the date of the balance sheet. This category includes cash, marketable securities such as commercial paper and government obligations, accounts receivable (or money not yet collected from customers to whom goods were shipped prior to payment), and inventories (which include raw materials, partially finished goods, and finished goods awaiting shipment to customers).

Fixed assets include a company's property, plant, and equipment. These represent holdings that are used over and over again to manufacture, display, warehouse, and transport a company's products. These assets are not intended for sale. The figure listed reflects the company's original cost of these assets (even though their current market value may be much higher) minus accumulated depreciation (an accounting concept that reflects the decline of an asset's useful value because of wear and tear from use and the passage of time).

Another category of assets includes prepayments and deferred charges. *Prepayments* represent advance payments for things such as insurance premiums or equipment rental, which still have time to run as of the balance sheet date. *Deferred charges* represent sums spent in advance for things such as research and development, introducing a new product, or moving a plant to a new location. Because it's expected that the benefits from these expenditures will be reaped in years to come, the cost is gradually written off over several years.

The final category of assets is *intangibles,* which represent items that have no physical existence yet may have substantial value to the company. These items might include patents for the exclusive manufacture of a product or an exclusive cable television franchise.

Liabilities

Liabilities are the financial obligations of a company, such as amounts owed to suppliers, salary and benefits owed to employees, taxes owed to the federal and state governments, as well as long-term debt. Liabilities are divided into current and long-term debts.

Current liabilities are corporate debts that will come due within the coming year. They include accounts payable (money the company owes to suppliers from whom it has bought goods), notes payable to banks or other lenders, and accrued expenses payable (salaries and wages owed to employees, fees to attorneys, and pension and insurance payments due). Because of its size and importance, federal income tax payable is usually stated as a separate item. *Long-term liabilities* are debts due after one year of the date of the balance sheet, such as repayment of long-term bonds and mortgages.

Stockholders' Equity

Stockholders' equity is what's left after you subtract a company's total liabilities from its total assets. In a well-run company, stockholders' equity should increase year after year as the company takes whatever profits remain after paying out dividends and plows them back into the business.

Key Financial Ratios

Investors should use the balance sheet to determine some key financial ratios that are commonly used to ascertain a company's soundness.

One of the important pieces of information you can glean from the balance sheet, for example, is a company's *net working capital*. This figure shows the difference between the company's total current assets and its total current liabilities, and indicates what would be left over if the company's current debts were to be paid off. Net working capital represents available money that the company could spend on expansion or reinvest in the business, so it should be growing, rather than declining, if the company is healthy.

Another way to determine if a company is sound financially is to calculate its *current ratio*. You divide current assets by current liabilities. Many analysts believe that for an industrial company, a current ratio of 2 to 1 is adequate. This means that for each $1 of current liabilities, there should be $2 of current assets.

Other tests of a company's financial health include determining the adequacy of a company's "quick" assets (ones that could be quickly converted into cash in an emergency) and its inventory turnover (or how quickly goods are bought and sold each year).

The Income Statement

Sometimes called the *Statement of Profit or Loss*, this report shows how much the company made or lost over the past year by adding up all its sources of revenue and then subtracting all its expenses. Basically, it is a moving picture of the company's operating activities over the period and provides guidance about how well the company may do in the future. Looking at a single year is not enough, however. To make a judgment about past and future trends, you need to examine the record for a series of years, even though the latest report provides the freshest evidence of a company's performance.

The first item to look for is *net sales,* which is the most important source of revenue a manufacturing company receives from its customers for goods or services sold (this item is called operating revenues for a railroad or utility). From this figure, the company then subtracts the cost of sales and operating expenses. These represent the cost of goods sold (such as raw materials and factory overhead), depreciation (the decline in the value of corporate assets because of wear and tear), and selling and administrative expenses (such as salaries, promotion, and office expenses).

When you subtract all the sales and operating costs from a company's net sales, you get its *operating profit (or loss).* This key figure tells you how well the company's core business has done. The company's operating profit provides the starting point for calculating a number of ratios that can help you determine whether purchasing stock in the company is a smart investment.

To figure out a company's *operating profit margin,* divide the operating profit by net sales. If, for example, profits were $1.1 million and net sales were $11 million, the operating margin of profit would be 10 percent. Or, to put it another way, for each $1.00 of sales, the company made $.10 in gross profit from operations. Compare this figure with the company's profit margin in previous years. Increases in the profit margin are desirable and often indicate better operating efficiencies or a more profitable customer base. You can also compare the company's profit margin with that of its competitors; if the company profit margin equals or exceeds that of its peers, it's a healthy sign.

After a company's operating profit is determined, add in other income, such as dividends and interest earned by the company. You then get the company's *total income.*

From total income, you subtract the company's interest expense on its outstanding debt and a provision for federal income tax due. This gives you the company's *net income* for the year, which is the amount available to pay dividends on the company's preferred and common stock and to reinvest in the business. Sometimes, the company's board of directors will decide to continue to pay dividends to stockholders even if the company only breaks even or shows a loss for the period; in such cases, the money comes from earnings that accumulated in prior years.

Many stockholders are more concerned with net income (or net income per share of the stock) than they are with the dividend. But a company's net income is not always the most helpful piece of information a stockholder can have.

For one thing, net income in a given year can be affected by "extraordinary items," nonrecurring events that stand out from the company's usual income and expenses or from its customary activities. These items might include a major accounting charge (for future health insurance or retirement benefits, for example), expropriation of company properties in a foreign country by a foreign government, a special charge to reflect the cost of downsizing the company, or the sale of securities at a big capital gain. These special one-time events can drastically impact a company's net earnings and are therefore separately listed before net earnings per share.

Another important measure of a company's performance is its *return on equity,* which tells you how efficiently the company is using its resources. It is computed by dividing a company's common stock equity (or its net worth) into its net income (after the company has paid its preferred stock dividends but before it has paid its common stock dividends). To discern trends, compute the company's return on equity for several consecutive years and then compare its numbers to that of the competition.

The final item you should check is the *accountants' letter* at the end of the annual report. Usually, independent auditors will not quibble with how management has kept the books and will attest that the financial results are in accordance with "generally accepted accounting principles." But, sometimes, the accountants disagree with the way management has handled its financial reporting and may qualify their opinion. If you see the phrases "subject to" or "except for," they should send you scurrying to the footnotes, where some of the really vital information about a company is often found. For example, you might learn that the company has a number of major lawsuits pending against it, or that it has granted extremely generous stock options and retirement packages to the same management responsible for current poor earnings.

Finally, bear in mind that reading just one annual report is not enough. You must compare the results and ratios with those of previous periods, so you'll have to review past annual reports as well. Be on the lookout for things such as a decline in receivables and net sales, which can indicate that demand for a company's products is languishing, or an increase in the debt-to-equity ratio, which may indicate that a company's borrowing is too heavy for the current state of its business. Serious massaging of the numbers is best left to the pros, but there is plenty of valuable information that even novice investors can glean from annual reports.

8

INVESTING IN BONDS

Bonds are the mirror image of stocks. Instead of owning a piece of the company, you are loaning the company (or the federal government, or a federal, state, or local government agency) funds to operate the enterprise, buy new equipment, or build or improve existing facilities. Bonds are IOUs, and you as the lender are taking the risk that the borrower might default or not have the financial wherewithal to repay the funds on a certain date as promised.

In return for the use of your money, the borrower agrees to pay you a fixed dollar amount of interest at regular intervals until the bonds mature. For this reason, bonds are called *fixed-income investments*.

The conventional wisdom used to be that bonds were the safest of all investments, particularly suitable for widows and orphans. They were considered safe and secure, with a guaranteed rate of return and little risk. But these days, the bond market is almost as vulnerable as the stock market to fluctuations triggered by changes in the world economy.

For one thing, interest rates have been on a roller-coaster ride over the past few decades, soaring to record highs in the early 1980s and then dropping to near-record lows in the early 1990s. Because bond prices move in opposite directions from interest rates, people who sell their bonds before maturity often have enormous capital gains (or losses) on their holdings, depending upon where in the cycle they bought and sold. Even investors who hung on to their holdings have seen continued inflation erode the value of the principal they got back when their bonds ultimately matured.

A few bankruptcies among big municipal borrowers have made the possibility of default far less remote than once was thought. And a rising wave of bond calls—that is, forced redemptions before maturity— have deprived some investors who bought high-yield bonds in the 1980s of the lofty interest rates they expected to receive for decades. These people have been forced to scour the investment landscape for alternative investments that yielded far less.

Despite these problems, bonds still have a place in everyone's portfolio.

HOW THE BOND MARKET WORKS

When companies or government agencies need to raise cash, they try to interest the public in lending them money by *floating*, or selling, bonds. Their goal is to raise the required amount of money at the lowest possible interest rate. You, as an investor, hope to earn the highest possible interest rate with the least risk.

With newly issued bonds, underwriters—typically big brokerage houses—help structure the deal by determining the maturity and repayment terms of the securities. They then offer the bonds to the general public. With previously issued bonds, there is a secondary market operated by brokerage houses in which investors can buy and sell their holdings.

If you buy a bond at a price that equals its face value, you are said to buy it at *par*. If you buy a bond at a price that is less than its face value, you buy it at a *discount*. And if you buy it at a price that is more than its face value, you buy it at a *premium*.

The interest generated by a bond is sometimes referred to as the bond's *coupon.* In the past, bonds were issued with detachable coupons that represented scheduled interest payments. Every six months, bondholders would "clip" their coupons and then turn them in to receive their interest payments. But such bonds, known as bearer bonds (because they are assumed to belong to the person who holds or "bears" them), are no longer issued.

Today, most bonds come in either registered or book entry form. *Registered bonds,* as their name implies, carry on their engraved certificates the names of the bond owners or the owners' agents (such as banks or brokers); they cannot be resold without an endorsement or a change in the issuer's books. *Book entry bonds* are similar to registered bonds, except there is no actual certificate. Instead, a printed or electronic bookkeeping entry is put on the issuer's books, and you automatically receive statements of periodic interest payments.

Even though you can buy some bonds for as little as $1,000 each, professionals recommend against buying individual bonds unless you have a significant amount of money to invest—usually at least $100,000. The reason is twofold. First, most bonds are bought and sold in large quantities, often in round lots of $100,000 to $1 million, and the steep transaction costs of buying smaller amounts can whittle away at your net yield from the investment.

Second, with bonds as with stocks, it is important to have a diversified portfolio. Unless you can spread your fixed-income investments among several different types and maturities of bonds, you will be vulnerable to the possibility of interest rate swings and defaults.

Bond Mathematics

The first rule of fixed-income investments is that bond prices and interest rates move in opposite directions. If you buy a bond and interest rates later rise, your bond will fall in value. Conversely, if interest rates later fall, your bond will increase in value.

Why is this so? Let's assume that AT&T decides to issue 22-year $1,000 bonds at the prevailing interest rate of 8 percent. That means investors will receive $80 a year interest on the bonds. Now suppose that inflation heats up and interest rates rise by 2 percentage points in two years; now those bonds have 20 years to maturity.

AT&T then decides to raise more money by floating more bonds, but now the company must pay investors the prevailing rate of 10 percent. You decide you need cash and want to sell your old 8 percent bonds. But nobody wants to pay full price for them because it's now possible to get comparable bonds that yield 10 percent and generate $100 a year in interest income.

So you wind up selling your old bonds for less than you paid for them. Their value declines by 17.1 percent and you pocket only $829 each for bonds you bought for $1,000 each (see Table 8.1). This means you have sold your bonds at a discount; the silver lining is that the loss you suffered on the deal can be deducted as a capital loss.

Suppose instead that, two years after your initial purchase, interest rates have fallen by 2 percentage points. The new AT&T bonds pay only 6 percent and produce only $60 of income a year. This makes your old 8 percent bonds, which produce $80 of income annually, very attractive investments. You would be able to sell the bonds for a premium over their face value and receive $1,231 each (see Table 8.1). This profit is a capital gain and must be reported as taxable income.

Interest Rate Risk and Reinvestment Risk

The impact of interest rate changes on bond prices is called *interest rate risk*. It is an important consideration for investors who do not expect to hold their bonds until maturity, but rather to trade them in the secondary market. Interest rate risk is also an important consideration for people who purchase bond mutual funds. These funds are constantly replenishing the securities in their portfolios, and the net asset value of the funds' shares will vary according to changes in interest rates. Of course, if you plan to hold your bonds until maturity, you don't have to worry about the impact that interest rate changes will have on the value of your holdings.

You do have to worry, however, about the interest rate at which you can reinvest your semiannual interest payments from those bonds. This is called *reinvestment risk*. Let's return to the example of the 8 percent

Table 8.1 Percentage Change in Bond Prices

Percentage Change in Bond Prices If Interest Rates Change by 1%

Years to Maturity	Zero Coupon		5% Coupon		6% Coupon	
	Rates Rise	Rates Fall	Rates Rise	Rates Fall	Rates Rise	Rates Fall
1	−0.9	0.9	−0.9	0.9	−0.9	0.9
5	−4.6	4.9	−4.2	4.4	−4.1	4.3
10	−9.1	10.1	−7.4	8.1	−7.1	7.7
15	−13.4	15.5	−9.8	11.2	−9.2	10.4
20	−17.4	21.2	−11.5	13.6	−10.6	12.5
25	−21.3	27.2	−12.8	15.7	−11.7	14.1
30	−25.0	33.5	−13.8	17.3	−12.4	15.4

Percentage Change in Bond Prices If Interest Rates Change by 2%

Years to Maturity	Zero Coupon		5% Coupon		6% Coupon	
	Rates Rise	Rates Fall	Rates Rise	Rates Fall	Rates Rise	Rates Fall
1	−1.9	1.9	−1.9	1.9	−1.8	1.9
5	−9.1	10.1	−8.3	9.2	−8.1	8.9
10	−17.4	21.3	−14.2	17.1	−13.5	16.3
15	−24.9	33.6	−18.3	24.0	−17.2	22.4
20	−31.8	47.1	−21.3	29.9	−19.7	27.3
25	−38.0	62.1	−23.4	35.0	−21.4	31.4
30	−43.6	78.5	−24.9	39.3	−22.6	34.7

7% Coupon		8% Coupon		9% Coupon		10% Coupon	
Rates Rise	Rates Fall	Rates Rise	Rates Fall	Rates Rise	Rates Fall	Rates Rise	Rates Fall
−0.9	0.9	−0.9	0.9	−0.9	0.9	−0.9	0.9
−4.0	4.2	−3.9	4.1	−3.8	4.0	−3.7	3.9
−6.8	7.4	−6.5	7.1	−6.2	6.8	−5.9	6.5
−8.6	9.8	−8.1	9.2	−7.6	8.6	−7.2	8.1
−9.9	11.5	−9.2	10.6	−8.5	9.9	−8.0	9.2
−10.7	12.8	−9.8	11.7	−9.1	10.7	−8.4	9.8
−11.3	13.8	−10.3	12.4	−9.4	11.3	−8.7	10.3

7% Coupon		8% Coupon		9% Coupon		10% Coupon	
Rates Rise	Rates Fall	Rates Rise	Rates Fall	Rates Rise	Rates Fall	Rates Rise	Rates Fall
−1.8	1.9	−1.8	1.9	−1.8	1.9	−1.8	1.8
−7.9	8.7	−7.7	8.5	−7.5	8.3	−7.3	8.1
−13.0	15.5	−12.4	14.8	−11.9	14.2	−11.4	13.5
−16.2	20.9	−15.3	19.6	−14.5	18.3	−13.7	17.2
−18.4	25.1	−17.1	23.1	−16.0	21.3	−15.0	19.7
−19.7	28.3	−18.2	25.7	−16.9	23.4	−15.8	21.5
−20.6	30.9	−18.9	27.6	−17.4	24.9	−16.2	22.6

Table 8.1 Percentage Change in Bond Prices (Continued)

Percentage Change in Bond Prices If Interest Rates Change by 3%

Years to Maturity	Zero Coupon		5% Coupon		6% Coupon	
	Rates Rise	Rates Fall	Rates Rise	Rates Fall	Rates Rise	Rates Fall
1	−2.8	2.9	−2.8	2.9	−2.8	2.9
5	−13.3	15.6	−12.1	14.2	−11.8	13.8
10	−24.9	33.7	−20.3	27.0	−19.5	25.7
15	−34.9	54.6	−25.9	38.7	−24.4	36.0
20	−43.6	78.8	−29.6	49.2	−27.6	44.8
25	−51.1	106.7	−32.2	58.7	−29.6	52.5
30	−57.6	139.0	−33.9	67.4	−30.9	59.0

Source: *American Association of Individual Investors Journal*

AT&T bonds. Even though you will receive $80 a year from those bonds for 22 years, your actual "yield to maturity" will depend upon the rate you can earn on that $80 of interest, year after year. If interest rates drop by 2 percent two years after you buy the bonds, your yield to maturity will fall to 7.2 percent. If interest rates rise by 2 percent, your yield to maturity would rise to 9.2 percent. The only time you don't have to worry about reinvestment risk is if you purchase zero-coupon bonds.

The rule of thumb is that the longer the maturity of the bond, the greater the interest-rate risk. Here's why. Long-term bonds (those with maturities of 20 years or more) pay interest over a longer time span than short-term bonds (ones with maturities of 5 years or less). So a rise in interest rates will have a greater impact on their extended stream of future income payments than it will on bonds with a brief stream of future income payments.

Given the gyrations of the bond market over the late 1980s and early 1990s, it seems almost futile to even try to predict where interest rates

7% Coupon		8% Coupon		9% Coupon		10% Coupon	
Rates Rise	Rates Fall	Rates Rise	Rates Fall	Rates Rise	Rates Fall	Rates Rise	Rates Fall
−2.7	2.9	−2.7	2.8	−2.7	2.8	−2.7	2.8
−11.5	13.4	−11.3	13.1	−11.0	12.8	−10.7	12.4
−18.6	24.5	−17.9	23.3	−17.2	22.3	−16.5	21.3
−23.0	33.5	−21.8	31.4	−20.6	29.4	−19.5	27.5
−25.7	41.0	−24.0	37.6	−22.5	34.6	−21.2	32.0
−27.3	47.1	−25.4	42.5	−23.6	38.5	−22.0	35.1
−28.3	52.1	−26.1	46.3	−24.2	41.5	−22.5	37.4

might be in 2015. To compensate investors for the uncertain course of future interest rates, as well as for the fact they are tying up their money for a substantial period, long-term bonds usually carry a higher coupon than short-term bonds. But holders of long-term bonds may incur big losses if rates later increase and they need to sell before maturity.

Assume, for example, you bought 7-year $1,000 bonds from AT&T yielding 6 percent, and rates rose two years later by 2 percentage points. If you sold at that point, you'd get only $919 for each bond and would incur an $81 capital loss per bond. But if you bought 32-year bonds, with a higher yield of 8 percent, and rates rose two years later by the same 2 percentage points, you'd get only $811 for each $1,000 bond and would suffer a $189 capital loss per bond (see Table 8.1).

The point is, when interest rates are relatively low, you should think twice before you invest in longer-term maturities because of their higher yield. If you must sell those bonds before maturity and interest rates have risen in the interim, their higher yield will be offset by the much lower prices the old, low-yielding bonds will command.

The Importance of Total Return

The combination of yield and price changes is the *total return* of a bond. If you plan to sell your bonds before maturity, or if you own shares in a bond mutual fund whose net asset value fluctuates constantly, total return—not yield—should be the benchmark by which you evaluate your investment performance.

To calculate total return, add the interest payments you have received and the price change of the bond you have, and divide that number by the original price of the bond.

Let's return to the above example in which you bought a 7-year bond with a 6 percent coupon at par and then sold it two years later at an $81 loss after rates had risen 2 points. Your total return on that investment would have been 3.9 percent (a loss of $81 plus earnings of $120 divided by $1,000).

Compare this to the second case, in which you bought a 32-year bond with an 8 percent coupon at par and then sold it two years later at a $189 loss after rates had risen 2 points. Your total return would have been a negative 2.9 percent (a loss of $189 plus earnings of $160 divided by $1,000).

Clearly, in this situation, you would have done far better with a shorter-term, lower-yielding bond than with a longer-term but higher-yielding security.

If Your Bond Is Called

A bond call occurs when the issuer redeems the bond before it is scheduled to mature. A call typically happens when rates have fallen sharply, thus enabling the issuer to refinance the debt at much lower cost.

Bond calls are bad news for investors. People who thought they had their savings locked up at an attractive rate get their money back sooner than they expected and must find someplace else to reinvest the proceeds—probably at a much lower rate than they expected to get. For example, if you had counted on getting 8 percent for 20 years and the bond is called after 10 years, you may now be able to reinvest the proceeds at only 5 percent.

Before you buy, find out whether a bond has a call provision or a call feature. Typically, bonds can't be called before a certain amount of time has elapsed—usually 5 or 10 years, depending on the issuer. It's especially important to find out about the possibility of a call if you are purchasing a premium bond (a previously issued bond whose interest rate is higher than prevailing rates and thus sells for more than its face value). If a premium bond has a call feature, it's possible that it can be redeemed only a week after you buy it, for less than you paid for it.

Corporations and municipalities call bonds all the time. On occasion, even the federal government can call bonds. In late 1991, the U.S. government made its first bond call in three decades. It redeemed almost $2 billion of high-yielding Treasury bonds that weren't scheduled to mature for almost two more years.

Ascertaining Credit Risk

Once you buy a bond, regardless of whether it is from a Fortune 500 corporation, an obscure start-up company, a large municipality, or a local school district, you become a creditor. As such, you are now subject to *credit risk*—the possibility that the borrower will be late in its interest or principal payments, or that it may default and not repay its obligations at all. In recent years, the incidence of default has gone from an unlikely possibility to a real problem to be reckoned with, particularly among municipalities.

Defaults occur among corporate borrowers as well. One way to guard against them is to be choosy about the type of issuer you do business with. The best way to check out an issuer's creditworthiness is to find out what kind of grades it is getting from the three major credit-rating agencies: Moody's, Standard & Poor's, and Fitch Investors Services. Even though the systems and symbols are not identical, their ratings range from AAA for the healthiest and most stable companies, to the B ratings of medium-grade debt issued by less stable companies, all the way down to C-rated bonds, which carry little likelihood of achieving investment-grade status.

Don't be blinded by higher interest rates. If you want to be sure of getting back all the money (plus interest) that you've lent to an issuer, stick with a borrower that is top-rated, even though the rate it pays will almost always be below that of a lesser-ranked borrower.

Pre-Refunded Bonds

One way to protect yourself against both credit risk and bond calls with municipal bonds is to buy pre-refunded bonds or bonds that are escrowed to maturity. These types of bonds are created when a municipality sells new bonds to "refund" older, higher-coupon bonds when the next call date comes up. Meanwhile, the municipality uses the proceeds of the offering to buy U.S. government securities.

If the bonds are scheduled to be redeemed at the first possible call date, they're called *pre-refunded*; if they're allowed to run until maturity, they're called *escrowed-to-maturity*. Since both types of bonds have already been "called," in effect, you don't have to worry about early redemption. Furthermore, because the money that will eventually be paid to you is invested in securities that are backed by the full faith and credit of the U.S. government, you're getting a powerful form of insurance.

Insured Bonds

Another way to protect yourself is to purchase bonds that are commercially insured. You should know, however, that bond insurance is not an ironclad guarantee. It is only a commitment by a corporation to pay in the event of a default, and it is not necessarily backed by money in the bank. Also, some bond issuers purchase insurance because they don't qualify for a top credit rating. Having the insurance enables some of these issuers to garner ratings they probably otherwise would not get, thus making their bonds more marketable.

Types of Bonds

Corporate Bonds

Corporate bonds are IOUs issued by companies of all sizes, from Fortune 500 giants to small start-up operations. The bond maturities run the gamut from short-term (1 to 5 years), intermediate-term (5 to 10 years), to long-term (10 to 20 years). Although corporates are considered more risky than government bonds, highly-rated corporates carry little risk. The interest they pay is fully taxable.

Even though you don't participate in the issuing company's profits and growth the way you would if you were a shareholder, you do have certain protections as a bondholder. For one thing, you are entitled to receive your interest payments before the company spends the money on anything else. And in the event of a bankruptcy, you must be paid in full before the stockholders. It could take years to get your money, however, and you may not get back everything you invested.

Convertible Bonds

Convertible bonds are hybrids. They are corporate bonds that pay almost as much interest as regular bonds but can be converted into a predetermined amount of common stock of the issuing company at any time during their life. The value of the underlying shares—the conversion value—is less than the face value of the convertible when it's issued. But if the underlying stock soars, the price of the convertible should increase too, though not quite as much.

Companies often issue convertibles when low stock prices make it unattractive for them to issue common stock, or when interest rates are so high that it's too costly to float regular bonds. Because convertibles generally trade at a premium to their face value, you're usually better off selling them in the open market than converting them to the underlying common stock.

Junk Bonds

Sometimes called unrated or noninvestment-grade bonds, junk bonds are securities issued by corporations in such shaky financial shape that they can't convince anyone to lend them money except at much higher rates than comparable companies are paying. Junk bonds can be issued by "rising stars" (small companies that lack the operating history or financial strength to qualify for investment-grade status), "fallen stars" (former blue-chip companies that are experiencing hard times), or companies trying to borrow heavily in order to finance or fend off a takeover or to refinance previously incurred takeover debt at lower rates. The high rates paid by these borrowers may be tempting, so make sure you know what you're getting into before you charge into junk bonds, and be sure you're willing to absorb their above-average risk.

Municipal Bonds

Municipal bonds represent a huge segment of the bond market, dwarfing the corporate bond market. They are issued by more than a million political entities, ranging from local school districts to major cities and states. The revenues they raise are used to finance all types of new construction, from schools, hospitals, and stadiums to sewage systems and roads. Their maturities vary widely, from 1 month to 30 years. Because the interest they pay is exempt from federal taxes and, in some cases, from state and local taxes as well, municipal bonds can pay lower interest rates than comparable corporate bonds. Their tax-exempt status makes municipals especially attractive to investors in high tax brackets.

Treasury Securities

Treasury securities are the way the U.S. government finances the national debt. Since they are fully backed by the government, Treasuries are considered the safest of all fixed-income investments. Because of their safety, however, they pay relatively low interest rates.

Treasuries come in a wide variety of maturities, ranging from short-term Treasury bills that mature in 3 months, 6 months, or 1 year, Treasury notes that mature in 2 to 10 years, and 30-year Treasury bonds. Savings bonds, which are issued at deep discounts to their face value, are another type of Treasury security. Even though the interest produced by Treasury securities is subject to federal income taxes, it is exempt from state and local income taxes. Their safety and partial tax exemption can make Treasuries very attractive to individual investors.

Agency Securities

Agency securities are bonds issued by various agencies of the U.S. government. The most popular of these are bonds issued by various mortgage packagers, such as the Federal National Mortgage Association (*Fannie Mae*), the Government National Mortgage Association (*Ginnie Mae*), and the Federal Home Loan Mortgage Corporation (*Freddie Mac*). The interest on these bonds is fully taxable, although the interest on the bonds of some other agencies, such as the federal government's Financing Corporation (FICO), is exempt from state and local taxes. Because these bonds generally do not have the same broad backing as U.S. Treasury securities, they are considered to be marginally more risky and thus pay marginally higher interest rates than Treasuries.

Zero-Coupon Bonds

Zero-coupon bonds are issued at deep discounts from their face value. Instead of paying out interest in cash every six months, as conventional bonds do, zeros pay "phantom" interest. You never actually get to put your hands on the money, but the interest on taxable zeros is imputed to you annually, and you must pay taxes on it unless you hold it in a tax-deferred account such as an IRA or Keogh, or unless the zero itself is a tax-free municipal variety. The cumulative value of that interest is reflected in what you receive when you redeem the bonds for their full face value at maturity.

Zeros can be issued by corporations or municipalities. They can also be backed by U.S. Treasury securities, where they are known by trade names such as CATs or TIGRs—names bestowed on them by the brokerage houses that package the bonds.

One advantage of zeros is that they eliminate the problems of reinvestment risk, or how to reinvest the interest you receive from conventional bonds every six months. The rate you receive on a zero is locked in for its life. As long as you hold the bond to maturity, you receive that rate regardless of where rates move in the future. But because the price of a zero coupon bond is much more volatile than that of a regular bond, however, you may suffer a significant loss if rates have risen and you have to sell before your zero matures.

More on Treasuries

Probably the best way for small investors to enter the individual bond market is to purchase Treasury securities issued by the U.S. government. These securities come in a wide range of maturities, ranging from 13-week Treasury bills to 30-year Treasury bonds. They are sold by auction at regular intervals during the year.

There are three main types:

• *Treasury bills.* Also known as T-bills, these securities have maturities of three months (13 weeks) or six months (26 weeks) or a year (52 weeks). Instead of receiving interest payments, you pay less than their face value and get back the full amount when they're due.

• *Treasury notes.* These securities, which mature in two to ten years, pay interest semiannually.

• *Treasury bonds.* These securities come in 30-year maturities and pay interest semiannually.

Safety is a major advantage of Treasuries. They are considered risk-free because the return of your principal, plus interest, is guaranteed by the federal government. Another plus is their liquidity. Treasury securities are traded around the world and are easy to sell quickly in the secondary market should you need to redeem them before they reach maturity. Also, Treasuries have an important tax advantage. The income they produce is exempt from state and local income taxes (though it is subject to federal income taxes). As a result, their net after-tax yield to you is higher than fully taxable bank CDs paying the same rate.

How to Buy from the Factory Store

It's possible to buy Treasuries through a bank or a broker, but you'll pay a commission that can range between $50 and $60 for each transaction. You can do it yourself, at no cost, through a Treasury Direct account. This account is automatically opened for you the first time you buy these securities directly from the government's factory store.

The interest payments on your Treasury investments can be automatically deposited in your checking or savings account, and you can ask to have your bills or notes reinvested automatically when they mature. They can only be reinvested in the same type of security, however. So while you can roll over one six-month bill into another, you cannot roll over that same bill into a longer-term note. (At this writing, the Treasury says it is working toward giving investors that additional flexibility.)

To set up an account, obtain a *tender*, or bid form, from one of the 37 Treasury Direct servicing offices around the country (see Appendix). The one-page form is easy to complete. You will be asked whether you wish to submit a competitive or noncompetitive tender. Check the box marked *noncompetitive*. This will ensure that you receive the average rate accepted at the auction in which you are bidding. A competitive bid is one that specifies the exact rate you're willing to accept; if you set the rate too high, your bid may be rejected.

You must also fill in the amount of your tender. The lowest amount of Treasury bills you can purchase initially is $10,000; additional purchases can be in multiples of $1,000. Payment must be by certified check or bank teller's check. The minimum purchase for two- and three-year notes is $5,000; additional purchases must be in multiples of $1,000. Longer-term notes and bonds can be purchased in minimum units of $1,000 and multiples of $1,000 thereafter. Ordinary personal checks are acceptable for purchases of Treasury notes and bonds.

Treasury auctions have a regular schedule. Three- and six-month bills are auctioned every Monday. One-year bills are auctioned every four weeks, on Thursdays. Two- and five-year notes are auctioned once a month toward the end of the month. Three- and 10-year notes are auctioned quarterly, early in February, May, August, and November, and 30-year bonds are sold twice a year, in February and August.

To participate in an auction, you can either submit your bid by mail or show up in person on the day of the auction at the Federal Reserve Bank or branch serving your geographic area (or if you live in the Washington, D.C., area, at the Bureau of Public Debt). If sent by mail, your bid must be postmarked one day before the auction.

Treasury securities are issued in book entry form, which means that you don't receive actual certificates. Instead, computer records of what you own are maintained by the Treasury. With notes and bonds, the interest you earn on the securities is automatically credited to your bank account every six months.

With Treasury bills, there is an added wrinkle since they are sold on a discount basis, or for less than their full face value of $10,000 each. Result: The quoted rate you receive is a price representing the bill's discount from its face value, and your real return on the investment is actually higher.

Assume, for example, that you purchase a one-year bill at a rate of 5 percent. This means that the bill will sell at a 5 percent discount from its face value, or $9,500. Even though you've sent off a check for $10,000, the local Federal Reserve bank will wire the $500 difference to your bank right after the auction. At maturity, you will receive the full $10,000. So, you will have earned $500 on an investment of $9,500, for a "coupon equivalent" yield of about 5.26 percent ($500 ÷ $9,500). This higher effective yield, coupled with the fact that the interest income from bills and notes is exempt from state and local income taxes, often makes Treasury bills much more attractive investments than comparable bank CDs paying the same rate.

Treasury Direct is designed for buy-and-hold investors. If you expect to trade in Treasuries—buying and selling them before maturity—this program is not for you. Even though it is possible to sell Treasury Direct securities before they mature, the process is cumbersome and time-consuming, and by the time you're done, it may no longer be an opportune time to sell in the bond market.

U.S. Savings Bonds

Years ago, savings bonds were considered wallflowers, languishing on the side while people pursued more exciting and glamorous investments. But with the steep decline in interest rates during the early 1990s, investors began to appreciate the many virtues of Series EE bonds, as savings bonds are technically called.

Special Tax Treatment One important virtue of EE bonds (the only type of savings bonds that is sold for cash today) is their favorable tax treatment. The interest that accumulates on them is exempt from state and local income taxes (but generally subject to federal taxes), unlike the interest on bank savings accounts, money market funds, and CDs, which is fully taxable. Furthermore, the interest income produced by savings bonds is not taxed year after year but instead accumulates on a tax-deferred basis and is taxed only when you redeem the bonds at maturity.

In addition, some people may be able to exclude this accumulated interest income from their federal tax if they cash in the savings bonds to pay for the higher education expenses of their children, their spouse, or another dependent. This exemption applies to EE bonds purchased after 1989, and *only* if family income falls within certain limits. For 1994, married couples filing jointly with modified adjusted gross incomes of $61,850 or less, including the proceeds of their savings bond redemptions, can exclude all the accumulated interest from the bonds. The exclusion is gradually phased out for couples with incomes above that level until it disappears entirely for those with modified AGIs of $91,850 and above. For singles, the limit is $41,200, and it disappears for those with modified AGIs above $56,200. (These limits may be raised significantly if a technical corrections bill pending before Congress is enacted.)

Ease of Purchase Savings bonds are also easy to buy. They are issued at deep discounts to their face value, at half the amount they can be redeemed for at maturity. They can be purchased at banks and credit unions for as little as $25 each. No charge or commission is involved. You can also buy savings bonds through a payroll deduction plan at work, but bonds purchased in this way must have a minimum face value of $100 (which means they will cost you $50). The maximum denomination of EE bonds is $10,000 (actual cost: $5,000), and you are allowed to purchase up to $30,000 worth of bonds a year (actual cost: $15,000).

Safety A third advantage of savings bonds is their safety. Backing by the "full faith and credit" of the U.S. government means there is no possibility of default. Nor is there a possibility of a bond call.

Interest Rates and Maturities Another advantage of EE bonds lies in the way interest on them is calculated. If rates decline after you buy the bonds, the government guarantees your rate will not fall below a certain minimum floor. If rates later rise, your rate will float upward to be set at 85 percent of the rate that five-year Treasury securities earned during the period you owned the bonds. It's a win-win situation. Here are the details.

Twice a year, each May 1 and November 1, the Treasury sets the market-based rate linked to Treasury securities with five years remaining before maturity (to get the current rate, call 800-4US-BOND). The guaranteed minimum rate is changed infrequently, usually on May 1 and November 1. In March 1993, however, citing the continued steep decline in interest rates, the government abruptly announced it was immediately dropping the guaranteed rate from 6 percent (where it had stood since 1986) to 4 percent. To qualify for this minimum guaranteed rate, you must hold your savings bonds for at least six months, effective with the lowering of the guaranteed rate to 4 percent; to get the market-based rate, you must hold the bonds for at least 5 years.

The maturity date of savings bonds is determined by the tax-free rate they pay; the higher the rate, the shorter the maturity. For example, at the current 4 percent rate, it will take EE bonds 18 years to reach maturity; under the former 6 percent rate, the bonds matured in 12 years.

HH Bonds Series EE bonds (the successor to the original Series E bonds issued during World War II) are the only savings bonds sold today for cash. One other class, Series HH bonds, can be acquired only in exchange for EE bonds, E bonds, and Savings Notes (also called Freedom Shares, sold between 1967 and 1970). Because they pay interest twice a year, series HH bonds are ideal for people such as retirees who want a steady stream of income. You must report the interest you get from HH bonds each year, although you can continue to defer taxes that built up on Series EE bonds before they were converted.

Tax-Free or Taxable Bonds?

At first glance, taxable corporate bonds may appear to be better investments than nontaxable municipal bonds because they offer higher yields. But the only way to determine whether you'd be better off with a corporate or a muni bond is to compare apples to apples. This means

KNOWING WHEN TO SELL SAVINGS BONDS

Correctly timing your savings bond purchases and redemptions is important. The rule of thumb for newer bonds is to buy at the end of the month and to sell at the beginning. That's because the issue date of the bond is simply recorded as the month and year of purchase, so you receive interest for the whole month even if you bought it near the end.

Be careful when you redeem older Series E bonds, however. An original E bond may increase in value during a month other than the one in which it was purchased. If you redeem an E bond in the "wrong" month, you may lose some of the interest you otherwise would have received.

To sort things out, request a *Table of Interest Accrual Dates,* which shows the two months in which Series E and EE bonds rise in value. This table is available from the U.S. Savings Bond Division, Department of the Treasury, Washington, D.C. 20226, (202) 377-7715. Also request a *Table of Redemption Values,* which shows you how much your bonds are worth and how much interest has accrued on them. Separate tables for Series E, Series EE, and Savings Notes are available at nominal charge from the Superintendent of Documents, U.S. Government Printing Office, Washington, D.C. 20402, (202) 783-3238.

you must compare the yields of both investments on either a before-tax or after-tax basis. (See Table 8.2 on page 160 for a comparison of taxable and tax-free equivalent yields for investors in different federal tax brackets.)

Assume, for example, you are in the 28 percent federal tax bracket and trying to decide whether it's better to purchase a municipal yielding 6 percent or a corporate bond yielding 8 percent. To determine the tax-free equivalent yield, or what the corporate bond would have to yield in order to equal the yield of the municipal bond, divide the yield of the tax-free investment (in this case 6 percent) by 1 minus your tax rate of 28 percent, or .72. The result—8.33 percent—is greater than the 8 percent yield of the taxable investment you're considering, so you would be better off with the municipal.

Table 8.2 Tax-Exempt/Taxable Yield Equivalents for 1994

Single Return	$0–$22,750	$22,750–$55,100	$55,100–$115,100	$115,100–$250,000	over $250,000
Joint Return	$0–$38,000	$38,000–$91,850	$91,850–$140,000	$140,000–$250,000	over $250,000
Tax Bracket	15%	28%	31%	38%	39.6%
Tax-Exempt Yields (%)		Taxable Yield Equivalents (%)			
2.0	2.4	2.8	2.9	3.1	3.3
3.0	3.5	4.2	4.3	4.7	5.0
4.0	4.7	5.6	5.8	6.3	6.6
5.0	5.9	6.9	7.2	7.8	8.3
6.0	7.1	8.3	8.7	9.4	9.9
7.0	8.2	9.7	10.1	10.9	11.6
8.0	9.4	11.1	11.6	12.5	13.2

Source: *The Handbook for No-Load Fund Investors* (see References and Resources)

To do this calculation in reverse, so you can determine the taxable equivalent yield of an investment, multiply the yield of the taxable investment (in this case 8 percent) by 1 minus your federal tax rate, or 0.72. The result is 5.76 percent, which means that any tax-free bond with that yield or better will equal the yield of the corporate bond.

Table 8.3 What Tax-Free Yields are Worth

Tax-Free Yield	Tax-Equivalent Yield (Federal Taxes Only)	Tax-Equivalent Yield if Free from State Taxes							
		CA	CT	MA	MI	NJ	NY	OH	PA
4%	5.80	6.51	6.07	6.59	6.08	6.23	6.61	6.23	5.96
5%	7.25	8.14	7.59	8.23	7.60	7.79	8.27	7.78	7.45
6%	8.70	9.77	9.11	9.88	9.11	9.35	9.92	9.34	8.95
7%	10.14	11.40	10.62	11.53	10.63	10.91	11.57	10.90	10.44
8%	11.59	13.03	12.14	13.18	12.15	12.47	13.23	12.45	11.93

Tax-equivalent yields are based on a 31% federal tax rate. New York rates include New York City rates.

Source: *The Handbook for No-Load Fund Investors* (see References and Resources)

You must go through a similar exercise to determine if you are better off investing in municipal bonds issued by your own state, where the income is exempt from federal, state, and local taxes, or in the securities issued by municipalities in other states, which are exempt from federal but not state and local taxes. To compare the net after-tax yields of two similar issues, multiply the yield on the out-of-state bond by 1 minus your state tax rate, and compare that with the yield on the local bond.

Suppose, for example, that you live in California (which imposes an 11 percent tax on residents) and are trying to decide between a non-California bond with a yield of 7 percent and a California bond with a yield of 6.6 percent. After paying California taxes, your net yield on the out-of-state bond would be 6.23 percent (7 percent multiplied by .89, or 1 minus 11 percent). Since the California bond yields more than that, or 6.6 percent, it would be the better investment.

The same approach can be used to compare the relative advantage of a single-state municipal fund with a municipal fund that invests nationwide. Just substitute the average yield of each fund for the yield of a single bond.

The Importance of Diversification

One drawback of concentrating your municipal investments in securities issued by a single state is that you become more vulnerable to any economic problems encountered by that state. In California, for example, a severe recession coupled with a cutback in property taxes led dozens of municipalities to default on millions of dollars of bonds in the early 1990s, dealing a severe blow to investors. So, even though you may reduce your net after-tax yield by purchasing municipal bonds that are issued by states other than the one in which you live, you may be safeguarding your principal by such geographical diversification.

Also, should you need to sell before maturity, you may find it difficult to sell municipal bonds, particularly those concentrated in one geographic area. Municipal bonds are less liquid (that is, less easy to sell in the secondary market) than comparable corporate bonds. Treasury securities are the most liquid of all.

SUCCESSFUL BOND INVESTING:
BUILDING A BOND LADDER

One of the best ways to increase bond yields is to construct a *bond ladder*. First, divide the money you intend to invest in the bond market into several different bundles. Then, rather than having all the bonds come due at the same time, stagger the maturities so that each bundle has a slightly longer maturity date than the next. You will wind up with a blended interest rate that is higher than what you would get if you invested in a money market fund or a bank account, or if you concentrated your holdings at the short (and safest) end of the maturity spectrum.

The most cost-effective way to construct a bond ladder is with Treasury securities. Reason: You can buy the securities directly from the government at no additional cost, rather than going through a broker and having to pay a commission on the transaction.

Assume, for example, that you had $100,000 to invest in bonds in early 1993 and decided to put all that money into Treasury securities. You could invest $10,000 each in 10 different Treasuries ranging from 1-year bills, 2-, 3-, 4-, and 5-year notes, all the way out to 10-year notes. The yield would have ranged from 3.6 percent on the 1-year bills upward to 6.7 percent on the 10-year notes, producing an average first-year yield for the entire portfolio of 5.5 percent. This percentage would be significantly higher than the 3 percent or so you would have earned had you invested in a money market fund.

Each year thereafter, you would be able to roll over one-tenth of the money in your bond portfolio into new bonds paying current interest rates. At the end of the first year, for example, when the 1-year bill matured, you would have several options about how to reinvest your principal. If you wanted to continue the ladder into a second decade, you could reinvest the proceeds in a 10-year note. Or, if you wanted a shorter investment horizon at that point, you could reinvest the proceeds in a 5-year note.

Bond ladders protect you in two ways: If interest rates go down, you will have locked in the old, higher rates for at least part of your bond portfolio. If rates climb, you will have some new money to invest every year at the higher rates.

Bond ladders are ideal for conservative investors, such as retirees or parents of children about to enter college, who plan to hold the bonds until maturity because they want a reliable stream of income to meet future needs. They aren't suitable for aggressive traders, who expect to sell before maturity and realize capital gains.

HOW TO SELECT A BOND MUTUAL FUND

For small investors, purchasing bonds via mutual funds is probably the best route. That's because it's impossible to get the diversification you need in a bond portfolio unless you have at least $50,000 or $100,000 to invest. With a bond mutual fund, your money is pooled with thousands of other small investors, and the portfolio manager then makes purchases on behalf of the fund shareholders.

Bond funds come in all shapes and sizes. There are long-term corporate bond funds and short-term municipal bond funds. Some funds invest only in gilt-edged U.S. Treasury securities; others specialize in high-yield junk bonds. Some funds invest in the securities issued by municipalities in just a single state; others invest in bonds issued by municipalities all across the nation.

Types of Mutual Bond Funds

Regardless of the types of securities involved, bond funds are structured in two ways:
- *Open-end funds*, which are the type most people purchase, theoretically have no limits on their expansion. If they are performing well and investors' money comes flooding in, these funds can accept an unlimited number of additional shareholders. They simply enlarge their portfolios by investing new shareholder money in additional securities.
- *Closed-end funds* have a fixed number of shares that are offered only once to the public. The doors are then closed forever, and the original shares are traded like stocks in the secondary market.

One drawback is that most bond funds, of either variety, do not have a set maturity date. Even though their holdings may be concentrated in bonds of different types and maturities, such as long-term corporate bonds or short-term municipal bonds, the fund managers generally don't sit on the sidelines just waiting for these bonds to mature. Rather, most bond funds are actively managed, which means that the portfolio managers are constantly fine-tuning their holdings, keeping some, dumping others, and replacing them with new securities.

The result is that bond fund shareholders can't count on getting a fixed interest rate or a stable price per share for their holdings. (The exception is money market mutual funds, which have a set value of $1 per share.) You may get more (or less) than you invested, depending upon what point in the interest rate cycle you bought and sold your shares.

Duration

One way to gauge a bond fund's volatility during periods of fluctuating interest rates is to check the average maturity of securities in its portfolio. But *duration* provides an even sharper measure of a fund's sensitivity to interest rate changes. One measure of a bond's (or a bond fund's) life, duration is a mathematical calculation of how long a bond (or bond fund) must be held to receive its stated yield (assuming the bond was bought at par), no matter what happens to interest rates.

To get a rough idea of the impact that future interest-rate changes will have on a bond fund, multiply the fund's duration by the rise or fall in interest rates. Say, for example, Big Bucks Bond Fund had a duration of 4.5 years at the end of the first quarter of 1994. If interest rates then rose by one percentage point, then Big Bucks would lose about 4.5 percent in principal value. If rates fell by one percentage point, the fund would gain about 4.5 percent.

Morningstar Mutual Funds, a Chicago organization that tracks mutual fund performance, now publishes duration figures for corporate and government bond funds, and plans to provide such information for the bond portions of hybrid funds, such as balanced funds and asset-allocation funds, that invest in both bonds and stocks. But duration information is not yet available on municipal and international bond funds from Morningstar because it is more difficult to obtain the necessary data.

Advantages of Bond Funds

Why invest in a bond fund? There are two reasons: diversification and professional management. Perhaps you have $35,000 to invest and decide to put it all in bonds issued by a neighboring city. The bonds pay a terrific rate compared to similar investments, and the interest income you get is exempt from federal, state, and local taxes.

Now assume that the city, whose economy is linked to a big aerospace manufacturer, runs into trouble because the federal government decides to cut back on defense spending. Hundreds of jobs are lost, the city's expected tax revenues fail to materialize, and the city defaults on the bonds. You might recover some of your money someday, but right now you're in deep trouble.

If you had put that $35,000 in a multi-billion-dollar bond fund that had purchased some of those same bonds, chances are that you might not even notice the default. For one thing, those holdings probably made up a mere fraction of a percent of the fund's entire portfolio, so the impact on the fund's earnings would be slight at most. Also, because the fund is managed by investment professionals backed up by a research staff, the managers were probably aware of the city's impending problems early on and got rid of the bonds before the city's troubles became public knowledge.

Bond Fund Charges

Unlike stock funds, which reflect the stock-picking acumen of their individual portfolio managers, bond funds are pretty much all alike. Because these funds do not buy and sell their holdings as frequently as stock funds, their expenses are much lower (see Chapter 9). And when you're buying a plain-Jane product, your goal should be to get it at the cheapest price.

With open-end funds, that means not paying a load (or sales charge) to a broker. Especially when rates are low, a sales charge of 4 or 5 percent may be more than you're earning on your money. You'll also want a fund whose management expenses are modest and total no more than 1 percent of its assets, preferably less. One way to go may be to purchase a bond index fund, one that buys a basket of bonds that mimic a given bond average and is passively managed.

Closed-end bond funds tend to sell at discounts after their initial public offering. So, with a new fund, you should wait to buy until after the offering. With an established fund, wait until the discount is larger than its historic average. You can find the prices of closed-end funds in the stock listings of many newspapers. For example, *The Wall Street Journal* publishes a weekly list showing the premium to, or discount from, net asset value at which each fund is trading.

UNIT INVESTMENT TRUSTS

Investment trusts are a diversified portfolio of bonds that are packaged by brokerage houses and then resold to individual investors, usually in units of $1,000 each. The selling point of these arrangements is steady monthly income.

With UITs, brokers assemble a set basket of securities (usually tax-free municipals) and then just sit tight for the remainder of the term of the trust.

Once assembled, the bonds are not "managed" (that is, securities are not bought and sold the way they are in open-end bond mutual funds) but are rather left untouched until they mature. The idea is that investors will benefit from a buy-and-hold strategy and are not subject to the volatility and risks of short-term trading. Meanwhile, you can count on earning a steady monthly income generated by the underlying bonds in the portfolio and getting your principal back when the trust expires, usually in 20 or 30 years.

Critics maintain, however, that many bonds put into unit investment trusts are of dubious quality and ordinarily would not be touched by professional investors. They also say that having a nonmanaged portfolio is a questionable virtue in today's bond market, which is every bit as volatile as the stock market. Not only can defaults reduce a unit trust's advertised yield, but so can any bond calls, since the bondholders wind up getting part of their principal back early and then have to worry about how to reinvest the money in a low-yield environment.

Perhaps the biggest drawback is the commission, usually 4 percent of the selling price, that brokers collect when they sell a unit investment trust to a small investor. Critics maintain that 4 percent seems like a steep price to pay for a nonmanaged portfolio, especially when you can purchase a managed no-load fund with no sales charge at all.

MORTGAGE-BACKED SECURITIES

Mortgage-backed securities represent ownership in a specific group of home mortgages. Probably the best known of these are certificates issued by the Government National Mortgage Association (nicknamed *Ginnie Mae*).

A Ginnie Mae certificate represents your interest in the cash flow of a pool of government-insured mortgages. Each month, you receive a check that represents a combination of interest and principal payments from homeowners in the pool, which typically totals about $2 million at the time the loans are packaged together. Similar mortgage loans are assembled by the Federal National Mortgage Association (*Fannie Mae*) and the Federal Home Loan Mortgage Corporation (*Freddie Mac*). The securities issued by all three of these mortgage associations are top-rated, but only Ginnie Maes are directly guaranteed by the federal government.

Ginnie Maes, however, do have risks. During times of declining interest rates, many homeowners may decide to refinance their old high-rate mortgages with new lower-rate ones. You, the lender, may wind up getting a larger than expected check (representing the prepayment of some of your original principal). Receiving more money than you had expected sounds attractive, but it means you must now decide how to reinvest this money—which you thought was locked up at a certain rate for a certain period of time—at a lower interest rate than you had reckoned on.

CMOs

To counter the problem of mortgage prepayments, the securities industry created an investment called a *collateralized mortgage obligation*
(CMO). CMOs separate the mortgage pools into different *tranches,* or
slices, with fixed rates of interest payable at different periods. The
tranches are organized in a long line. People at the beginning of the
line, holding the shortest tranches, get paid first, whereas people near
the end of the line get paid only after most of the people ahead of them
have already received their money. Tranches near the head of the line
have lower yields, but they are less volatile than the ones near the end
that have higher yields.

If you buy into a 10-year tranche, for example, you would receive
payments that consist mostly of interest for about 10 years, then get
back your principal over the next year and half or so. Even with a CMO,
you can't know for sure how fast the mortgages will be paid off. If interest rates plummet, your 10-year tranche could be paid off a few years
early. And if rates soar, you might have to wait for an extra year or two
to get your principal back.

Most importantly, individual investors are usually the last to be
offered CMOs. If some good deals are around—typically the less
volatile short-term tranches—they are usually snapped up by large
institutional investors. As is the case with many unit investment trusts,
the least desirable CMOs (what's left after the institutions have picked
over the crop) are packaged and then resold to less financially sophisticated individual investors.

9

INVESTING IN MUTUAL FUNDS

FOR many Americans, mutual funds have supplanted direct ownership of stocks. There are now over 4,000 mutual funds—nearly twice the number of stocks traded on the New York Stock Exchange—and assets of mutual funds now exceed $1.7 trillion.

Mutual funds are investment companies that pool investors' money to purchase a diversified portfolio of securities, typically stocks, bonds, or money market instruments, or combinations of these different types of assets. Investors share in a fund's income, expenses, profits, and losses, in proportion to the number of shares they own in the fund. Because those securities can (and do) fluctuate in value, the value of your investment is not fixed, the way the original deposit is in a savings account. Instead, the value of your shares can rise or fall daily, depending upon the value of the securities in the fund's portfolio.

When you buy a mutual fund, you purchase instant diversification and professional management. Instead of having to assemble a diversified portfolio of securities yourself, you turn over the chore to someone else. The fund is run by a portfolio manager (usually just one person, but sometimes a team) who makes investment decisions based on information provided by a cadre of research analysts.

Because of their size, mutual funds buy and sell huge blocks of many different types of securities. Instead of buying 50 or 100 shares of stock at a time, for example, a fund may buy 10,000 or 20,000 shares. This means that the fund's brokerage costs (expressed as a percentage of the value of the securities traded) are much lower than the commissions you would pay if you were trading similar securities on your own. And unlike individual investors, who often buy and then forget about the stocks they own, mutual fund managers are expected to monitor the performance of their holdings constantly, comparing them to similar securities, to the markets as a whole, and to the performance objectives of the individual fund, in order to determine which securities to keep and which to sell.

TYPES OF MUTUAL FUNDS

The vast majority of mutual funds—and the ones largely discussed in this chapter—are the open-end type. *Open-end* means that a fund can accept an unlimited number of shareholders, using the money from new investors to purchase more securities (although this usually happens only if the fund does well and gets new inflows of cash). A few funds may voluntarily close their doors to new investors after they reach a certain size because they fear the fund has become too large and unwieldy to invest nimbly.

One drawback of open-end funds occurs when the funds fall into disfavor and are swamped with redemption orders by shareholders who want to bail out. This overwhelming number of redemptions may force fund managers to dispose of securities in their portfolios at precisely the wrong time in the market cycle.

The second type of fund is the *closed-end fund*. A closed-end fund generally issues a set number of shares just once, when it begins business. Thereafter, the fund is traded like stock on major stock exchanges, and you must pay a brokerage commission when you buy or sell its shares. Instead of buying shares in just one company, though, you buy shares in the basket of companies that the closed-end fund has accumulated in its portfolio.

Most closed-end funds tend to trade at discounts to the underlying value of the securities in their portfolios—in effect, you're buying a basket of securities for less than they're worth. Newly introduced funds usually trade at premiums—that is, for more than their underlying value. The premiums reflect the cost of bringing the funds to market, and the prices usually decline after several months.

MUTUAL FUND FAMILIES

Although some mutual funds are individually operated and not affiliated with other funds operated by the same management company, many others are part of mutual fund "families." These groups handle many different types of funds, but consolidate record keeping, marketing, and trading under one management umbrella. Investors then have the opportunity to pick and choose among the menu of funds offered by a particular fund family, and have greater flexibility in shifting their holdings from one fund to another. There are more than 100 no-load fund families and more than 150 load fund families. The biggest no-load groups such as Dreyfus, Fidelity, T. Rowe Price, and Vanguard, operate dozens of different funds and have tens of billions of dollars under management.

Purchasing a mutual fund that belongs to a large family makes it easy to switch to different funds within the group should market conditions or your personal investment objectives change. You might wish to trade a chemical fund for a banking fund, for example, or sell a growth fund and temporarily park the proceeds in a money market fund. If your fund family has telephone switch privileges, all you need to do is pick up the phone. If you are trading funds run by unrelated sponsors, it can take weeks before the transaction is completed by mail.

You can also use a discount broker to speed up switches between unrelated fund sponsors. But not all discount brokers offer this service, and there may be a charge for it, although some fund families are waiving the fees.

HOW TO BUY MUTUAL FUNDS

In order to buy a fund, you usually have to call or write to the fund adviser and obtain a *prospectus*. A prospectus is a legal document containing information on a fund's fees, risks, and investment objectives, as well as 1-year, 5-year, and 10-year performance data.

In 1993, the Securities and Exchange Commission (SEC) proposed permitting investors to buy funds by clipping coupons from ads in newspapers, magazines, or direct-mail promotions and sending in the coupons with their checks. This approach, called *off-the-page sales*, brings mutual funds in line with no-load funds that sell directly to the public, and with load funds that are marketed through brokers who are not required to show investors prospectuses prior to purchase.

It's too early to tell whether the SEC experiment will be successful. But many investors are intimidated by the daunting legal language and dense financial data in prospectuses and fail to read them, so the change may have little impact.

If you do read the prospectus, here's what to look for.

How to Read a Prospectus

Many prospectuses begin with a synopsis, or short summary, that describes the particular fund in question. Be on the lookout for any "special considerations" or "risk factors" that may be noted in the summary; this information will tell you about the fund's more unusual investments that may make it unsuitable for your needs. Here's an example (including the capital letters) culled from the prospectus of an aggressive growth fund: "THE FUND MAY INVEST IN SUBSTANTIAL SHORT-TERM TRADING, AND MAY INVEST UP TO 10 PERCENT OF ITS ASSETS IN RESTRICTED SECURITIES. THESE INVESTMENT POLICIES INVOLVE SUBSTANTIAL RISK AND MAY BE CONSIDERED SPECULATIVE." If you're nearing retirement and concerned about preserving your principal, those words should make you think twice before buying. You would probably feel more comfortable with a fund that did not have such a speculative bent.

It's also important to examine a fund's *expenses* when reading a prospectus. Expenses include the management fee, up-front and deferred sales charges, and other fees and operating costs. The fee table in a prospectus illustrates the effect of these expenses on a hypothetical investment over various time periods.

The prospectus should also provide a table on *per-share income and capital changes,* allowing you to review the fund's investment results on an annual basis for the last 10 years—or for the life of the fund, if it has been in existence for less than 10 years.

A fund's *portfolio turnover rate* tells you the annual rate at which a fund buys and sells its holdings. If a fund has a 100 percent turnover rate, that means all the fund's stocks are sold and replaced within a 12-month period. A 200 percent turnover rate means that the fund retains its stocks for an average of only 6 months. There's no correlation between performance and turnover rate: Just because a fund has a high turnover rate doesn't mean that it will do better (or worse) than a fund with a low turnover rate. But there *is* a correlation between a high turnover rate, particularly in a bull market, and your tax bill. Since a high turnover rate generally means that a fund will convert more "paper" (or unrealized) profits into actual (or realized) profits, you as a shareholder will have to pay your share of incomes taxes on those gains.

One of the most important sections of the prospectus is the *general description,* which provides a detailed discussion of a fund's objectives, policies, and types of investments. This will tell you, for example, whether you're looking at a conservative, broadly diversified fund that concentrates on dividend-paying blue chips, or a highly aggressive fund that has placed all its bets on a single emerging industry (perhaps biotechnology) and uses sophisticated trading techniques to boost performance.

For example, a fund that says it "seeks long-term growth of capital through investing in common stocks of small, rapidly growing companies" would be classified as an aggressive growth fund, while a fund that says it seeks "long-term growth of capital and reasonable current income" would be classified as a more conservative growth-and-income fund. A "value" fund, one that looks for companies that are cheap relative to their underlying assets, might say it looks for stocks with a "lower than average ratio of market price to book value."

The prospectus also explains *how to buy and redeem,* or sell, shares in a fund. It states the minimim initial investment amounts, which usually range from $250 to $3,000, and subsequent minimum investments, which can be as low as $100. The prospectus will also discuss things such as wire or telephone privileges, exchange privileges within a fund family, and special automatic purchase or withdrawal plans. The prospectus usually includes an application for the fund.

Categories of Mutual Funds

Mutual funds are divided into two broad groups: stock (equity) funds and bond (fixed-income) funds. Within those two groups, there are as many as 30 different categories, depending upon how they are subdivided. In the equity fund area, for example, the types of funds range from aggressive growth funds that concentrate on speculative new companies, to more conservative balanced funds that split their holdings between dividend-paying stocks and bonds, to international funds that invest around the globe. Similar divisions exist in the bond fund area, with funds that specialize in corporate securities, others that concentrate on tax-free municipals, and still others that purchase international securities.

Classifying funds is an art, not a science. The category in which a fund is placed depends upon the organization that is doing the classifying, and it is often a matter of degree. Although there is no one "best" fund for your needs, you should start your research by seeking a category that appears to match your current objectives. If you are just starting your career, for example, it may be appropriate to tilt your holdings toward stock funds and to choose at least one aggressive growth fund. On the other hand, if you are nearing retirement, it may be better to split your holdings between stock and bond funds and to limit your stock holdings to the more conservative types of growth funds.

The quickest way to determine which category a fund falls in is to check the daily mutual fund tables in *The Wall Street Journal,* which uses 27 different investment objective categories based on classifications developed by Lipper Analytical Services, Inc. These categories, which are furnished in abbreviated form, appear immediately after a fund's name. For example, the *Dreyfus Growth Opportunity Fund* is found under the Dreyfus group of funds abbreviated as *GthOp* and is followed by the notation *GRO* (which stands for growth). The group's *New Leaders Fund,* abbreviated as *NwLd,* is followed by the notation *SML* (which stands for small company growth).

You can also obtain this information by reading financial newsletters or visiting the library and consulting standard mutual fund reference works, such as the *Morningstar Mutual Fund Sourcebook, CDA/Wiesenberger Mutual Funds Update,* or *Standard & Poor's/Lipper Mutual Fund Profiles.* These references contain enormous amounts of information on fund performance, dividend history, performance objectives, and sales charges. They also provide telephone numbers (most of which are toll-free) for individual funds.

How Many Mutual Funds Should You Own?

Since many funds have initial minimum investments that range up to $3,000, the answer depends to a large extent on how much you have to invest. If you have $5,000 or so, then one or two funds is probably adequate. But if you have $50,000 or $100,000, 5 or 10 funds might be more appropriate. The goal is to have a diversified portfolio of funds, which include both stock and bond funds, so that you'll have some protection against the inevitable ups and downs in different financial markets. With stock funds, it's wise to own funds that represent both growth and value investment styles, and to own at least one fund that invests in foreign markets. With bond funds, it's wise to own funds with different average maturities, so that you are protected against sudden fluctuations in interest rates.

Even mutual funds require monitoring, and you should check the performance of your funds against the market averages and against the averages of funds with similar objectives at least once a quarter. If that seems like too much work, you'll probably want to keep the number of funds you own to a minimum. You may find that a *balanced* fund (which owns a combination of stocks and bonds) or an *asset allocation* fund (which owns a variety of different investments, such as real estate and gold, as well as stocks and bonds) suits your needs because it shifts most of the investment decision-making from you to the fund managers.

Stock Funds

Stock funds hold ownership stakes in hundreds of different companies. They run the gamut from the riskiest aggressive growth funds, which invest in new start-up companies, to the most conservative income funds, which concentrate on dividend-paying blue-chip stocks but may also own a generous amount of bonds for price stability.

Over the long haul, stocks (and stock funds) offer the best chance for you to achieve significant wealth, and some portion of your portfolio should be devoted to them, even if you're retired. From 1944 through 1993, a 50-year period, stocks rose by more than 12 percent a year, while fixed-income investments such as government bonds and Treasury bills hovered between 4.6 and 5.6 percent and barely kept pace with inflation (see Table 9.1). Stock funds include the following choices.

Table 9.1 Long-Term Historical Returns*

	68 years 1/1/26–12/31/93	50 years 1/1/44–12/31/93
Common stocks (S&P 500)	10.33%	12.30%
Corporate bonds (long-term)	5.58	5.57
Government bonds (long-term)	5.03	5.24
Treasury bills	3.67	4.61
Inflation (Consumer Price Index)	3.13	4.35

*Compound annual returns with income reinvested

Source: *The Handbook for No-Load Fund Investors* (see References and Resources, p.251)

Aggressive Growth Funds

Aggressive growth funds aim for the greatest possible profits in the shortest possible time. They promise the greatest rewards and entail the greatest risks for individual investors. Sometimes known as "maximum capital gain," "capital appreciation," or "performance" funds, they invest in speculative stocks, often those of small or emerging companies with unknown track records or no track records at all. The dividend-paying ability of stocks in their portfolios is unimportant. These companies may have great prospects for success, but they also have a substantial chance of failure. Aggressive growth funds are very volatile, often leading all other types of stock funds in bull markets and doing extremely poorly in bear markets.

Aggressive growth funds may also engage in adventurous trading techniques—such as selling short, buying on margin, and using options and straddles—in an effort to give profits an added burst of adrenaline. These funds make for great cocktail party conversation (as long as they're doing well), but they are not for the faint of heart.

How do you know if the fund you're considering is an aggressive growth fund? It might describe its objectives in the following manner: "Seeks significant capital appreciation by investing in securities, primarily common stocks, that management believes are more aggressive and carry a greater degree of risk than the market as a whole. . . ."

Growth Funds

If aggressive growth funds make you nervous, you may be more comfortable with growth funds, sometimes known as long-term growth funds. The investment policies of these funds are more conservative than those of aggressive growth funds, though these differences are often a matter of degree. The emphasis here is on long-term growth rather than short-term profits. These funds tend to hold the stocks of larger, well-established companies and don't turn their portfolios as frequently as aggressive growth funds. Nor do they tend to use speculative trading approaches.

Growth funds usually follow one of two different investment styles. *Growth* managers look for companies with prospects of rapid earnings growth—the target increase is usually at least 15 percent a year—and do not search for companies that pay out steady or increasing dividends. *Value* managers look for stocks whose prices are relatively cheap compared to what these managers think the companies are really worth. Such funds often have the word "value" in their name and tend to own stocks with lower price/earnings ratios, lower price-to-book ratios, and higher dividend yields than pure growth funds.

These two investment styles act like a seesaw: When one is up, the other is down. So it's a smart idea to own both types of funds if you have enough money to meet the minimum investment requirements. This will increase the diversity of your portfolio, as well as the likelihood that at least one segment of your investment portfolio will be performing well at any given time.

Although both growth and value stock funds are less volatile than aggressive growth funds, they are not immune from market ups and downs. They tend to do well during bull markets but can suffer major price declines during bear markets. These funds are for investors with relatively long time horizons—at least six or seven years—who want to see their investments grow faster than inflation but who also can tolerate periodic peaks and troughs in the funds' performance.

Here's how a pure growth fund might describe itself: "Primary objective is capital appreciation, and secondary objective is current income. Invests in readily marketable common stocks of established companies. In many cases, dividends are paid on these investments, but the amount of dividends is not a major factor in selecting stocks. . . ."

A value fund might say "Seeks common stocks with lower than average ratio of market price to book value," or "invests in undervalued securities."

Growth-and-Income Funds

Growth-and-income funds are for conservative investors who want long-term growth of capital plus a reliable stream of income. You know you're dealing with a growth-income fund if the prospectus says its aim is to provide you with a "reasonable" return on your money by investing in common and preferred stocks of established companies. Growth-and-income funds have higher dividend yields than either growth or aggressive growth funds, and this steady dividend component helps to reduce their volatility. They do not engage in the speculative trading techniques used by their riskier cousins.

Here's how a typical growth-income fund might state its objectives: "Seeks long-term growth of capital, a reasonable level of current income and an increase in future income through investments in income-producing equity securities that have prospects for both growth of capital and dividend income."

Income Funds

Despite their name, income funds invest a major portion of their assets in stocks (but only income-producing stocks) and the rest in convertible securities and bonds. On the risk spectrum, these funds are considered less volatile than growth funds but more risky than bond funds. Their dividend yield is typically greater than other diversified stock funds but less than long-term bond funds. There are several different types of income funds, all with slightly different investment objectives. All are appropriate for conservative investors, particularly retirees, who rely upon a steady stream of dividend income but also want some exposure to the stock market in order to protect their money against the effects of inflation.

Equity-income funds Equity-income funds aim for liberal current income; capital gains are typically secondary. Such a fund might describe itself as follows: "Goal is high current income and capital appreciation, with primary emphasis on income and secondary emphasis on capital appreciation."

Balanced Funds

Balanced funds try to "balance," or combine, equity and fixed-income investments in a single portfolio. Their prospectuses usually require them to maintain a fixed ratio of stocks to bonds—often 60 percent stocks to 40 percent bonds. Balanced funds are a smart idea for novice investors who feel they lack the expertise to split their holdings between stocks and bonds, and would rather turn the job over to a fund portfolio manager. They're also a good idea for people who don't have the necessary money to meet the minimum investment requirements of several different mutual funds.

Asset Allocation Funds

Sometimes known as *flexible portfolio funds,* asset allocation funds typically invest a set range of their portfolios in five or six different asset classes, such as stocks, bonds, real estate, gold and mining, and international securities. The idea is to create one broadly diversified fund with ownership interests in a wide spectrum of financial markets that generally do not move in lockstep with the U.S. stock market.

Convertible Securities Funds

Convertible securities funds invest in *convertibles*—bonds or preferred stock that can be exchanged for the common stock of the company that issued them. Companies usually sell convertibles when the stock market is down and it is difficult to issue new common stocks, or when long-term interest rates are so high that it is too expensive to issue new bonds. The conversion feature is an attempt to persuade investors to accept below-market interest rates in hopes that the underlying stock will increase in value and that the bonds will follow suit.

International and Global Funds

International and global stock funds have a major portion of their holdings outside U.S. borders. The increasing popularity of these funds reflects the growth of foreign stock markets in recent years. About two-thirds of the world's publicly traded stocks and nearly the same percentage of bonds are now registered outside the United States. Given the continuing challenge that American industry faces in world markets, it's probably smart to own at least one international fund.

There are two major types. *International funds* (sometimes called foreign funds) invest exclusively overseas; *global funds* invest both in the United States and abroad. Some international funds specialize in certain regions, such as the Pacific Rim, Latin America, or Western Europe. Others limit themselves to single countries, such as Mexico, Thailand, or Switzerland; because of their lack of liquidity, such single-country funds are usually organized as closed-end funds.

The advantage of international and global funds is that they offer you greater diversification than an all-U.S. portfolio. The world's stock markets don't necessarily move in tandem; in fact, during many recent years, the performance of foreign exchanges has far outstripped the performance of the domestic stock market. Investing in these funds is also advantageous when there is a drop in the value of the U.S. dollar compared to other currencies; this makes stock holdings in those currencies more valuable. Conversely, international funds can suffer when the dollar appreciates against other currencies. Management and transaction fees tend to be higher with these funds than with domestic funds because it is more costly and complicated to trade overseas holdings.

Sector Funds

Sector funds limit their portfolio holdings to a particular industry, or sector. Just name an industry, and there's probably a sector fund for it. There are bank funds, S&L funds, chemical funds, health-care funds, biotechnology funds, utility funds, communications funds, transportation funds, aviation funds, real estate funds, precious metals funds, and so on. Some sector funds can post dazzling returns when their industry is shining but dismal returns when that industry falls out of favor. Health-care funds, which were stars in the late 1980s and early 1990s but strikeouts a few years later, are a prime example of the volatility of sector funds.

These funds are for traders who are able to devote the time to following a particular sector and have the psychological makeup to jump in and out of different industries on short notice. The best time to buy a sector fund is when it's at the bottom of the performance lists, but that requires a stronger stomach than many people have. Conversely, the best time to sell is when your fund is steaming along, leaving other funds in its dust. This, too, requires more resolve than most people can muster. If you're most comfortable pursuing a buy-and-hold investment philosophy, you will probably find that owning a sector fund causes too much anxiety.

Socially Responsible Funds

Socially responsible funds have spurned investments in industries of which they disapprove. Their investment blacklist may include companies involved in military-related manufacturing, nuclear power, alcohol, tobacco, and gambling. Some funds won't invest in companies that do business in South Africa. Others won't buy stock in companies that pollute the environment. Still others won't invest in businesses that engage in unfair labor practices.

Of course, what entails socially irresponsible behavior is an individual decision. You may consider U.S. Treasury obligations to be a relatively benign investment, but there's even a fund that avoids purchasing these securities on the grounds that the money they raise can be used to finance defense spending.

Even if you agree with the aims of socially responsible funds, you need to consider whether buying them is a wise investment. The record, while far from black-and-white, indicates you'll probably pay a price for your conscience. Even though socially responsible funds occasionally lead the pack, several studies have shown that they tend to lag the performance of average equity funds by anywhere from 1 percentage point to 10 percentage points a year. If you want to back certain causes, you may do better by investing in a "neutral" fund, such as an index fund, and using some of your profits to make a charitable donation to organizations whose goals you support.

Index Funds

For many people, the mention of index funds evokes a yawn. That's because these funds, which assemble portfolios of stocks or bonds that mimic a given market index, aren't actively traded; once the securities are acquired, they usually aren't touched unless certain stocks are added or dropped from the index. These funds simply aim to passively match the composition and performance of securities in the index they track; they do no better and no worse (except for some modest transaction charges) than the index on which they are modeled. Because their holdings are turned over infrequently, index funds tend to have exceptionally low management fees and much smaller commission costs, operating expenses and capital gains distributions than their more actively managed cousins. This gives them a powerful edge that belies their modest demeanor.

You might think that given their ho-hum objective, the performance of index funds would be eclipsed by funds managed by professional money managers, who are paid big salaries to outsmart the market. But the fact is that since the first index fund was introduced in 1976, it has provided better returns than most professionally managed stock funds. Index funds may be boring, but they have made money for their shareholders. For this reason, some financial advisers say that index funds should make up the core of individual investors' holdings in the stock market.

Critics of index funds say that in a prolonged bear market, which these funds have not yet experienced, such funds can lose money for their shareholders. Detractors also maintain that investors should not have to settle for the "average" returns of index funds. But the passive investing approach of index funds may seem much more attractive when you consider that only one-third of general equity mutual funds managed to exceed the performance of the Standard & Poor's 500 stock index over the decade ended December 1991.

The original index fund, started by the Vanguard Group, is modeled on the Standard & Poor's 500 Composite Stock Price Index, which represents about 70 percent of the total market value of American stocks. It clones the S&P 500 by buying all 500 companies in proportion to each company's market capitalization (that is, its number of shares outstanding multiplied by its market price). The result is that the fund is tilted toward large company stocks and contains fewer small company stocks. This fund proved so popular that other fund families introduced their versions, too, and those versions proved so popular that there now are about 70 index funds on the scene (see Table 9.2).

Table 9.2 Index and Passively Managed Funds

Fund	Index
S&P 500 Funds	
CA Inv Tr-S&P 500 Index	S&P 500
DFA U.S. Lg Co+	S&P 500
Dreyfus Peoples Index	S&P 500
Federated Max-Cap	S&P 500
Fidelity Market Index	S&P 500
IBM Lg Co Index+	S&P 500
Portico Equity Index	S&P 500
Price, Rowe Equity Index	S&P 500
Seven Seas S&P 500 Index	S&P 500
Stagecoach S&P 500 Stock	S&P 500
Vangd Index 500	S&P 500
Vangd Index Growth	S&P 500
Vangd Index Value	S&P 500
Woodward Equity Index	S&P 500
Other large company indexes	
ASM Fund	DJIA
DFA U.S. Large Cap Value	
Drey-Wilsh Lg Co Gro	Wilshire 5000
Drey-Wilsh Lg Co Value	Wilshire 5000
Lexington Corporate Lenders Trust	
Schwab 1000	
Vangd Index Total Market	Wilshire 5000
MidCap Indexes	
CA Inv Tr-S&P MidCap Index	S&P MidCap 400
Dreyfus Peoples MidCap	S&P MidCap 400
Federated Mid-Cap	S&P MidCap 400
Gateway Mid-Cap Index	S&P MidCap 400

Comments	Total Return	
	1993	5 yrs (ann)
500 large and medium size companies	9.8	—
500 large and medium size companies	9.8	—
500 large and medium size companies	9.5	—
500 large and medium size companies	9.5	—
500 large and medium size companies	9.6	—
500 large and medium size companies	9.6	—
500 large and medium size companies	9.1	—
500 large and medium size companies	9.4	—
500 large and medium size companies	9.6	—
500 large and medium size companies	—	—
500 large and medium size companies	9.9	14.3
174 companies w/hi price/book ratios	1.5	—
326 companies w/low price/book ratios	18.2	—
500 large and medium size companies	9.8	—
Dow look-alike	13.3	—
Listed stocks with high book value relative to market value	—	—
Growth companies w/$725 million + market caps	−0.7	—
Value companies w/$725 million + market caps	13.3	—
23 blue chip corporations	17.6	14.0
1000 largest U.S. companies	9.6	—
Broadest index available	10.6	—
Medium-size stocks with medium market caps of approx $800M	12.9	—
Medium-size stocks with medium market caps of approx $800M	13.5	—
Medium-size stocks with medium market caps of approx $800m	11.2	—
Medium-size stocks with medium market caps of approx $800M	5.2	—

Table 9.2 Index and Passively Managed Funds (Continued)

Fund	Index
Seven Seas S&P MidCap Index	S&P MidCap 400
Vangd Index Extended Mkt	Wilshire 4500

Small Cap Indexes
DFA U.S. Small Cap Value	
DFA U.S. Small Co	
DFA U.S. Small Co	
Drey-Wilsh Sm Co Gro	Wilshire 5000
Drey-Wilsh Sm Co Val	Wilshire 5000
Federated Mini-Cap	Russell 2000
Gateway Small-Cap Index	Wilshire Small Cap
IBM Sm Co Index	
Schwab Small Cap Index	
Vangd Sm Cap Stk# SC	Russell 2000

Specialized Indexes
Benham Gold Eq Index	
DFA Real Estate Sec+	
Domini Social Equity Fund	
Dreyfus Edison Electric	
IBM Utility Index	Russell Utility
Rushmore Amer Gas Indx	

International Indexes
DFA Continental Sm Co	
DFA Japan Small Co	
DFA Lg Cap Int'l	
DFA Pacific Rim Small Co.	

Comments	Total Return	
	1993	5 yrs (ann)
Medium-size stocks with medium market caps of approx $800M	13.0	—
All companies except S&P 500	14.5	14.2
Listed stocks with high book to market value	—	—
Bottom half of listed stocks	13.7	—
Bottom 2 deciles of listed stocks	21.0	13.3
Growth companies w/$70–$725 million market caps	15.7	—
Value companies w/$70–$725 million market caps	11.2	—
Small companies with avg market cap of $180 million	15.3	—
250 small size companies	—	—
Russell 3000 excluding S&P 500 stocks	11.3	—
1000 companies with capitalization from $150M–$600M	—	—
Small companies with avg market cap of $180 million	18.7	13.0
30 North American mining companies	81.2	9.0
REITs	—	—
400 social stocks, half drawn from S&P 500	6.5	—
Members of the Edison Electric Institute (electric companies)	10.5	—
121 large utility companies	13.3	—
Members of the American Gas Assoc.	16.6	—
Small companies on European continent	25.3	6.0
Bottom half Tokyo Stock Exchange stocks	14.2	−3.6
Large companies in Europe, Australia & Far East	25.9	—
Small companies in Singapore, Hong Kong, Australia, Malaysia	—	—

Table 9.2 Index and Passively Managed Funds (Continued)

Fund	Index
DFA U.K. Small Co	Financial Times Index
Schwab Int'l Index	
Vangd Int'l Indx-Europe	MSCI-Europe
Vangd Int'l Indx-Pacific	MSCI-Pacific
Wright Equifund - Belgian/ Luxem	
Wright Equifund - Dutch	
Wright Equifund - Hong Kong	
Wright Equifund - Italian	
Wright Equifund - Japanese	
Wright Equifund - Nordic	
Wright Equifund - Spanish	
Wright Equifund - Swiss	

Bond and Balanced Indexes

Fund	Index
IBM U.S. Treas Index	Salomon Bros. U.S. Treasury Index
Laurel Bond Market Index	Lehman Bros Govt/Corp Bond
Stagecoach Bond Index	Lehman Bros Govt/Corp Bond
Vangd Balanced Index	Wilshire/Salomon
Vangd Bond Index - Inter Bond	Lehman Bros Inter Corp/Govt Bond
Vangd Bond Index - Long Bond	Lehman Bros Lg Corp/Govt Bond
Vangd Bond Index - Short Bond	Lehman Bros Sh Corp/Govt Bond
Vangd Bond Index - Tot Bond Mkt	Lehman Bros Aggregate Bond Index

Source: *The Handbook for No-Load Fund Investors*

Comments	Total Return	
	1993	5 yrs (ann)
Bottom half of United Kingdom index	30.6	2.4
350 large companies excluding U.S. & South Africa	—	—
Morgan Stanley large cap European stocks	29.2	—
Morgan Stanley large cap Pacific stocks	35.5	—
Substantially all publicly traded companies in country	—	—
Substantially all publicly traded companies in country	19.5	—
Substantially all publicly traded companies in country	84.3	—
Substantially all publicly traded companies in country	11.5	—
Substantially all publicly traded companies in country	—	—
Substantially all publicly traded companies in country	—	—
Substantially all publicly traded companies in country	21.6	—
Substantially all publicly traded companies in country	—	—
U.S. Treasury notes and bonds with remaining maturities of 1+ yrs	13.3	—
	—	—
	—	—
60% Vanguard Total Market Fund, 40% Bond Market Fund	10.0	—
5–10 year maturities	—	—
10+ year maturities	—	—
1–5 year maturities	—	—
	9.7	10.8

Some of the new funds split the old broad-based indexes into growth stocks, with fast-growing earnings, and value stocks, with share prices that appear cheap in relation to the companies' assets or earnings. There are now large-company growth-index funds and small-company growth-index funds, and large-company value-index funds and small-company value-index funds. There's even an index fund that uses hedging programs to minimize losses in flat or down markets. (See Table 9.2.)

There are also overseas index funds that buy baskets of stocks based on Morgan Stanley's Europe, Australia, and Far East (EAFE) Index. But these funds often incur high costs because they buy stocks on foreign exchanges and do business through foreign brokers.

Part of the appeal of the early index funds was their simplicity. You simply selected a fund that copied the broad market, and that was that. Now, with the influx of so many new, more complex index funds, it may be as difficult to choose one as it is to choose a more specialized equity fund.

Bond Funds

Bond funds invest in fixed-income obligations, or debt, issued by corporations, municipalities, federal agencies, and governmental bodies. There are more than 1,000 such funds. The interest income they produce may or may not be taxable, depending upon the type of securities in a fund's portfolio. Unlike stock funds, where star portfolio managers can have a major impact on performance, the differences between bond funds are less striking. So, once you determine what type of bond fund you want, it makes sense to choose one that does not impose any sales or distribution charges and has a low expense ratio. The differences in performance among bond funds are greatly affected by the presence or absence of these charges.

A major distinction between owning individual bonds and bond funds (see Chapter 8) is that individual bonds have a set interest rate and fixed maturity whereas bond funds (except for certain zero-coupon bond funds) do not. This distinction can be a plus or a minus. With a bond, you can count on getting a fixed amount of interest at regular periods until the bond matures; at that point, you can redeem the bond for its face value. With bond funds, your interest income and per-share price constantly fluctuate. If there is a sustained rise in interest rates, you will eventually receive more interest income but the market value of your holdings will also fall. Conversely, when there is a sustained decline in interest rates, you will eventually receive less interest income but the value of your holdings will also increase.

In selecting a bond fund, it's important to look beyond a fund's yield and to focus on its *total return.* The concept of total return reflects a fund's yield as well as changes in its per-share price. When interest rates rise, for example, a long-term bond fund may generate more interest income but may also suffer a sharp decline in the current market value of securities in its portfolio. The result may be a yield in the double digits but a negative total return. Even though you may be receiving hefty dividend income, the value of your principal is diminishing. This may not trouble you if you are investing your income and plan to hold on to your shares for a long time. But if you think you may need to sell soon, you probably will be better off purchasing a shorter-term bond fund, which has a lower yield but a positive total return.

There are many types of bond funds. They include funds that specialize in corporate bonds, municipal bonds, government bonds, international bonds, and money market instruments.

Corporate Bond Funds

Corporate bond funds invest primarily in the debt of corporations, though they may hold some government securities as well. The interest income you earn from corporate bond funds is fully taxable.

When you purchase a corporate bond fund, you need to consider two major issues:

• *What quality do you want?* The most conservative funds, which restrict their investments to bonds issued by top-rated corporations, also have the lowest yields. If you want a higher return, you will have to assume additional risk by purchasing a fund that invests in the debt of lower-rated companies. The riskiest funds invest in *junk bonds,* securities that have received low ratings—or no ratings at all—from the major rating agencies. These funds, which can usually be identified by the words "high yield" in their name, can offer extremely attractive yields, but the risk of default is also high. Because their performance is so closely tied to the financial fortunes of the company that issued them, junk bonds behave more like stocks than bonds. So, a junk bond fund should really be considered a substitute for a stock fund.

• *What maturity do you want?* The shorter the maturity, the less chance of big price swings in your holdings of the fund. But the yield on your investment will usually be lower than if you had purchased a fund with a longer maturity. This presents the classic trade-off between risk and reward. The shorter the maturity, the less the risk—and the less the reward.

Municipal Bond Funds

Municipal bond funds can invest in the debt issued by hundreds of thousands of states, local governments, communities, and agencies around the nation. The interest they generate is exempt from federal tax, which makes them attractive investments for people who are in the 28 percent tax bracket or above. If your municipal fund sells some securities from its portfolio at a profit, however, it will realize capital gains and your share of those gains will be fully taxable as it would be with any other bond fund. Although the yield on municipal bond funds is generally less than that on corporate bond funds, the spread between the two sometimes narrows to the point where municipal funds represent a good buy, even for people in low brackets.

There are also single-state municipal funds that invest in the securities issued by localities in a particular state; if you live in that state, the interest income they produce is usually exempt from state and local taxes, as well as from federal taxes. While total escape from income tax may seem alluring, you should be aware of one potential drawback of single-state funds: They are not as diversified as general municipal bond funds. If your state's economy falters and there is a wave of defaults, the interest income and value of your fund could be negatively affected.

Table 9.3 Dollar-Cost Averaging in a Stock Fund

Year Ended 12/31	Total of $100 Monthly Investments	Shares Purchased*	Average Cost Per Share	Fund's Price Range		Cumulative Market Value of All Shares Owned*
				Lowest	Highest	
1980	$1,200	110.492	$10.91	$ 9.66	12.79	$1,288.34
1981	1,200	98.971	13.05	11.15	17.45	3,655.13
1982	1,200	72.829	18.93	14.58	27.23	7,133.52
1983	1,200	85.095	21.37	15.88	25.53	7,105.26
1984	1,200	191.156	13.89	11.38	19.35	8,674.17
1985	1,200	102.474	16.57	14.97	18.60	12,189.15
1986	1,200	146.894	16.79	15.14	18.94	13,839.52
1987	1,200	179.203	16.18	15.76	18.87	18,429.42
1988	1,200	287.480	18.23	17.45	20.84	22,636.79
1989	1,200	263.968	18.67	17.10	25.17	27,817.20
1990	1,200	161.086	18.78	17.37	20.60	31,936.39
	$13,200	1,699.648	$16.67	$ 9.66	$27.23	$31,936.39

*Reflects reinvestment of all dividend and capital gain distributions made during the period. This table is a hypothetical illustration intended to demonstrate the effects of dollar-cost averaging; it is not intended to indicate future results for a specific security or fund.

Source: T. Rowe Price Associates

Government Bond Funds

Government bond funds, which invest in obligations of the federal government and its agencies, represent the ultimate in credit safety. That's because the securities in many of their portfolios are backed by the "full faith and credit" of the U.S. government (others carry a less sweeping and less explicit guarantee). So, you generally don't have to worry about the possibility of default the way you do with corporate and municipal bond funds. This makes government funds ideal for conservative investors who want to preserve their capital and are willing to sacrifice some yield for that peace of mind. But not even government bond funds are immune from fluctuating interest rates, so your interest income and the per-share price of your holdings will still vary, depending upon market conditions.

A subcategory of government funds are Treasury funds (see Chapter 8), which restrict their purchases to ultrasafe U.S. Treasury obligations: bills, notes, and bonds. But they differ in terms of their average maturity. Short-term Treasury funds have a maturity of 1 to 5 years and the lowest yields; intermediate-term funds have a maturity of 5 to 10 years and somewhat higher yields; and long-term funds have maturities of 10 years on up and boast the highest yields. The interest income that Treasury funds produce is generally free from state and local tax but is subject to federal tax.

Other government funds invest in securities issued by government agencies, such as the Government National Mortgage Association (nicknamed Ginnie Mae). These obligations represent pools of mortgages that Ginnie Mae buys from lenders around the country and then packages for resale to investors (see Chapter 8). Each month, investors receive income dividends that represent interest income from those mortgages as well as repayment of some of their principal. During periods of declining interest rates, homeowners often refinance their old high-rate mortgages, and shareholders in Ginnie Mae funds wind up getting a much bigger chunk of their principal back than they had expected. The problem is that they must find someplace else to invest that money, but at much lower rates than they had anticipated when they first purchased the fund. Because they are considered slightly riskier than Treasury funds, Ginnie Mae funds have a slightly higher yield.

International Bond Funds

A relatively new entry on the mutual fund front, international bond funds invest in the bonds of foreign companies and governments. Introduced in the late 1980s, international bond funds try to take advantage of yields that may be higher outside U.S. borders than within. These funds gain an additional advantage when the U.S. dollar weakens against the foreign currencies of the bonds they own because those holdings are worth more in dollar terms; on the other hand, they suffer when the dollar appreciates against these currencies.

The advantage of international bond funds is that they increase the diversification of your portfolio and allow you to take advantage of the nvest. If you divide the $850 sales charge by the $9,150 you invest, you wind up paying an effective brokerage commission of 9.3 percent on your investable funds. That's quite a cut off the top of your hard-earned money, and the fund will have to perform mighty well to offset that hefty sales charge.

Most load funds impose a sales fee only on the initial amount you invest, and in recent years the average load has declined from 8.25 percent to between 4 and 5 percent. Many funds will also reduce a high load the more money you invest, though there are many variations. An 6.5 percent load might shrink to 6 percent on an investment of $25,000, to 4 percent on an investment of $50,000, and to 3 percent on an investment of $100,000. But beware of the handful of funds that add insult to injury, and impose loads not only on your initial investment but also on the dividends and capital gains that you reinvest in the funds' shares rather than taking them out in cash.

Explaining Expenses

All mutual funds have operating expenses, but these costs can vary considerably and may have a major impact on fund performance. The biggest component is the management fee, which covers the salaries of fund personnel, the cost of office space and facilities, and the cost of managing the portfolio. (But brokerage costs, which can be a huge expense, are considered capital items and therefore are not included in fund operating expenses. Instead, these costs are simply deducted from the value of the fund's holdings in the same way they would be if you were buying and selling stocks on your own.)

Sometimes, as a marketing effort aimed at attracting new shareholders by temporarily boosting yields, funds—particularly money market funds—will temporarily reduce or waive the management fee. This concession can be a powerful inducement to buy a fund, but you must be on the lookout six months or a year down the road when the fund may have attracted its target number of shareholders. Gambling that most people will decide it's too much trouble to switch, fund managers may decide to start imposing management fees. For most funds, combined

growing importance of foreign bond markets, which do not always move in the same direction as the U.S. bond market. But you also become subject to the risk of foreign currency fluctuations, which can overwhelm the actual return on bonds in their portfolios. If you can tolerate some risk and uncertainty in your bond fund holdings, you might consider placing a modest portion of your fixed-income assets in an international bond fund.

Money Market Funds

Introduced about 20 years ago, money market funds invest in short-term money market instruments, such as jumbo bank certificates of deposit, U.S. Treasury bills, U.S. government agency securities, and municipal securities. Unlike bond funds, whose per-share price can vary, money market funds have a fixed price of $1 per share. Because they usually offer check-writing privileges (although the minimum size of the check may be as high as $500), money market funds are an attractive alternative to bank money market accounts. They usually pay somewhat higher rates but are not covered by federal deposit insurance. However, no money fund shareholder has yet lost a penny.

The safest money funds are the government-only ones, which restrict their holdings to obligations issued by the U.S. Treasury and certain government agencies. Their yield is usually below that of regular money market funds; however, it's often exempt from state and local taxes. Then there are tax-exempt money market funds, which purchase only obligations issued by state and local governments. Even though the interest income they produce is exempt from federal tax, their yield may be so low that only top-bracket investors come out ahead. There are even single-state money funds, whose interest income is exempt from state and local as well as federal tax. But because the yield of these funds is lower yet, they too are usually suitable only for top-bracket investors who reside in that state.

LOADS VERSUS NO-LOADS

Mutual funds are sold two ways, through brokers or directly to the public. Funds sold through brokers typically impose a load, or front-end sales charge, that can range between 4 and 8.5 percent; these are known as *load funds*. Funds sold directly to the public and promoted through advertising do not impose any sales charges and are known as *no-load funds*. In addition, there are *low-load funds* (generally the best-performing funds of some no-load families, such as Fidelity), which impose sales charges that usually range between 2 and 3 percent. Banks are also starting to sell mutual funds to the public; their funds may or may not impose sales charges (see Chapter 6).

There is a continuing debate as to whether load or no-load funds offer a better deal for investors. Load fund proponents argue that fund performance, not the sales charge, is what matters most. If a load fund is outperforming its peers, the presence of a sales charge is immaterial, they say. That's true, up to a point. Let's assume that a fund is up by 1,000 percent over a five-year period, compared to a rise of only 100 percent by its competitors. If you can be assured that this fund will continue to outperform its competition by the same margin (a big if), then a sales charge of 8.5 percent is indeed insignificant, considering your past and future profits.

But research indicates there's no correlation between performance and the presence (or absence) of a load. Load funds, on average, turn in about the same performance as no-load funds. If chances are good that some no-load funds in the universe can achieve a 1,000 percent increase in performance, why pay 8.5 percent for something you can get for nothing? Put another way, if all other things are equal, then the presence of a load can reduce the amount of profits you personally pocket (see Chart 9.1). This is particularly so in the case of bond funds, where the stock-picking acumen of the portfolio managers of an issue does not play as large a role as it does with stock funds and you are essentially buying a commodity. When you buy a commodity, you want to purchase it as cheaply as possible. Why pay a name-brand price (by paying a load) for a generic product? With bond funds, differences in performance are usually traceable to loads and high expense ratios.

To illustrate how pernicious the impact of a load can be, let's examine the case of a fund with an 8.5 percent load. This charge is actually understated, because it is expressed as a percentage of your total pur-

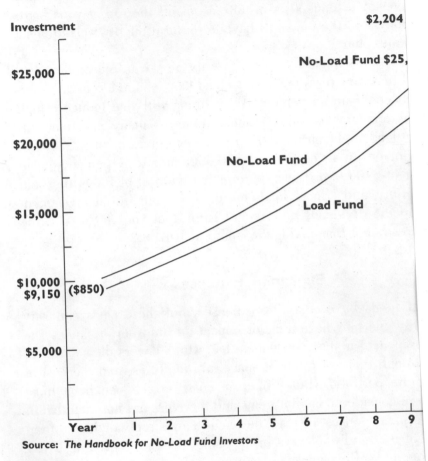

**Chart 9.1 Comparison of $10,000 Investment in Two Mutual [
Each Growing 10% Per Year, Compounded Annually**

Source: *The Handbook for No-Load Fund Investors*

chase price (that is, the amount you invest in the fund *plus* charge) rather than as a percentage of just the amount you inve: do the mathematics, you will see that an 8.5 percent load worl be 9.3 percent of the amount you invest.

Here's why. Assume you want to put $10,000 into a fund wit percent load. From that amount, $850 goes straight to the sales zation that sold you the fund. That leaves you with only $9

expenses range between 0.5 percent and 1.5 percent of average assets. Some funds have minuscule expense ratios of less than one-tenth of 1 percent, and some stock funds have top-heavy expense ratios exceeding 5 percent. Expense information is contained in tabular form in the fund prospectus.

12b-1 Fees and Other Charges.

A recent development, particularly among funds sold by brokers, is the growth of *12b-1 plans*. These plans are named for a 1980 SEC rule that permits funds to pass along their marketing and distribution costs to investors by collecting an annual fee from the fund's net assets. Such fees are now collected by more than half the mutual funds in existence and have ranged as high as 1.25 percent of fund assets. These costs can adversely affect your net return because they are subtracted every year, even if you do not make any additional purchases.

These 12b-1 fees are usually coupled with another new marketing strategy. A few funds have always imposed redemption fees of 1 to 2 percent to deter short-term trading; these fees were eliminated after an investor held a fund for six months or more. Now, many funds sold by brokers impose *contingent deferred sales charges* of as much as 5 to 6 percent if investors redeem their shares within the first year; the charge usually declines by 1 percentage point a year for the next five or six years and disappears after that.

A fund that imposes both a 4 percent contingent deferred sales charge and a 1.25 percent 12b-1 fee may appear more attractive than one that comes with a 6.5 percent up-front load, but shareholders end up paying about the same in total charges over the long term.

The government is beginning to establish some limits on the maximum amount of charges that can be imposed by a fund. Effective July 1993, the total sales charges—including the initial load, any contingent deferred sales charges, and any 12b-1 charges—generally may not exceed 7.25 percent. Funds that require fees that exceed the 7.25 percent ceiling will have to return any excess fees to the fund. In addition, 12b-1 fees are now capped at 0.75 percent, with an additional 0.25 percent permitted as a service fee. Funds that charge only a front-end load can continue to charge up to 8.5 percent.

HOW MUTUAL FUNDS ARE PRICED

The worth of a mutual fund is reflected in its net asset value, or *NAV*. The NAV is determined at the end of each trading day by adding up all a fund's securities, cash, and other assets, subtracting any liabilities, and dividing the resulting figure by the number of shares outstanding. In effect, net asset value is the liquidation value of a fund if it were to sell everything at the end of the day and divide the proceeds among its shareholders.

Current market prices of most mutual funds are listed in the financial sections of many newspapers. In general, the first listing will show the net asset value, or price at which fund shares can be sold back to the fund. This is sometimes called the *sell* or *bid* price. If a fund charges a redemption fee, it will be reflected in the NAV. The second column will list the *offer, buy,* or *ask* price, which is what you must pay to purchase shares in the fund. With a load fund, the offer price includes the fund's maximum sales charge; with a no-load fund, it does not. No-load funds carry the designation *NL*.

MUTUAL FUND DISTRIBUTIONS

A typical mutual fund makes two kinds of payments to its shareholders: income dividends and capital gains. The source of dividends is the fund's investment income from its holdings of stocks and bonds. *Income dividends* represent the fund's net income, or what is left after the fund's operating expenses have been subtracted from its earnings. Mutual funds are not allowed to retain their net income for future expansion or reserves, but must pay out virtually all of their earnings to shareholders each year. Depending upon the type of fund, income dividends are paid monthly (many bond funds), quarterly (some index funds), or semiannually or annually (many stock funds).

Capital gains occur when a mutual fund sells securities from its portfolio at a profit. The fund then distributes a pro rata share of the profits from these sales to shareholders. The timing of these distributions varies, but many stock funds make capital gains distributions once a year, typically in December.

Shareholders have the option of receiving their dividends and capital gains in cash or reinvesting them in additional shares. While many shareholders of bond funds need the income and take the dividends in cash, four out of five shareholders of stock funds reinvest their capital-gains distributions. Either way, both the dividends (unless they represent income from tax-free municipal bond funds) and capital gains are considered income, and you must pay tax on them regardless of whether or not you actually get your hands on the money.

If your goal is long-term growth of your investments and you don't need the income produced by your fund, the best idea is to reinvest both dividends and capital gains. That way, you will reap the considerable benefits of long-term compounding.

THE POWER OF COMPOUNDING

Many mutual fund shareholders don't realize that reinvested dividends are a major component of their total return on stock funds. This is illustrated by Chart 9.2, which shows the results of investing $10,000 in the Standard & Poor's 500 Stock Index at the start of a 20-year period ending December 31, 1993.

During that time, the principal (amount you invested) would have grown by almost $38,000 and you would have received almost $16,000 in cash dividends. The total value of your investment would have approached $64,000, including your original $10,000. But if you had reinvested your dividends and not taken them in cash, the total value of your investment would have grown to more than $110,000—74 percent more than without reinvestment.

The results are even more dramatic over longer time periods. If you had invested $10,000 in the S&P 500 at the end of 1950, you would have accumulated almost $246,000 by year-end 1990, including about $84,000 in cash dividends. If the dividends had been reinvested, the total value of your investment would have grown to more than $800,000. And the value of shares you acquired with your reinvested dividends would have exceeded $653,000, accounting for 80 percent of your total return on the original $10,000 investment.

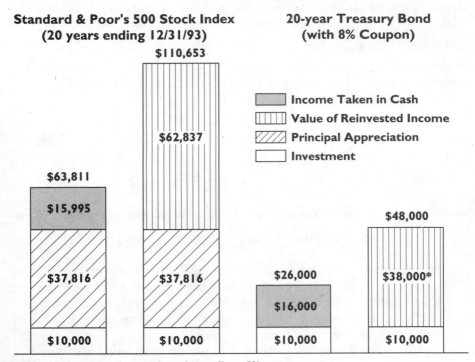

Chart 9.2 The Power of Compounding Stock Dividends
($10,000 Investment)

*Assumes income reinvested semiannually at 8%
Source: T. Rowe Price Associates

HOW TO MEASURE PERFORMANCE

Once you've found a fund that matches your investment objectives, you need to scrutinize its performance. Three- and five-year performance figures are usually sufficient. But it's also important to look at a fund's more recent performance (over the last three to six months) because that may be more predictive of how it will do over the next year than a record compiled more than a decade ago.

The goal is to find a fund that has performed well over recent history, within its particular category. Past performance is not an absolute guar-

HOW TO READ MUTUAL FUND LISTINGS

To check on how a mutual fund is doing, turn to the mutual fund listings in your daily newspaper. (These listings typically appear close to other tabular material, such as listings of individual stocks traded on the major stock exchanges.) To find your fund, first look under the name of the sponsoring company, which is listed alphabetically in boldface print. This is the company, such as Fidelity, T. Rowe Price, or Vanguard, that is running the fund; all funds operated by the same company appear under the sponsor's name.

To illustrate, we're using a snippet of mutual fund listings that appeared in the April 5, 1994, edition of *The Wall Street Journal*.

	Inv Obj.	NAV	Offer Price	NAV Chg.	— Total Returns —		
					YTD	4 wks	1 YR R
Fidelity Invest:							
Contra	GRO	29.77	30.69	−0.35	−2.8	−5.3	+10.1 A
EmrMkt	ITL	16.18	NL	−0.61	−17.9	−10.2	+35.9 A
MagIn	GRO	68.87	71.00	−0.85	−2.8	−6.3	+13.7 A

• The first column gives the name of the fund, which is often abbreviated. In this case, we are looking at three different funds sponsored by Fidelity Investments: ContraFund, Emerging Markets Fund, and Magellan Fund.

An e after the fund name stands for ex, or ex-distribution, which means the fund declared a capital-gains distribution.

An f indicates the price is for the previous day.

A p indicates a fund has a 12b-1 plan, which imposes annual fees for marketing and distribution costs.

An r after the fund name indicates the fund charges a redemption fee or a contingent deferred sales charge when you sell your shares.

An s indicates a fund has split its shares or has declared a stock dividend.

A t indicates the fund has both a 12b-1 plan and a redemption fee or a contingent deferred sales charge (ouch!).

An x after the fund's name stands for ex-dividend, which means it declared a cash or income dividend.

• The second column gives the investment objective of the funds, as defined by Lipper Analytical Services, Inc. In the case of Contra and Magellan, the objective is growth (GRO); in the case of Emerging Markets, it is international. This information on fund objectives does not appear in all newspapers, however.

• The third column gives the fund's *net asset value,* or NAV. This is the dollar amount that the fund would pay you for one share in the fund if you wanted to sell it back that day, minus any deferred sales charges. Sometimes, this is listed as the "sell" or the "bid" price. The net asset value of a fund is calculated by adding up the value of all of the fund's holdings and dividing by the number of shares in the fund at the end of each business day. The net asset value of Magellan is $68.87, for example.

• The fourth column gives the *offer price,* which reflects the sales commission you must pay to buy a load fund; it represents the net asset value plus any sales charges. Sometimes, this is listed as the "buy" or "ask" price. Some funds quote the same price in the *NAV* and the offer price; this means they assess no up-front charges but instead impose a fee when you sell.

In this case, you must pay $71.00 to purchase a share of Magellan, a low-load fund, even though you would get only $68.87 a share if you were to sell it back to the fund. The fund sponsor pockets the difference.

The term *NL* indicates that the fund is a no-load fund that does not impose a sales charge when you buy or sell. If you were an investor in Fidelity's Emerging Markets Fund (EmrMkt), one of its pure no-load funds, you would pay $16.18 to purchase a share of the fund—exactly what you'd get if you sold a share of the fund.

• The fifth column shows the change, if any, in the fund's net asset value between the close of business from one day to the next. In this case, the net asset value of Fidelity's ContraFund fell by $0.35 a share, to $29.77, over the most recent one-day trading period.

antee of future performance, but it's the only way to compare how well funds have served their existing shareholders.

Mutual fund performance is usually measured by the yardstick of *total return.* This concept reflects price increases or decreases in fund shares (that is, changes in a fund's net asset value), as well as any capital gains or dividends that the fund has distributed to shareholders during a specific period. Performance figures often differ, depending on how the organization calculating the returns treats capital gains and income dividends. Some analyses assume reinvestment of both items but not necessarily on the same dates, whereas others just assume reinvestment of capital gains.

You can obtain information on the total return of dozens of different mutual funds by reading newsletters (see "References and Resources") that regularly track the industry, financial magazines, and daily newspapers. Many newspapers have expanded the statistical data they carry on mutual funds to meet the growing interest of individual investors. *The Wall Street Journal,* for example, now provides total return data on hundreds of mutual funds for different time periods, and gives them letter-grade performance rankings that range from A (the top 20 percent) to E (the bottom 20 percent).

Morningstar Mutual Funds (available in many libraries) uses a star system, ranging from five stars for funds in the top 10 percent to one star for funds in the bottom 10 percent.

When evaluating performance, be alert to changes in the top management of a fund. The outstanding performance of a fund often reflects the ability of the portfolio manager who chooses the securities that the fund buys and sells. This was the case, for example, with Fidelity's Magellan Fund, which owed much of its remarkable record to the legendary stock-picking talents of former portfolio manager Peter Lynch. If that person departs and someone else takes over the helm, it's possible that fund performance will suffer.

Over the years, there have been repeated proposals that funds be required to disclose to shareholders a change in top management. These recommendations have been vigorously contested by the mutual fund industry, but the SEC recently mandated that funds must disclose portfolio managers in the prospectus. Because these documents can be up to a year old when you receive them, ask who the current manager is before purchasing a fund. And you should know that some funds, in an attempt to skirt this new rule, now say they are run by a team rather than an individual manager.

Tax Consequences

Despite the basic simplicity of the mutual fund concept, the tax consequences of buying, owning, and selling them can be bewildering.
Indeed, unraveling the tax impact of a mutual fund's distributions and
sales is probably the single biggest drawback to owning these funds.
For one thing, many people believe that if they sell one mutual fund
and use the proceeds to buy another fund within the same family, no
taxes will be due on any profits. Not true. Any sale of a mutual fund is
considered a "taxable event," even if the proceeds remain within the
same group of funds. Figuring the amount of the gain (or loss) can be a
major headache, particularly if you have reinvested dividends and
capital gains over the years and are selling just part of your fund
holdings.

How to Calculate a Gain

You can use three different ways to figure your gain or loss on the sale
of mutual fund shares:

Specific-Share Method Under this approach, which gives you
maximum flexibility in figuring your gain or loss, you must identify the
particular shares you are redeeming and notify the fund in writing at
the time you make the sale. This method can be a real plus if you
bought shares in the fund at different times and at different prices.
Specifying shares with the highest acquisition cost, or basis, will
produce the smallest profit and the smallest tax bill (or, if the fund has
declined in value, the largest loss).

Assume you own 1,000 shares of Fat Cat Fund, which has a current
net asset value of $40. You bought 500 shares of the fund on March 15,
1990, at $30 a share, and another 500 shares of the fund a year later on
March 15, 1991, at $35 a share. If you tell the fund that you want to sell
the 500 shares purchased on March 15, 1991, at $35 a share, your gain
will be only $5 a share, or $2,500.

First-In-First-Out Method You can use this method if you don't
identify specific shares. This approach assumes that you are selling

shares in the same order in which you bought them. Using the above example, your gain would be figured on the first shares you bought at a price of $30 each. Your gain would thus be $10 a share, for a total profit of $5,000.

Average-Cost Method Under this approach, you calculate your total investment in the fund and divide it by the number of shares you own. You then use the resulting average tax cost to determine your gain or loss. Again, using the above example, your average cost per share would be $32.50 and your taxable gain would come to $7.50 a share, or $3,750. (A variation of this method distinguishes between gains on long-term shares, which are taxed at a maximum rate of 28 percent, and gains on short-term shares, which are considered ordinary income and can be taxed at rates as high as 39.6 percent.)

If you use the average-cost or the specific-share method, you must state that on Schedule D (Capital Gains and Losses) of your federal income tax return. And once you've used this method, you must continue to use it for all transactions in the same fund, unless you get written permission from the IRS to switch to another method.

These examples make it seem relatively simple to figure out your gain or loss when selling a mutual fund. But this simplicity is deceiving because the examples don't take into account any dividends or capital gains that have been *reinvested* in additional shares over the period you have owned the fund. The only way to calculate the impact of such reinvestments is to plow through piles of old statements. And the difficulty increases if you have sold some of your fund holdings bit by bit, rather than redeemed them all at once. Partial redemptions are a major problem for people who own bond funds and have used the check-writing privileges of these funds to gradually cash out part of their holdings as the need arises.

Because there have been so many complaints about the difficulty of calculating taxes on sales of mutual funds, Congress has proposed that funds be required to send shareholders annual reports showing not only the value of any shares they redeemed during the year, but also the tax basis of those shares. This proposal sounds good, but there is one catch: What you and other mutual fund investors will be shown on such reports is the *average* basis of the shares you hold. As noted above, the average-basis method can result in a higher tax bill than the specific-identification method.

The timing of payouts of capital-gains and dividend distributions can also be confusing. With many stock funds, capital-gains distributions are declared (or announced) in December but not paid out to shareholders until January. This delay can be particularly frustrating because you are liable for income taxes on this distribution in the year that it was declared, even though you don't receive the money until the following year. Timing also plays an important tax role in the purchasing of mutual funds.

Timing Your Mutual Fund Purchases

Never, ever buy mutual funds before an upcoming distribution of dividends and capital gains (unless you're buying for a tax-favored retirement account). The reason is that you'll wind up paying unnecessary taxes on your own money. Here's why: Mutual funds are unique in that they temporarily deposit any undistributed income dividends and realized capital gains (profits from the sale of securities in their portfolios) in the fund's pool of assets. When a fund makes a distribution, it subtracts the money it pays out as income dividends and capital gains from assets in this pool. That, in turn, reduces the fund's net asset value by the amount of the distribution. This is known as "going ex-dividend," or "ex-distribution."

Even though the fund's share price declines by the amount of the distribution, that doesn't mean you have lost money. The price change represents the amount of the distribution you have received. It's like taking from one hand and giving to the other. In making this simple transfer, however, you become liable for income taxes on the amount of the distribution, regardless of whether you owned the fund for a day or 10 years and a day. So, it's much better to wait to purchase a fund until *after* the fund's ex-dividend (or ex-distribution) date.

Let's take the case of the hypothetical Market Wizard Fund. You pay $10 a share and invest $1,000 in the fund on April 15. That same day, the fund goes ex-dividend and declares a capital-gains and dividend distribution of $1 a share to shareholders of record as of April 16. The fund's net asset value immediately drops by $1, to $9 a share. You now own 100 shares worth $9 each and also receive $100 in dividends and capital-gains distributions. The total value of your investment is unchanged. *But* (and this is a big *but*) you have also purchased a tax liability on the $100 of distributions you received, regardless of whether you took the distribution in cash or reinvested it in additional shares. If you had waited to purchase the fund until April 17, at the post-distribution price of $9 a share, you would have avoided the tax bill and would have been able to purchase 111.1 shares rather than just 100 shares.

Because many stock mutual fund distributions are declared in December, be careful about buying a stock fund late in the year. The idea is to avoid purchasing just before the ex-dividend (or ex-distribution) date. You can glean information on a fund's history of declaring distributions by reading certain newsletters, such as *No-Load Fund X* (see References and Resources), that track this data. Or call the fund and ask when it is planning to make a distribution. Some funds may be willing to provide this information, although they are not required to do so.

Tax Effectiveness

A relatively new concept is that of a mutual fund's "tax effectiveness." This reflects the accumulated gains of all the securities held in a fund's portfolio. Until the fund actually "realizes" these paper gains by selling the securities, the price appreciation of these holdings is not taxed. But when the fund eventually converts its paper gains into real gains by selling, the profits will, in turn, be distributed to investors. If you are an investor in a fund at the time these gains are realized, you will have to pay your share of taxes on the profits, even if some or all of those profits are from securities the fund bought well before you purchased shares in the fund.

In general, funds that frequently turn over their portfolios have a lower tax effectiveness than funds that hold on to their investments for long periods of time. (You can find information on a fund's portfolio turnover rate in the fund prospectus.) All other things being equal, you'll do better on an after-tax basis if you hold funds with a high turnover rate in your IRA or your Keogh account, where gains can accumulate tax-free until you start to withdraw your money at retirement.

If you're considering several funds for your regular (taxable) portfolio, you may wish to use their tax effectiveness as a tie-breaker to determine which fund to buy.

DOLLAR-COST AND VALUE AVERAGING

By reinvesting dividends and income, you are practicing a form of dollar-cost averaging. That means you are regularly buying shares of a fund, regardless of whether the market is up or down at the time you make your purchase. The advantage of this approach is that it often reduces the average cost of your shares below what you would have paid had you invested in one large lump sum. This is particularly true if you are prone to hop on the stock-buying bandwagon just as the market nears a peak and to bail out just when it hits bottom. Such inopportune timing means that you wind up buying high and selling low. You should be doing just the opposite. Dollar-cost averaging helps you to do that because you wind up purchasing more shares when prices are down and fewer shares when prices are up.

The following hypothetical example should drive home the point. Say you invested $100 a month in a mutual fund from 1980 through 1990. At the end of this period, your cumulative investment would have been $13,200, but because the share price of the fund was steadily rising, the market value of your holdings would have been almost $32,000, or more than twice that amount. The price you paid per share during that period ranged from a low of $9.66 to a high of $27.23. Because you wound up buying more shares in the fund when the price was low, and fewer shares when the price was high, your average cost per share was $16.67 and wound up between those two extremes.

A variation of this purchasing technique is called *value averaging*. Its developer, Harvard Business School professor Michael Edleson (see References and Resources), maintains it is potentially more profitable than dollar-cost averaging. Value averaging calls for the *value* of your holdings to increase by a set amount each month. Say, for example, you decide that the value of your portfolio should increase by $100 a month. In months when the value of your holdings declines, you must invest more than $100 to "replace" their lost value. In months when the value of your holdings increases, you invest less than $100 because capital gains have provided some of the "required" increase in value. Theoretically, you might even have to sell off some of your holdings (which could trigger unwanted taxes) if the value of your holdings increases so much that you exceed your value goal. The alternative is to delay making further purchases until the value of your portfolio subsides. Value averaging also requires that you increase the dollar amount of your goal every year or two to take into account the impact of inflation.

Automatic Investment Plans

These plans provide one of the easiest ways to periodically invest in the mutual fund of your choice. With an automatic investment plan, you can funnel fixed amounts from your bank account, your paycheck, even your Social Security check, into a mutual fund without lifting a finger. You simply complete a form authorizing the fund to take out a set amount at regular intervals, typically once a month or once a quarter. If you have trouble saving, this is an ideal solution. What you don't see, you don't spend.

There are two other advantages to this approach. First, it forces you to dollar-cost average. By ensuring that you invest regardless of whether the market is up or down, you wind up purchasing fewer shares of a fund when the price is high and more shares when the price is low. The result lowers your average price per share.

The second plus is that many funds that require fairly high minimum initial investments waive this rule for people who enroll in an automatic investment plan. Funds that normally require initial investments of $2,500 or $3,000 may allow you to put in only $50 or $100 at a time if you invest automatically. Subsequent minimum investments are often lower, too—sometimes less than half the regular required amount—if you use an automatic investment program.

Automatic Withdrawal Plans

The flip side of automatic investment plans, automatic withdrawal plans let you redeem a set amount of your mutual fund holdings at regular intervals. These plans can be ideal for retirees who want to regularly liquidate a portion of their holdings to help pay for living expenses. Most funds require that you have at least $10,000 invested, and suggest that no more than 6 percent be withdrawn annually so that you do not exhaust your capital. The minimum withdrawal is usually $50 a period. Checks can be sent directly to you, to your bank, or to a third party.

These plans are very flexible, and can be changed at any time. You can increase or decrease your withdrawals, discontinue them entirely, or liquidate all your holdings. Withdrawal plans can be set up with just about any type of mutual fund, but they are most appropriate for conservative growth or growth-and-income funds, which are likely to outpace inflation without suffering enormous price swings.

HOW TO SUCCEED WITH MUTUAL FUNDS

How does a novice investor narrow down the enormous range of choices among mutual fund investments? If you adopt the following approach, the task can be much less daunting:

• **Determine your own investment objectives.** Are you trying to accumulate money for a short-term need, such as a down payment on a house? Or are you trying to accumulate a retirement nest egg for decades from now?

• **Assess your tolerance for risk.** Do you have trouble sleeping at night if the stock you inherited from your Aunt Mabel loses 5 percent of its value overnight? Or can you shrug off such ups and downs and view your participation in the stock market as a long-term affair that is bound to run into rough seas?

• **Find a fund category that matches your investment goals.** If, for example, you're putting away money in order to purchase your first house, a short-term bond fund that is not apt to experience large price swings may be a good bet. But if you're stashing away money for retirement and have the stomach to ride the stock market's roller coaster, an aggressive growth fund that performs wonderfully in up markets—but sinks like a rock in down markets—may be perfect. You can afford to swallow some occasional price declines as long as you have decades before you're going to need to draw on that money.

• Look for funds within your investment objective category that have good long-term records. While past performance is no guarantee of a repeat in the future, it doesn't make sense to turn over your money to a fund that has consistently lagged its peers.

• If all other things are equal—that is, if you've found several similar funds with comparable performance ratings—choose a no-load fund (one that has no sales charge) or a low-load fund (one that has a low sales charge) with a modest expense ratio. The less of your investment that you have to give to the fund's sponsors, the more money there will be available to work for you.

But the absence of sales and distribution charges does not guarantee that your fund will produce returns that match or exceed those of its competitors. That's why you must also compare a fund's performance to that of other funds of the same type.

• If you're making a significant investment ($10,000 or more), don't do it all at once. Instead, dollar-cost average into the fund by spreading your investments over a period of time when the market is down as well as up. Chances are, your average cost per share will be lower than if you had bought it all at one time.

• Reinvest both income dividends and capital-gains distributions, unless you need the income to live on. Over time, the power of compounding on these reinvestments may be more significant than the performance of the fund itself.

• Keep tabs on your fund at least once every three months. Although mutual funds don't require the same amount of attention as individual stocks and bonds, you don't want to buy and forget the funds either. Otherwise, you might discover that your fund has lost much of its value—perhaps because it was invested in the wrong industry at the wrong time—while you were blissfully unaware.

• Consider selling a fund if it consistently lags the performance of funds with similar objectives over a period of several years. It's true that investment styles go in and out of fashion: Growth funds may be the rage for a few years and then be supplanted by value funds. But over time, these differences tend to smooth out. However, if you own a fund that regularly trails the competition in both down *and* up markets, you should probably bite the bullet and sell.

• Don't panic and dump all your holdings during steep market downturns. The worst time to sell is when hysteria sweeps investors. The market will inevitably recover (as people who unloaded their stocks during the enormous decline of 1987 discovered, much to their chagrin), although not always right away.

10

INVESTING IN INSURANCE PRODUCTS

THIS chapter comes near the end of the book because you shouldn't even think about purchasing insurance products unless you've thoroughly explored every other type of suitable investment.

There are several reasons why. First, even though the premise of most insurance investments seems simple, the products themselves can be extremely complicated to decipher. To make matters worse, the sales tactics of some agents are designed to obscure rather than clarify the nature of these investments.

Second, many more fees are attached to insurance products than to other types of investments. If you don't quite grasp all the ramifications of a particular insurance product you buy, and later decide to bail out, you may lose a bundle of money.

Third, the investment performance of insurance products often lags behind that of comparable investments.

Given all these negatives, you may wonder why anyone would want to purchase insurance products at all. The major reason is the tax advantage they offer. In fact, insurance investments have been touted as one of the few remaining tax shelters.

That's because the money you invest in these products, like the money you contribute to an IRA, Keogh plan, or 401(k) plan, accumulates interest or profits on a tax-free basis until you begin to withdraw the funds, presumably at retirement when you are in a lower tax bracket than you were when you made the initial investment. But unlike the money you use to fund IRAs, Keoghs, and 401(k) plans, which is either tax-deductible or pretax money, the money you use to purchase insurance products is usually after-tax money for which no deduction is available.

Once you start to withdraw the money (unless it is in the form of a loan or in a few other special cases), some portion of it becomes subject to tax. Furthermore, with certain types of insurance products, there are negative estate tax consequences that your beneficiaries would not face had they inherited assets such as stocks, bonds, or mutual funds.

If, after all this, you're still interested in insurance products, read on. There are two basic ways to go with insurance investments. You can purchase a cash-value insurance policy or an annuity.

With a *cash-value policy*—whole life, universal life, or variable life—you get a policy that combines a death benefit with a savings fund. In the early years of the policy, you pay a lot more for the insurance element than you would with term insurance (coverage that provides a death benefit but without any savings element). As more and more money is funneled into the savings fund portion of the policy, the cash value increases until, in the later years, you have accumulated a substantial tax-deferred nest egg.

With an *annuity*, you give the insurance company money now and it is used to purchase a guaranteed stream of income that is paid out to you (usually in the form of a monthly check), either right away or at some future date. You can structure the payments so you purchase the annuity with one big lump sum, or in gradual increments over a period of years. And you can structure the payouts so that you receive the money for your entire lifetime, for the joint lifetimes of you and your spouse (or some other beneficiary), or for some predetermined period.

Below are the details. Just bear in mind that while insurance products may be suitable for some people, they should never constitute the core of your financial holdings. Rather, they should be just a part of a well-diversified portfolio that holds many different types of assets.

LIFE INSURANCE POLICIES

A traditional whole life policy provides a set death benefit (the face amount of the policy). The policy is designed to cover you for life, hence the name. It also is known as a cash-value policy, reflecting the fact that the savings portion of the policy accumulates a cash value. You also don't need to renew a whole life policy each year, the way you do with a term insurance policy. As long as you pay the annual premiums, the policy remains in force.

Although the concept of an unchanging insurance cost may be attractive, the premiums in the early years of a whole life policy are set so high that you overpay for the amount of protection you get. That's because the chance of your dying at a young age is relatively small, so the cost of insuring your life is also relatively low. The portion of your premium that is not used to purchase a death benefit (and not used for heavy up-front costs, mainly agents' commissions) goes into the savings portion of your policy. In effect, a whole life policy is a type of forced savings plan.

The hitch is that for people in their thirties and forties, premiums for whole life policies are far higher than for comparable amounts of term insurance. In fact, a 35-year-old man might pay 10 times as much for $200,000 of whole life insurance as he would for the same amount of term insurance. (However, the premiums for term insurance generally increase year after year, until they outstrip the cost of whole life for people in their sixties, if they are able to purchase term insurance at all.)

The real problem is that because of the steep cost of whole life, many people can't afford to keep these policies in force beyond the first couple of years. In fact, more than one in five whole life policies lapses within the first two years, which leaves the former policyholders without coverage when they need the protection most. Furthermore, virtually the entire first-year premium is paid out as a commission to the insurance agent who sold you the policy, rather than funneled as a contribution to the cash-value portion of the policy. Indeed, surrender charges (discussed later) can run to 150 percent or more of one premium. So you could pay two years' premiums and have no policy value at all.

Now let's turn to the cash-value portion of the policy, which, after all, is why this type of insurance is discussed in a book on investing.

According to a study by an actuarial consulting firm, commissions and other distribution expenses of a whole life policy amount to 20 to 25 percent of the premiums paid over the life of a conventional policy. By contrast, the distribution costs of low-load insurance products (those with modest commission fees) run between 5 and 10 percent of the premiums paid. And distribution costs of no-load insurance products are negligible.

Two insurance companies sell no-load products without the typical agent salesforce: USAA Life, a subsidiary of the auto-insurance company, United Services Automobile Association, based in San Antonio, Texas, (800) 531-8000; and the much smaller Ameritas Life Insurance, based in Lincoln, Nebraska, (800) 552-3553. There are also two mutual fund groups that sell low-load variable annuities directly to the public: the Vanguard Group, (800) 522-5555, and Scudder Stevens & Clark, (800) 225-2470.

IS WHOLE LIFE A GOOD INVESTMENT?

Assuming you've got enough income to pay the premiums, you may well wonder how a whole life policy compares to other investments. In a 1979 landmark study, the Federal Trade Commission (FTC) found that the rates of return for dividend-paying insurance policies averaged 1.9 percent over ten years and 4.6 percent over 20 years. That was a pretty dismal return at a time when market rates averaged between 6.5 and 7.5 percent. A 1985 report by the FTC found that whole life policies had improved somewhat, but their rates of return were still below the market rates on other investments.

Actuaries determine a rate of return on insurance policies by calculating something called a *Linton yield*. The rate of return derived from the Linton yield depends upon the assumption made about a policy's cost of death protection. The lower the mortality charges used in a policy, the smaller the yield will appear to be; conversely, the higher the mortality charges, the higher the apparent yield. Linton yields are calculated for different time periods, and the results change dramatically the longer a policy is held.

In a 1986 study of life insurance policies, *Consumer Reports* found negative Linton yields at the end of a five-year period for policies studied. This reflected the fact that most whole life policies have miserable rates of return if you hold them for such a short period. That's because the expenses charged against the policies consume a big portion of your accumulated cash value. But if you hold the policies for 20 years, the rate of return for some policies ranks favorably with those of other comparable investments.

Obtaining the Linton yield for a policy you're considering can be difficult, if not impossible, depending upon the company. Insurance regulators don't require companies to disclose rates of return for their cash-value policies, and companies rarely give them out voluntarily. You can get the rate of return on a policy if it is included in a *Consumer Reports* periodic survey on the cost of life insurance. But if you are considering a company that was not studied or refused to participate in the survey, you're out of luck. Unless such a company discloses its rate of return, and you can double-check that rate, you probably are better off choosing a company that is more forthcoming.

To determine whether a whole life policy, in which the cash-value portion of the policy accumulates interest on a tax-deferred basis, is a better investment than some other fully taxable investment—such as a bond or a bank CD—you must take several factors into account:

- Your tax bracket
- The rate of return on the policy (which you usually can't find except by consulting the *Consumer Reports* study).
- The rate offered by the alternate investment. You then need to

calculate the after-tax return on the alternate investment, which is what you'd have left after paying federal and state taxes on the earnings it produced, to the after-tax return on the policy, which is what you'd have left after keeping the policy for a certain period of time and then paying federal and state taxes on the taxable portion of the cash buildup within the policy.

As you can see, making such a comparison is a daunting process and well beyond the capabilities of most ordinary mortals. One place to get help is the National Insurance Consumer Organization (NICO), a public interest group run by insurance professionals. Their advice, while not free, is modestly priced, as well as knowledgeable and unbiased. NICO will evaluate any proposal you get for a cash-value policy and tell you the interest rate that you would need to get on a comparable investment in order to do better. It will also calculate the current worth of your present cash-value policy. At press time, NICO charged $40 for the first analysis, and $30 for each additional analysis requested at the same time. To get an evaluation, send a stamped, self-addressed envelope and copies of your proposals, or, in the case of existing policies, projections of future policy values on the current dividend scale, to NICO, P.O. Box 15492, Alexandria, Virginia 22309.

Single-Premium Whole Life Insurance

More of an investment than life insurance protection, single-premium insurance is usually sold to affluent people who have a big chunk of money to invest and want a tax break.

Here's how it works. You make a one-time payment to an insurance company. The amount can be as little as $5,000 or as large as $25,000 or $50,000. In return, you get a specific amount of insurance for life, with no further payments due. You also receive a package of cash values that accumulates tax-free until the money is withdrawn. Under current law, that package of cash values is never taxed if the policy is held until death. Any withdrawals, including loans, are taxable; in addition, there is an income tax penalty on withdrawals before age 59½. Thus, this product is best suited to older people who want to pass along money to their heirs in a tax-efficient way.

With a traditional single-premium policy, the company agrees to credit interest to your cash values for a specific period, usually one year but sometimes as long as five years. Be sure that the company quotes you its lower net rate and not its higher gross rate. The net rate is what you'll earn on your cash values, and it reflects deductions by the company for such items as policy fees, mortality charges, and expenses.

With a *variable* single-premium policy (as with a regular variable life policy), you get to choose your own investments from a menu of stock funds, bond funds, and money market funds. Rather than earning a predetermined amount, your cash values will grow (or shrink), reflecting the performance of the investments you have selected.

It used to be that the biggest advantage of single-premium whole life policies was the ability to borrow against the accumulated cash value without paying any tax on your loans. In effect, you could use the growing cash values to generate a stream of tax-free income (though the loans had to be repaid if survivors were to receive the full death benefit of the policy).

In June 1988, however, the government tightened the rules. The new policies are now known as *modified endowment contracts*, and any loans or other withdrawals against them, up to the amount of money the policies have earned, are considered taxable income; again, tax penalties apply if money is withdrawn before age 59 ½.

An additional drawback is that these policies have severe cancellation penalties. If you want to back out during the first few years—perhaps because you've found a much better investment—you'll probably be hit with a surrender charge. These charges can be as much as 7 to 9 percent of the premium in the first year or so, but usually taper off and disappear by the end of the tenth year. Indecisiveness can be expensive with these policies. If you're investing $50,000, you don't want to sacrifice $4,500 just because you changed your mind. That makes these policies somewhat illiquid investments.

Universal Life Insurance

This is the insurance industry's chameleon product, and for a time it threatened the dominance of whole life policies. A universal life policy can be tailored to build cash values, to provide nearly pure term insurance, and to allow you to temporarily reduce premiums—or even eliminate them altogether.

The advantage of universal life over whole life is that the different elements of the policy are revealed for all to see. First, the company discloses the current interest rate it is crediting on the cash-value portion of the policy, information that is hard to get with whole life. Then, once a year, you receive a statement showing how much you earned on the cash value, how much was withdrawn to pay for the policy's expenses and the death benefit, and how much the cash value has increased.

The problem is that the advertised interest rate on the cash value portion of the policy may be misleading and is not comparable from company to company. The cost of a universal life policy reflects three factors:

• The interest rate that is credited to the cash-value portion of the policy

• The cost of the death benefit (sometimes called the mortality charge or the cost of insurance)

• The company's expenses. In determining what rate it will pay, each company concocts its own pricing mix—perhaps obscuring high expenses and mortality charges with an artificially high interest rate.

So, you can't automatically assume that the best deal is always with the company that pays the highest rate. You actually may be better off purchasing a policy from a company with a lower rate (but also with low expenses and low mortality charges).

The biggest selling point of universal life is its flexibility. You are free, within certain limits, to decide how much in premiums to pay. When money is tight, you can cut back in premiums for a month or two. If you get a bonus or an unexpected gift, you can increase your payments, thus fattening the cash-value portion of the policy. But this very flexibility can lull you into a false sense of security about the adequacy of the insurance protection you think you're getting. If you cut back on premiums at the same time that interest rates take a nosedive, and the rate you receive on your cash value plummets, it may turn out that you're no longer paying enough to keep the insurance portion of the policy in force.

For this reason, companies set a *target* premium for you to pay. This is the minimum premium that will keep the policy in force for your entire life and still allow you to accumulate a substantial cash value. A universal life policy behaves like a traditional whole life policy if you faithfully pay the target premium, year after year. Paying the target premium ensures that you won't be left without adequate coverage if interest rates suddenly change.

The concept behind universal life is simple to understand, but comparing different companies' policies is extremely tricky. Your best bet would be to check *Consumer Reports* most recent Ratings of universal life policies or to call on the services of NICO (see page 220).

Variable Life Insurance

Variable life policies shift the investment risk from the insurance company to you, the policyholder . The amount of the cash value buildup in a variable life policy is linked to the success or failure of mutual fund investments that you choose for yourself from among those offered by the insurer. If you're an investment ace and you select stock, bond, or money market funds that soar, so will your cash value. (However, the cash value won't rise as much as the underlying investments, because variable life expenses are generally higher than those of other types of cash-value insurance.) If you're an investment dud and the funds you pick drop, then the cash value—as well as the death benefit—could shrink.

The big mistake most people make with this type of policy is being too conservative. They tend to gravitate toward lower-yielding fixed-income investments, such as bond and money market funds, rather than higher-yielding investments in stocks. Stocks offer the only real chance that policyholders have to capitalize on variable life insurance, because investment and administrative expenses are higher with variable life than with whole life or universal life. So you have to be willing to gamble on the stock market—which historically has had much higher returns than bonds or money market instruments—for variable life to pay off.

There are two ways to purchase variable life. With *straight* variable life, you pay a fixed premium just the way you do with whole life. With *universal* variable life, which is much more popular, you can vary your premiums to suit your circumstances just the same way you can with regular universal life.

As with universal life, one danger is that if you reduce your premium payments—or even skip them altogether—you may wind up putting your death benefit in jeopardy. A few companies offer some protection against this possibility by guaranteeing that your policy will remain in force for a specific period if you agree to pay a minimum target premium during the first few years.

Again, trying to compare variable life policies can be next to impossible for the layperson. To get help in analyzing different policies at a modest cost, contact NICO (see page 220).

LIFE INSURANCE ANNUITIES

These have been likened to celebrity marriages, in which it's delightful to be courted and easy to tie the knot, but dreadfully expensive to call it quits. But they may play a role for affluent, conservative investors who want the security of knowing they'll receive a reliable stream of income down the road once they're retired.

You can buy annuities from a wide range of financial services providers, such as mutual funds, financial planners, banks, and insurance agents, but the ultimate guarantors of these products are insurance companies. And even though there are a staggering array of bells and whistles, annuities share two common characteristics: You purchase the annuity by plunking down pretax rather than after-tax dollars. That means you don't get a tax deduction for your investment. But once your money is inside the annuity, it compounds on a tax-deferred basis. That means you don't owe any income tax on the buildup in value until you start receiving a payout from the annuity; at that point,

HOW SAFE IS YOUR COMPANY?

It's increasingly important to be sure that your insurance company is financially strong. That may be easier said than done, however. Most of the major ratings agencies failed to predict the two largest failures in the history of the U.S. insurance industry: Executive Life and Mutual Benefit. Since there have been almost 150 insurance company failures in the last four years—twice as many as in the previous decade—the possibility that a company may go belly-up is far from remote.

The conventional wisdom is to choose a company that receives a top grade from one of the major rating agencies, such as A.M. Best, Moody's, Standard & Poor's, Duff & Phelps, or Weiss Research. Some of these agencies—notably Best—have been accused of being soft on companies and failing to alert the public to impending problems. On the other hand, Weiss has been accused of exaggerating company problems in an attempt to gain media attention. However, Weiss was the only rater to predict the failures of Executive Life and Mutual Benefit. If you'd rather be safe than sorry, you should carefully consider the Weiss ratings before signing on the dotted line.

If the company you choose does get into trouble, your state guaranty association may come to the rescue. All 50 states now have such associations, under which all the insurers doing business in a state agree to chip in and make good on the promises of a troubled insurer. The protection limits vary by state. The death benefit is usually capped at $300,000, although it may go as high as $500,000 or as low as $100,000. The amount you can collect on cash values and annuities is also limited, often to $100,000.

Death benefits and monthly payments from annuities that have begun when the insurer failed are usually paid promptly. But it can take years before policyholders can borrow from the policies, withdraw their cash values, or receive annuity payments that hadn't yet started.

only part of the payout (reflecting the earnings on your contribution) is taxable.

Types of Annuities

Here's a rundown of the different types offered by the industry:

• An *immediate* annuity is purchased with one payment. It then begins immediately to provide a stream of income for life, or for some other period.

• A *deferred* annuity is one you purchase with either a chunk of cash now, or a series of payments spread over a period of months or years. At a future date you can choose a stream of income for life or for some other length of time.

• *Split-funding* is a combination of immediate and deferred annuities. The immediate annuity provides current income and the deferred annuity provides a chance to accumulate money for the future.

• A *single-premium* annuity is one you buy with one lump sum. The minimum purchase amount is often $5,000, though many people invest as much as $25,000 or $50,000.

• A *flexible-premium* annuity is one in which you can vary the premiums. You might decide to pay $200 a month for 24 months, or fund it with a generous bonus check of $5,000 instead.

• A *fixed* annuity pays you a set interest rate on your money. The rate is "fixed" by the insurance company, but the company can unilaterally decide when that rate will change and can modify it as frequently as once a month.

• A *variable* annuity allows you to select investments from a menu of mutual funds that are wrapped inside an insurance contract. The insurance coverage is generally modest, usually a promise from the company that your heirs will receive the value of your original investment or the value of the annuity at your death, whichever is greater. The success (or failure) of the investments you choose within the annuity determines how much your money grows (or shrinks) and how large (or small) the eventual payout will be.

Weaving Your Way Through Variable Annuities

Variable annuities are the fastest growing segment of annuity sales, with $100 billion in assets. But a big problem with these products is that people are too conservative with their investments. Studies show that almost two-thirds of the money in these accounts is invested in low-yielding fixed-return accounts with underlying investments in bonds and similar securities, or in bond funds or money market funds. The trouble with this approach is that the puny yields of these "safe" investments can be swamped—or even wiped out—by the hefty assortment of fees that are attached to variable annuities. Result: Policyholders often wind up with negligible—or even negative—return on their investments.

In mid-1993, for example, the average one-year rate on fixed-return accounts for variable annuities was 4.67 percent, according to Morningstar, a Chicago firm that tracks the performance of mutual funds and annuities. But combined charges on such annuities were about 2 percent a year, reducing investors' net return by almost half. If you have your heart set on making a fixed-return investment through an annuity, you'd be better off putting your money into a fixed annuity, which generally has lower charges.

But the best course is to become a bit of a gambler and take a chance on investing in the stock market. Historically, stocks have had a far higher return than fixed-income investments or money-market securities. When shopping for a variable annuity, it's important to check the track record of *all* the mutual funds it offers. Unlike investing outside an annuity, where you are free to pick the best-performing mutual funds (or dump the worst-performing ones) as you please, within an annuity you can select only from the package of funds (technically known as subaccounts) available in the insurance contract.

Look for an annuity in which the basic stock, bond, and balanced funds are all strong performers, preferably with good track records that extend back at least three years. Don't be blinded by the exceptional performance of just one fund; that fund's portfolio manager may lose momentum or leave, and you may be stuck with the annuity's other mutual funds, which could turn out to be real laggards. That's not so unlikely. Research by Morningstar found that of the 10 largest variable annuities sold to individuals, most had mutual funds that were poor performers, though there were some exceptions.

Fees

Investors who are attracted by the tax-deferred buildup of earnings within a variable annuity can pay dearly for that privilege. There are a variety of fees connected with these insurance products that can take years of good investment returns to overcome. Often, you do better by investing outside the annuity, even though you must pay taxes each year on any profits. Consider the following variable annuity fees:

- *Annual Insurance Contract Charge.* This is the annual fee you pay to be in a variable annuity contract; it averages about 1.25 percent, according to Morningstar. It covers the death-benefit guarantee, company expenses, and the commission that is paid to the agent who sold you the contract.

The most popular variable annuities tend to have higher than average contract charges, with the highest charge reaching 1.5 percent. Variable annuities sold by two big mutual funds (Vanguard and Scudder) directly to investors, without brokers, tend to have the lowest contract charges, with the least expensive contract imposing a 0.55 percent charge.

- *Mutual Fund Fees.* These are the fees you pay for the management of the different mutual funds, or subaccounts, available in the insurance contract. They range from a high of 1.3 percent of average fund expenses (for international bond funds), to a mid-level of 0.69 percent (for stock funds), to a low of 0.53 percent (for money market funds), according to Morningstar. If you're thinking of investing in the international bond or stock markets, you'll probably do better outside an annuity, where you are not subject to such steep charges.

- *Surrender Fee.* This is the penalty you must pay to the insurance company if you take out your money before a certain number of years has elapsed. The average surrender fee is 7 percent in the first year, declining by one percentage point annually over seven years or so. But some surrender fees go as high as 9 percent.

You may run into a surrender fee if you bought a variable annuity with an exceptionally high initial rate and then found that the insurance company slashed the rate to less than the competition was paying after the initial guarantee period expired. If you yank out your money before age 59 ½, you are subject to an additional 10 percent IRS penalty on the earnings portion, as well as income tax on the money. The only way to avoid this is to shift the money directly into another annuity.

THE DARK SIDE OF VARIABLE ANNUITIES

No one likes to talk publicly about it, but some people are drawn to annuities (and certain life insurance policies) for less orthodox reasons than tax savings: Annuities enable them to hide assets from the long reach of state Medicaid officials, college financial aid officers, and creditors. While it may be perfectly legal to use annuities to shield assets for such purposes, this approach raises serious public policy issues. Many colleges, for example, don't count life insurance and annuities in their financial aid formulas. Some families stash money into these products in order to appear less wealthy, so their children will qualify for aid. But colleges are getting wise to this tactic, and increasingly are requiring parents to disclose such investments on their financial aid forms.

Many states exclude annuities and insurance policies from assets that can be seized in bankruptcies, so some people use these products to shield their assets from creditors. But the fastest growing use of annuities for this purpose may be to protect assets from being "spent down" by expensive nursing home stays. Some people shift their money into annuities so they appear poorer, and thus may be able to qualify for Medicaid. Result: the taxpaying public picks up the tab for their nursing home bills.

Who Should Buy A Variable Annuity?

Are you making the maximum contributions allowed to such tax-favored retirement savings plans as IRAs, Keogh plans, and 401(k) plans? Since deductions to these plans are usually tax-deductible and

thus cut the amount of income taxes you would otherwise have to pay, use them to the hilt before purchasing an annuity with pretax dollars. But if you do not qualify for deductible IRA contributions, a variable annuity may make sense. Other reasons to consider an annuity:

• You're in a high enough tax bracket to make investing in an annuity really worthwhile. At the least, you should be in the 28 percent bracket. Otherwise, you're tying your money up unnecessarily and subjecting yourself to stiff fees for a tax advantage that isn't worth very much.

• You can afford to keep your money tied up for a long time. Because of the steep fees connected with a variable annuity, it can take 15 or 20 years for the investment within the annuity to catch up with the performance of an investment outside the annuity, even though they may have identical returns along the way. That's a long time horizon indeed, and few people are in a position to lock up their funds for so far into the future, particularly because of the specter of higher inflation and uncertainty about future tax rates.

• You're prepared to take the plunge and purchase true growth investments, such as stocks or stock funds. That's the only way you're going to get the most out of your annuity dollar. If you're a timid, risk-averse investor, you're better off forgoing the dubious tax advantage of an annuity and instead purchasing Treasury bills (which have tax advantages of their own), bonds, or bank CDs outside the annuity. That way, you escape the special insurance company fees and charges.

11

AFTERWORD
Putting It All Together

CONGRATULATIONS. You've made it through to this point, and have waded through the intricacies of such formerly arcane matters as money-purchase pension plans, the kiddie tax, mortgage-backed securities, junk bonds, and closed-end mutual funds. You're comfortable with the basics of investing and can toss off some of the jargon to impress your bridge partners and golfing buddies.

All that's left is to do it. Yes, it is hard to get started. Establishing a Keogh plan or creating a Uniform Gifts to Minors Account for your baby does take work. So does putting your first $100, or $1,000, into a mutual fund. Simply figuring out which fund to buy, and then obtaining the prospectus and application, can seem like a daunting task if you've never done it before. It's so much easier to give in to the inertia factor—to that inner voice that says it's all right to just leave your money in a bank CD.

But what a shame to do nothing. By not acting, you are sacrificing an opportunity to build yourself a financially comfortable future. Everyone needs to accumulate wealth for some future purpose, whether it's for making the down payment on a first house, sending your daughter to an Ivy League school, or accumulating a nest egg so you can afford to take an early retirement package. The important thing is to get started.

If the notion of investing makes you nervous, start small. Make the most of tax-favored savings and retirement plans at work, and contribute the maximum allowed. If you still have funds available, put away a little each month into a mutual fund. Make it easy on yourself by using the automatic investment plans offered by many mutual fund families.

Don't worry if you make mistakes. It happens to everyone, even the pros. Rather than castigate yourself for what you should have done (but didn't), or what you did do (but shouldn't have), try to learn from your mistakes so you don't repeat them again and again.

Don't panic if your investments fail to soar in value right away. Remember, you're investing for the long term and need to be patient. Financial markets and investing styles run in cycles, and often the best time to buy is when something is out of favor . . . and down in price. Of course, if one of your holdings consistently lags its peers, it may be time to replace it with something else.

Diversify your holdings. First, make sure you have adequate cash reserves (parked in a money market fund or bank equivalent) that will enable you to meet any unexpected emergencies. Then spread what's left among stocks and bonds (or stock funds and bond funds). Since these two types of assets usually don't move in tandem, you'll be protecting at least part of your portfolio if one segment of the market goes into a tailspin. The actual mix of stocks and bonds you aim for depends upon your age, other financial resources, and your tolerance for risk. And consider putting some portion of your money into foreign stocks and bonds so you can participate in the economic growth of other parts of the world.

Don't spend weeks agonizing over which particular stock or mutual fund to buy. Research has shown that the most important factor in accumulating wealth is the type of asset category that you invest in, rather than the specific assets that you purchase within that category.

Don't be too conservative. It's tempting to stick with bonds and bank CDs that deliver a guaranteed stream of income, particularly after stock market declines on the magnitude of 1987's Black Monday. But histori-cally, stocks have provided a far better return (after adjusting for inflation and taxes) than bonds or cash investments. So rev up your confidence and venture into the stock market.

Index funds may be the best way to go. There's a growing body of evi-dence that suggests these mutual funds—which are designed to mimic the performance of broad groups of stocks—are an extremely cost-effective way for people to invest. Very few individual money managers have been able to outperform these indexes over the long term. And index funds have the additional virtue of imposing modest fees, because they are passively managed and are able to keep stock trading to a minimum.

Remember to periodically reevaluate both your investments and your investment needs. Markets and investing styles move in cycles. You don't need to bite your nails and dump your holdings if they decline in value, but you should definitely consider parting with them if they are regularly at the bottom of the performance lists. You may also need to change your investment plan as your personal circumstances change. If, for example, your spouse loses his or her job, you may need to tem-porarily curtail your investing. If, on the other hand, you receive an unexpected inheritance, you may have a lot more money available to invest—and may be able to take a few more risks—than you had origi-nally anticipated.

Be sure to keep informed. Read the business pages of your local newspaper and consider subscribing to specialized financial magazines to keep abreast of investing trends. Even though you're in this for the long haul, the world of finance is exquisitely sensitive to news develop-ments. You don't want to discover that the value of your portfolio has needlessly dwindled because you failed to act after adverse news about some of your holdings became public.

Above all, have fun. It can be rewarding—emotionally as well as finan-cially—to take control of your money and watch it grow year after year. For most of us, investing is just a means to an end, and not an end in itself. But taking responsibility for your investments is a challenge that matches any job. The payoff is the freedom to pursue whatever may inter-est you in the future, without worrying too much about how to pay for it.

APPENDIX

Federal Reserve Banks and Treasury Servicing Offices

For In-Person Visits

FRB Atlanta
104 Marietta Street, N.W.
Atlanta, Georgia
404-521-8657 (Recording)
404-521-8653

FRB Baltimore
502 South Sharp Street
Baltimore, Maryland
301-576-3300

For Written Correspondence

104 Marietta Street, N.W.
Atlanta, GA
30303

P.O. Box 1378
Baltimore, MD
21203

FRB Birmingham
1801 Fifth Avenue, North
Birmingham, Alabama
205-252-3141 Ext. 215
(Recording)
205-252-3141 Ext. 264

P.O. Box 10447
Birmingham, AL
35283

FRB Boston
600 Atlantic Avenue
Boston, Massachusetts
617-973-3805 (Recording)
617-973-3810

P.O. Box 2076
Boston, MA
02106

FRB Buffalo
160 Delaware Avenue
Buffalo, New York
716-849-5046 (Recording)
716-849-5030

P.O. Box 961
Buffalo, NY
14240-0961

FRB Charlotte
401 South Tryon Street
Charlotte, North Carolina
704-336-7100

P.O. Box 30248
Charlotte, NC
28230

FRB Chicago
230 South La Salle Street
Chicago, Illinois
312-786-1110 (Recording)
312-322-5369

P.O. Box 834
Chicago, IL
60690

FRB Cincinnati
150 East Fourth Street
Cincinnati, Ohio
513-721-4787 Ext. 334

P.O. Box 999
Cincinnati, OH
45201

FRB Cleveland
1455 East Sixth Street   P.O. Box 6387
Cleveland, Ohio   Cleveland, OH
216-579-2490   44101

FRB Dallas
400 South Akard Street   Securities Dept. Station K
Dallas, Texas   400 South Akard Street
214-651-6362   Dallas, TX 75222

FRB Denver
1020 16th Street   P.O. Box 5228
Denver, Colorado   Terminal Annex
303-572-2475 (Recording)   Denver, CO 80217
303-572-2470 or 2473

FRB Detroit
160 West Fort Street   P.O. Box 1059
Detroit, Michigan   Detroit, MI
313-964-6153 (Recording)   48231
313-964-6157

FRB El Paso
301 East Main   P.O. Box 100
El Paso, Texas   El Paso, TX
915-521-8295 (Recording)   79999
915-521-8272

FRB Houston
1701 San Jacinto Street   P.O. Box 2578
Houston, Texas   Houston, TX
713-659-4433   77001

FRB Jacksonville
800 West Water Street   P.O. Box 2499
Jacksonville, Florida   Jacksonville, FL
904-632-1179   32231-2499

FRB Kansas City
925 Grand Avenue
Kansas City, Missouri
816-881-2767 (Recording)
816-881-2409

P.O. Box 440
Kansas City, MO
64198

FRB Little Rock
325 West Capitol Avenue
Little Rock, Arkansas
501-372-5451 Ext. 273

P.O. Box 1261
Little Rock, AR
72203

FRB Los Angeles
950 South Grand Avenue
Los Angeles, California
213-624-7398

P.O. Box 2077
Terminal Annex
Los Angeles, CA 90051

FRB Louisville
410 South Fifth Street
Louisville, Kentucky
502-568-9232 (Recording)
502-568-9236 or 9238

P.O. Box 32710
Louisville, KY
40232

FRB Memphis
200 North Main Street
Memphis, Tennessee
901-523-7171 Ext. 225 or 641

P.O. Box 407
Memphis, TN
38101

FRB Miami
9100 N.W. Thirty-Sixth Street
Miami, Florida
305-593-9923 (Recording)
305-591-2065

P.O. Box 520847
Miami, FL
33152

FRB Minneapolis
250 Marquette Avenue
Minneapolis, Minnesota
612-340-2075

250 Marquette Avenue
Minneapolis, MN
55480

FRB Nashville
301 Eighth Avenue, North
Nashville, Tennessee
615-259-4006

301 Eighth Avenue, North
Nashville, TN
37203

FRB New Orleans
525 St. Charles Avenue
New Orleans, Louisiana
504-522-1659 (Recording)
504-586-1505 Ext. 293

P.O. Box 61630
New Orleans, LA
70161

FRB New York
33 Liberty Street
New York, New York
212-720-5823 (Recording)
212-720-6619

Federal Reserve
P.O. Station
New York, NY
10045

FRB Oklahoma City
226 Dean A. McGee Avenue
Oklahoma City, Oklahoma
405-270-8660 (Recording)
405-270-8652

P.O. Box 25129
Oklahoma City, OK
73125

FRB Omaha
2201 Farnam Street
Omaha, Nebraska
402-221-5638 (Recording)
402-221-5633

2201 Farnam Street
Omaha, NE
68102

FRB Philadelphia
Ten Independence Mall
Philadelphia, Pennsylvania
215-574-6580 (Recording)
215-574-6680

P.O. Box 90
Philadelphia, PA
19105

FRB Pittsburgh
717 Grant Street
Pittsburgh, Pennsylvania
412-261-7988 (Recording)
412-261-7863

P.O. Box 867
Pittsburgh, PA
15230-0867

FRB Portland
915 S.W. Stark Street
Portland, Oregon
503-221-5931 (Recording)
503-221-5932

P.O. Box 3436
Portland, OR
97208

FRB Richmond
701 East Byrd Street
Richmond, Virginia
804-697-8000

P.O. Box 27622
Richmond, VA
23261

FRB Salt Lake City
120 South State Street
Salt Lake City, Utah
801-322-7911 (Recording)
801-355-3131

P.O. Box 30780
Salt Lake City, UT
84130

FRB San Antonio
126 East Nueva Street
San Antonio, Texas
512-224-2141 Ext. 311
(Recording)
512-224-2141 Ext. 303 or 305

P.O. Box 1471
San Antonio, TX
78295

FRB San Francisco
101 Market Street
San Francisco, California
415-882-9798 (Recording)
415-974-2330

P.O. Box 7702
San Francisco, CA
94120

FRB Seattle
1015 Second Avenue
Seattle, Washington
206-442-1650 (Recording)
206-442-1652

Securities Services Dept.
P.O. Box 3567
Terminal Annex
Seattle, WA 98124

FRB St. Louis
411 Locust Street
St. Louis, Missouri
314-444-8602 (Recording)
314-444-8665

P.O. Box 14915
St. Louis, MO
63178

United States Treasury
Washington, DC

Mail Inquiries to:

Bureau of the Public Debt
Securities Transactions
Branch
1300 C Street, S.W.
Washington, DC
202-287-4113

Bureau of the Public Debt
Division of Customer
Services
300 13th Street, S.W.
Washington, DC
20239-0001

Mail Tenders to:

Device for hearing
impaired
202-287-4097

Bureau of the Public Debt
Department N
Washington, DC
20239-1500

GLOSSARY

Agency Securities Securities issued by U.S. government agencies or instrumentalities, such as the Federal National Mortgage Association, the Federal Farm Credit Bank, and the Federal Home Loan Bank. Because they are not direct obligations of the U.S. Treasury (although most of these securities are backed to some extent by the federal government), they pay a slightly higher rate of interest than comparable Treasury securities.

Annuity A guaranteed stream of income from an insurance company—either for your life, for the joint life span of you and a designated beneficiary, or for a preset period, such as 10 years. To purchase an annuity, you can make a single lump-sum payment or a series of periodic payments to the company.

Assets Items of value that you own, such as cash, bank accounts, CDs, stocks, bonds, real estate, and precious metals.

Asset Allocation An investment philosophy that spreads holdings among a variety of different asset classes, such as cash, stocks, bonds, real estate, and precious metals.

Balance Sheet A detailed listing of what a business owns (its assets), what it owes to others (its liabilities), and what the owners have invested (their capital) at a given point in time.

Bonds Debt securities, or loans, taken out by corporations or governments, in which they borrow money from others to finance expansion and operations. In return for the use of this money, bond issuers promise to pay investors an annual fixed rate of interest and to repay the full amount borrowed at maturity.

Bear Market A market in which prices are declining. You can have a bear market in stocks or bonds.

Bull Market A market in which prices are rising. A bull market can exist for stocks or bonds.

Callable Bonds Bonds that can be called, or redeemed, prior to maturity at the issuer's discretion. Bonds are typically called when interest rates have fallen sharply below the level that existed when they initially floated, thus enabling issuers to borrow more cheaply.

Capital Gain or Loss The profit or loss you get from selling property or securities. The tax treatment of these gains (or losses) has varied over the years. In 1994, the top rate on long-term capital gains (profits on the sale of assets that you held for more than one year) was 28 percent, while the top rate on ordinary income was 39.6 percent. This current 11.6 percentage-point differential is an incentive for top-bracket individuals to seek investments that generate long-term capital gains rather than interest and dividends.

Cash Equivalents Assets, such as money market funds or short-term bonds or notes or bond funds, that can be easily converted into cash.

Closed-End Funds Sometimes known as publicly traded funds, these are mutual funds that issue a set number of shares just once, when they begin business. Thereafter, the shares are traded on stock exchanges just like common stock, with prices determined by supply and demand.

Common Stock An equity security that represents an ownership interest in the company that is issuing the stock. As part owner of the company, you get to share in its profits (or losses).

Compounding The process of increasing your wealth by reinvesting interest, dividends, and profits. The growth in these reinvested amounts occurs at the same rate as the underlying securities, and can result in your assets multiplying at dramatic rates over time.

Contrarian An investor who does the opposite of what most other investors are doing at a particular time, for example, purchasing out-of-favor stocks.

Convertibles A type of stock or bond that can be converted, or exchanged for another type of security, subject to certain conditions.

Coupon The interest that is paid on a bond. Some older bonds were issued with detachable coupons that represented scheduled interest payments on the obligations; at the prescribed time, you would "clip" a coupon and send it in to receive your interest payment.

Debt Investment The purchase of bonds issued by corporations or governments.

Defined-Benefit Plan The traditional type of pension under which your company promises to pay you, once you retire, a specific dollar amount each year for the rest of your life.

Defined-Contribution Plan A more risky (from the employee's viewpoint) type of savings plan in which your company promises only to contribute a set amount each year toward your retirement. It does not guarantee it will provide a certain benefit once you stop working.

Distributions The payment of income dividends or capital gains that mutual funds pass along to their shareholders. Also, withdrawals of money from tax-qualified retirement plans, such as IRAs and Keogh plans.

Diversification The concept of spreading your investments among several different types of securities or assets to minimize the risks inherent in investing. The opposite of putting all your eggs in one basket.

Efficient Market The theory that stock market prices reflect the knowledge and expectations of all investors. Proponents of this theory maintain that any new information about a company is instantly reflected in the company's stock price. In effect, this makes it impossible for investors to consistently beat the market over time.

Equity Investment The purchase of common stock, or an ownership interest in a company.

Ex-Dividend For mutual funds, the date on which declared distributions (of dividends and capital gains) are deducted from the funds' net asset values. On the day that a fund goes ex-dividend, the closing net asset value per share is calculated minus the distribution.

Fannie Mae A nickname for the Federal National Mortgage Association, a government corporation that helps to finance mortgages.

Fixed-Income Investment The purchase of a bond, which pays a fixed amount of interest over a specified period of time.

Foreign Exchange Risk The possibility that the dollar will fluctuate against foreign currencies so that the value of your holdings of foreign securities will be reduced in terms of U.S. dollars.

401(k) Plan A corporate-sponsored savings plan that allows you to put away money for retirement or other purposes by investing pretax rather than after-tax dollars. Under this arrangement, you agree to defer part of your current salary by placing it in the plan, thus cutting your current income taxes.

Ginnie Mae A nickname for the Government National Mortgage Association, a government corporation that helps to finance mortgages.

Income Statement A document, sometimes called a profit-and-loss statement, which shows how much money a company made or lost over the past year by adding up all its sources of revenue and then subtracting all its expenses. What's left is the company's net income.

Index Fund A mutual fund that aims to match the overall investment performance of a large group of publicly-traded stocks or bonds contained in a given index, such as the Standard & Poor's 500 Composite Stock Price Index.

Individual Retirement Accounts Called IRAs, these plans were originally designed as retirement accounts for people who were not covered by pensions at work. Now available to those who are covered as well, though contributions may not be tax-deductible if you earn too much. IRAs permit you to contribute as much as $2,000 per year ($2,250 for couples with just one breadwinner). Earnings on these contributions accumulate tax-free until you withdraw them at retirement.

Investment Company A corporation, trust, or partnership in which investors pool their money to obtain professional management and diversification of their investments. Mutual funds are the most popular type of investment company.

IPO Acronym for Initial Public Offering, or the first time that shares in a privately held corporation are offered for sale to the general public.

Junk Bonds Low-quality, high-risk bonds that typically offer much higher yields than other bonds of comparable maturity.

Keogh Plan Also known as an H.R. 10 plan, this is a tax-favored retirement plan for self-employed individuals and their employees.

Liquidity The ability to easily convert an asset into cash with minimal impact on its price. Assets that are difficult to convert to cash quickly, such as real estate partnerships, are considered illiquid.

Load Fund A mutual fund whose shares are sold by brokers or salespeople and which imposes a sales charge. Load funds generally have sales charges that range between 4.75 and 8.5 percent of the net asset value.

Low-Load Fund A fund with a front-end sales charge of 3 percent or less. It may be sold directly to the public, or marketed through brokers or other sales personnel.

Mortgage-Backed Securities Securities created from pools of mortgages that are packaged together and then sold as bonds. The monthly interest and principal payments on the underlying mortgages are then passed through to individual investors.

Mutual Fund An investment company that pools individuals' money and uses it to assemble a portfolio of securities that is managed by a professional adviser.

Net Asset Value (NAV) The value of a mutual fund's total assets—that is, its securities, cash, and any accrued earnings—divided by the number of shares in the fund.

No-Load Fund A mutual fund that sells its shares at net asset value without imposing any sales charges. However, some such funds may impose redemption or 12b(1) fees.

Odd Lot An order of less than 100 shares, or an amount of shares that is not in even multiples of 100. Commission costs on odd-lot purchases (or sales) are often higher, expressed as a percentage of the total dollar amount of the transaction, than on round-lot purchases (or sales).

Open-End Fund A traditional mutual fund that allows you to make additional investments or cash out the shares you already own, whenever you wish. The fund can accommodate an unlimited number of new shareholders, which is why it's called open-end.

Pension Max Short for pension maximization, a risky approach that calls for taking your pension in a form that will not continue payments to your spouse if you die first. The supposed advantage is that while you're alive, you receive a much larger monthly pension check than you would if you took the ordinary form of a pension payable to a married couple. With the extra money, you purchase a life insurance policy that will presumably provide income for your spouse after your death.

Portfolio All the securities, such as stocks, bonds, certificates of deposit, money market funds, and mutual funds, that represent your personal investments.

Preferred Stock Stocks that pay a set dividend that will never rise or fall. These investments behave more like bonds than stocks.

Price/Earnings Ratio The price of a stock divided by its earnings per share over the most recent 12-month period. A p/e ratio is a kind of popularity index that can indicate the desirability of holding a particular stock, or can compare it to other companies in the same industry.

Principal The amount of money that you put into—and have at risk—in an investment.

Profit-Sharing Plan A savings plan in which your employer contributes a percentage of profits to your personal account. Profits are not required for contributions, however, and a company is not obligated to make contributions on a regular basis.

Prospectus An official booklet that describes a mutual fund and offers its shares for sale. Required by the Securities and Exchange Commission, the prospectus provides information on subjects such as the fund's investment objectives and policies, the fund's financial history, and how to buy and sell its shares.

Proxy A document that allows shareholders who do not attend the annual meeting of a company or a mutual fund to vote on various matters that are put before shareholders, such as the election of directors.

Real Estate Investment Trust Sometimes nicknamed REIT, this is a publicly traded company set up to manage a portfolio of real estate or mortgages for shareholders.

Redemption Fee A charge imposed by some mutual funds when you redeem, or sell, shares.

Round Lot Shares of common stock that are bought (or sold) in multiples of 100.

Series EE Bonds The traditional U.S. savings bonds that can be bought at half their face value. You receive a guaranteed minimum rate if you hold them for at least six months, or a market-based rate if you hold them for at least five years. Interest income may be free from federal, state, and local tax if the proceeds are used to pay for your child's college education, and if your income is below certain limits.

S&P 500 The Standard & Poor's 500 Composite Stock Price Index, which tracks the movements of 500 large and medium-sized companies. The S&P 500 represents about 70 percent of the market in terms of market value and is a widely followed barometer of stock market behavior.

Taxable Equivalent Yield What you need to earn on a taxable investment, such as a bank CD or corporate bond, to equal what you would earn on a tax-free investment, such as a municipal bond. The higher your tax bracket, the higher the taxable equivalent yield needed to match the return of a tax-free investment.

Tax-Free Equivalent Yield What you need to earn on a tax-free investment, such as a municipal bond, to equal what you would earn on a taxable investment, such as a bank CD. The higher your tax bracket, the lower your tax-free equivalent yield (because you'll be keeping more for yourself and paying out less to Uncle Sam).

Term Insurance Life insurance that provides only a death benefit and has no savings element.

Total Return A calculation that measures the performance of a stock, bond, or mutual fund, taking into account dividend or interest payments as well as price changes of the security.

Treasury Securities Short-term bills, intermediate-term notes, and long-term bonds that are issued by the U.S. Treasury Department. They are backed by the full faith and credit of the U.S. government, and the interest income they produce is free from state and local taxes but subject to federal income tax.

12b(1) Plan An arrangement that permits a percentage of a mutual fund's assets to be paid to the fund's distributor in order to cover sales and marketing costs.

Unit Investment Trust An unmanaged portfolio of securities, typically bonds, that is liquidated after a specific period.

Universal Life A type of whole life insurance (see below) that separates the insurance and savings elements of the policy and allows you to decide how much to pay in premiums each year.

Variable Life Another type of whole life insurance (see below) that links the death benefit and cash value of the policy to the investment performance of stocks, bonds, or money market securities that you invest in.

Volatility The relative rate at which a security tends to move up or down in price as compared to an average or index of other securities. A highly volatile asset category, such as stocks, usually rises or declines far more than an asset category such as cash.

Whole Life Traditional life insurance that has a savings element as well as an insurance element. Part of the premium is for a death benefit that is paid to your beneficiaries if you die, and part is invested in a savings account that accumulates interest on a tax-deferred basis. You can borrow against this accumulated cash value in a pinch, or take it in cash when you no longer need the policy.

Yield Sometimes called return, this is the income you receive from a bond or mutual fund, expressed as a percentage of the security's current market price. Yield is typically computed on the basis of one year's income.

Yield to Maturity The yield earned on a bond over its full life, including any capital gains (or losses) that result because the bond was bought at a discount from (or premium to) its face value.

Zero-Coupon Bonds Bonds that are issued at deep discounts to their face value and have no semiannual coupons. Instead, so-called "phantom" interest is imputed to bondholders annually, and the return on the bonds is the difference between the purchase price and redemption price (as long as the bonds are held to maturity). Zeros backed by U.S. Treasury obligations often go by trade names, such as TIGRs and CATs.

REFERENCES AND RESOURCES

Readers who want more detailed information should consult the following sources:

Chapter 4: Investing for College

Leider, Robert and Anna. *Don't Miss Out: The Ambitious Student's Guide to Financial Aid.* Octameron Associates, P.O. Box 2748, Alexandria, Va. 22301; (703) 836-5480.

Chapter 5: Investing for Retirement

Dickman, Barry, and Lieberman, Trudy. *How to Plan for a Secure Retirement.* Consumer Reports Books, 101 Truman Ave., Yonkers, N.Y. 10703.

Protecting Your Pension Money: A Pension Investment Handbook, The Pension Rights Center, 918 16th St. N.W., Washington, D.C. 20006. The mutual fund family T. Rowe Price Associates publishes two excellent planning kits. *The Retirees Financial Guide* is for people who are already retired or plan to retire in the near future; *The Retirement Planning Kit* is for those who expect to retire within the next five years. Both are available free by writing to T. Rowe Price Investment Services, P.O. Box 89000, Baltimore, Md. 21289-0220, or by calling (800) 541-8460.

Chapter 7: Investing in Stocks

Directory of Companies Offering Dividend Reinvestment Plans. Evergreen Enterprises, P.O. Box 763, Laurel, Md. 20725; (301) 953-1861.

Edleson, Michael. *Value Averaging.* International Publishing Corporation, 625 N. Michigan Ave., Suite 1920, Chicago, Ill. 60611.

Lynch, Peter. *Beating the Street.* Simon & Schuster, Rockefeller Center, 1230 Avenue of the Americas, New York, N.Y. 10020.

Chapter 9: Investing in Mutual Funds

Bogle, John. *Bogle on Mutual Funds.* Richard D. Irwin, 1333 Burr Ridge Parkway, Burr Ridge, Ill. 60521, 800-634-3966.

Herzfeld, Thomas. *Herzfeld's Guide to Closed-End Funds.* McGraw-Hill, 1221 Avenue of the Americas, New York, N.Y. 10020; (800) TJH-FUND.

L/G No-Load Fund Analyst is a varied package of materials, including a monthly newsletter on no-load funds, quarterly statistical tables, comprehensive annual reports on a small selected group of funds, and four model portfolios of funds for different investment objectives. L/G Research, 4 Orinda Way, Suite 230-D, Orinda, Calif. 94563; (510) 254-9017.

Morningstar Mutual Funds is an extensive analytical service that reports on 1,240 selected load and no-load funds, giving a detailed description of each (available in many libraries and brokerage offices). Address: 225 W. Wacker Drive, Chicago, Ill. 60606. Telephone: 800-876-5005.

Morningstar also publishes a more general monthly, *Mutual Funds Performance Report,* which provides no analysis but tracks 3,400 different funds and lists the leaders and laggards in different fund categories. In addition, it publishes *Morningstar Closed-End Funds,* which provides data on 268 closed-end funds.

The No-Load Fund Investor is a monthly newsletter that covers almost 900 no-load and low-load funds, provides three model portfolios, and publishes an annual handbook of no-load funds, *The Handbook for No-Load Fund Investors.* Address: P.O. Box 318, Irvington-on-Hudson, N.Y. 10533. Telephone: 914-693-7420.

No-Load Fund X is a monthly newsletter that monitors the performance of no-load and low-load funds. Address: 234 Montgomery Street, San Francisco, Calif. 94104-2994. Telephone: 415-986-7979.

Chapter 10: Investing in Insurance Products

Annuity & Life Insurance Shopper is a quarterly publication that provides rates and the performance of more than 250 companies offering annuities. Address: 81 Hoffman Rd., Englishtown, N.J. 07726. Telephone: (800) 872-6684.

Daily, Glenn. *The Individual Investor's Guide to Low-Load Insurance Products.* International Publishing Corporation, 625 N. Michigan, Suite 1920, Chicago, Ill. 60611.

The Editors of Consumer Reports Books with Trudy Lieberman. *Life Insurance.* Consumer Reports Books, 101 Truman Ave., Yonkers, N.Y. 10703.

Hunt, James. *Taking the Bite Out of Insurance: How to Save Money on Life Insurance.* The National Insurance Consumer Organization, 121 N. Payne St., Alexandria, Va. 22314.

Morningstar Variable Annuity/Life Performance Report is a monthly report that tracks the performance of more than 12,000 variable-type insurance products.

INDEX

growing importance of foreign bond markets, which do not always move in the same direction as the U.S. bond market. But you also become subject to the risk of foreign currency fluctuations, which can overwhelm the actual return on bonds in their portfolios. If you can tolerate some risk and uncertainty in your bond fund holdings, you might consider placing a modest portion of your fixed-income assets in an international bond fund.

Money Market Funds

Introduced about 20 years ago, money market funds invest in short-term money market instruments, such as jumbo bank certificates of deposit, U.S. Treasury bills, U.S. government agency securities, and municipal securities. Unlike bond funds, whose per-share price can vary, money market funds have a fixed price of $1 per share. Because they usually offer check-writing privileges (although the minimum size of the check may be as high as $500), money market funds are an attractive alternative to bank money market accounts. They usually pay somewhat higher rates but are not covered by federal deposit insurance. However, no money fund shareholder has yet lost a penny.

The safest money funds are the government-only ones, which restrict their holdings to obligations issued by the U.S. Treasury and certain government agencies. Their yield is usually below that of regular money market funds; however, it's often exempt from state and local taxes. Then there are tax-exempt money market funds, which purchase only obligations issued by state and local governments. Even though the interest income they produce is exempt from federal tax, their yield may be so low that only top-bracket investors come out ahead. There are even single-state money funds, whose interest income is exempt from state and local as well as federal tax. But because the yield of these funds is lower yet, they too are usually suitable only for top-bracket investors who reside in that state.

LOADS VERSUS NO-LOADS

Mutual funds are sold two ways, through brokers or directly to the public. Funds sold through brokers typically impose a load, or front-end sales charge, that can range between 4 and 8.5 percent; these are known as *load funds*. Funds sold directly to the public and promoted through advertising do not impose any sales charges and are known as *no-load funds*. In addition, there are *low-load funds* (generally the best-performing funds of some no-load families, such as Fidelity), which impose sales charges that usually range between 2 and 3 percent. Banks are also starting to sell mutual funds to the public; their funds may or may not impose sales charges (see Chapter 6).

There is a continuing debate as to whether load or no-load funds offer a better deal for investors. Load fund proponents argue that fund performance, not the sales charge, is what matters most. If a load fund is outperforming its peers, the presence of a sales charge is immaterial, they say. That's true, up to a point. Let's assume that a fund is up by 1,000 percent over a five-year period, compared to a rise of only 100 percent by its competitors. If you can be assured that this fund will continue to outperform its competition by the same margin (a big if), then a sales charge of 8.5 percent is indeed insignificant, considering your past and future profits.

But research indicates there's no correlation between performance and the presence (or absence) of a load. Load funds, on average, turn in about the same performance as no-load funds. If chances are good that some no-load funds in the universe can achieve a 1,000 percent increase in performance, why pay 8.5 percent for something you can get for nothing? Put another way, if all other things are equal, then the presence of a load can reduce the amount of profits you personally pocket (see Chart 9.1). This is particularly so in the case of bond funds, where the stock-picking acumen of the portfolio managers of an issue does not play as large a role as it does with stock funds and you are essentially buying a commodity. When you buy a commodity, you want to purchase it as cheaply as possible. Why pay a name-brand price (by paying a load) for a generic product? With bond funds, differences in perfor-mance are usually traceable to loads and high expense ratios.

To illustrate how pernicious the impact of a load can be, let's exam-ine the case of a fund with an 8.5 percent load. This charge is actually understated, because it is expressed as a percentage of your total pur-

**Chart 9.1 Comparison of $10,000 Investment in Two Mutual Funds
Each Growing 10% Per Year, Compounded Annually**

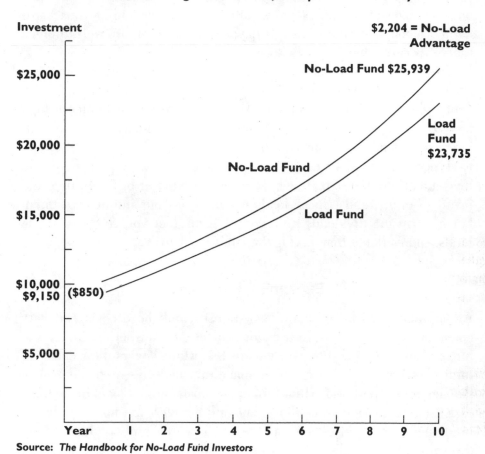

Source: *The Handbook for No-Load Fund Investors*

chase price (that is, the amount you invest in the fund *plus* the sales charge) rather than as a percentage of just the amount you invest. If you do the mathematics, you will see that an 8.5 percent load works out to be 9.3 percent of the amount you invest.

Here's why. Assume you want to put $10,000 into a fund with an 8.5 percent load. From that amount, $850 goes straight to the sales organization that sold you the fund. That leaves you with only $9,150 to invest. If you divide the $850 sales charge by the $9,150 you invest, you wind up paying an effective brokerage commission of 9.3 percent on your investable funds. That's quite a cut off the top of your hard-earned money, and the fund will have to perform mighty well to offset that hefty sales charge.

Most load funds impose a sales fee only on the initial amount you invest, and in recent years the average load has declined from 8.25 percent to between 4 and 5 percent. Many funds will also reduce a high load the more money you invest, though there are many variations. An 8.5 percent load might shrink to 6 percent on an investment of $25,000, to 4 percent on an investment of $50,000, and to 3 percent on an investment of $100,000. But beware of the handful of funds that add insult to injury, and impose loads not only on your initial investment but also on the dividends and capital gains that you reinvest in the funds' shares rather than taking them out in cash.

Explaining Expenses

All mutual funds have operating expenses, but these costs can vary considerably and may have a major impact on fund performance. The biggest component is the management fee, which covers the salaries of fund personnel, the cost of office space and facilities, and the cost of managing the portfolio. (But brokerage costs, which can be a huge expense, are considered capital items and therefore are not included in fund operating expenses. Instead, these costs are simply deducted from the value of the fund's holdings in the same way they would be if you were buying and selling stocks on your own.)

Sometimes, as a marketing effort aimed at attracting new shareholders by temporarily boosting yields, funds—particularly money market funds—will temporarily reduce or waive the management fee. This concession can be a powerful inducement to buy a fund, but you must be on the lookout six months or a year down the road when the fund may have attracted its target number of shareholders. Gambling that most people will decide it's too much trouble to switch, fund managers may decide to start imposing management fees. For most funds, combined